# AL DENTE

FOODS AND NATIONS is a new series from Reaktion that explores the history – and geography – of food. Books in the series reveal the hidden history behind the food eaten today in different countries and regions of the world, telling the story of how food production and consumption developed, and how they were influenced by the culinary practices of other places and peoples. Each book in the Foods and Nations series offers fascinating insights into the distinct flavours of a country and its culture.

Already published

*Al Dente: A History of Food in Italy*
Fabio Parasecoli

*Beyond Bratwurst: A History of Food in Germany*
Ursula Heinzelmann

# Al Dente

## A History of Food
## in Italy

Fabio Parasecoli

REAKTION BOOKS

Published by Reaktion Books Ltd
33 Great Sutton Street
London EC1V 0DX, UK

www.reaktionbooks.co.uk

First published 2014
Copyright © Fabio Parasecoli 2014

Printed and bound in China
by Toppan Printing Co. Ltd

A catalogue record for this book is available from the British Library

ISBN 978 1 78023 276 8

# CONTENTS

# The Food of Italy:
# Beyond Myths and Stereotypes

> It is not down in any map; true places never are.
> Herman Melville, *Moby Dick*

Tiramisu. Spaghetti. Pizza. These items have become so pervasive that they come across as tired stereotypes. Even if many global consumers are not fully aware of their origin, Italian food is undoubtedly among the most palate-pleasing culinary traditions of the world. Its influence and appeal are increasing not only in the kitchen, but also in popular culture. A contemporary book about the recent developments in u.s. cuisine carries the title *The United States of Arugula: How We Became a Gourmet Nation*, focusing on the fashionable (and now ubiquitous) Italian green as a symbol of cosmopolitanism and culinary innovation.[1] In the past three decades Italian cuisine has gained status as well as notoriety. It is not only served at family-style eateries, ice cream parlours and pizza shops: high-end Italian restaurants are now listed among the most prestigious establishments in major cities worldwide, receiving heartfelt accolades from both critics and patrons. tv shows and magazines are full of Italian recipes, all claiming authenticity, and culinary professionals become celebrities banking on their Italian origins. As Italian cuisine acquires new relevance, scores of travellers flock to the epicentre of it all: Italy. They come to unearth yet undiscovered traditions, to visit villages and farms off the beaten track and to savour unique products. They lounge in countryside villas while taking a break in between cooking classes with world-renowned chefs, or scout out mom-and-pop establishments to enjoy 'authentic' local cuisine. So what is all the fuss about? How did Italian food manage to become what it is today? Why does it speak to so many people all over the world? Where does the apparently endless

Unusual pasta types such as *trofie* from Liguria are attracting the attention of food enthusiasts all over the world.

variety of local and regional cuisines come from? How did the dazzling – and, frankly, quite confusing for many – assortment of wines, cheeses, breads, vegetables and salamis come to be?

## Building the Mystique

When people find out I am from Italy, a question they frequently ask is: 'So, what's your favourite Italian restaurant?', which is usually followed by 'Do you cook every day?' The assumption that I have a deep and innate connection with good food points to the widespread notion that Italy is, indeed, a special place when it comes to eating and the pleasures of the table. The world seems to be so in love with Italian food that many tend to think of it as exquisitely traditional, almost timeless, untouched by the events that have shaped what many consider a broken food system. Foodies are enraptured by its endless diversity and its capacity to intrigue and to always offer something new and 'hot'. Tourists and travellers, often pleasantly surprised by their meals and the warm manners that surround them, end up projecting healthy amounts of romanticism on to dishes and ingredients, enriching Italian food with their own desires and longings. Writers also do their bit to perpetuate the myth. Besides cookbooks, non-fiction works like Frances Mayes's *Under the Tuscan Sun* have played an important role in solidifying perceptions, expectations and biases about Italian food. Although Mayes herself points out that 'it is easy for foreigners to idealize, romanticize, stereotype, and oversimplify local people', she often gets very close to doing precisely that.[2]

> The rhythm of Tuscan dining may throw us off but after a long lunch outside, one concept is clear – siesta. The logic of a three-hour fall through the crack of the day makes perfect sense . . . My idea of heaven is a two-hour lunch with Ed, I believe he must have been Italian in another life. He has begun to gesture and wave his hands, which I've never seen him do. He likes to cook at home but simply throws himself into it here.[3]

Exposed to the influence of the environment and enthralled by the inevitable languor that apparently possesses everything and everybody in Italy, the foreign protagonists of Mayes's story slowly change their behaviour. Time seems to lose its weight and its rigidity, melting into

The Tuscan landscape plays an important role in the mystique of the Italian countryside and its food.

## The scandalous fame of extra-virgin olive oil

Extra-virgin olive oil is certainly among the most sought-after of Italian products and a symbol of the Mediterranean diet. Each variety of olive, or cultivar, differs in size, taste and growing periods, creating a multiplicity of local varieties. Following the increasing appreciation for the cultural and economic value of the product, in recent years the profession of olive-oil taster has been publicly recognized, and also the more refined consumers are now aware of the impact of elements such as growing areas, cultivar and harvesting times. Small productions, difficult to purchase and frankly quite expensive, enjoy unprecedented success. Nevertheless, for everyday use, most consumers still buy mass-produced olive oils, sensitive to prices more than just quality.

Often referred to as 'liquid gold', both for its unique hue and its commercial value, extra-virgin olive oil has been the focus of rural and trade policies aimed at guaranteeing its origin and its quality. In fact, the sector is plagued by a long history of adulteration and counterfeiting. Olive oil is classified in different grades according to extraction methods, taste and oleic acid content, with extra-virgin olive oil having an acidity lower than 0.8 per cent, with an absolutely perfect taste. However, many producers argue that these measurements are not enough to limit the sales of cheap 'deodorized' oils, which are chemically purified to get rid of smells connected with defective production.

But the problem goes well beyond grades. Other vegetable oils – including hazelnut – have been bottled and sold as

the pleasure of extended lunches and long naps, which are considered as essential to the natives' lives as their gestures and flair for pleasure – especially of the culinary kind.

The genre of the food memoir has become quite prevalent in popular culture, relating the adventures and human development of the foreigner who arrives in Italy and establishes a new, sensual connection with his or her true self through eating and other assorted messy, noisy pleasures. Italy is not the only place of course, as any location with exotic

*Taggiasca* olives from Liguria are renowned for producing high-quality extra-virgin olive oil.

extra-virgin olive oil, both for the national and the international markets. Taking advantage of laws that do not require the indication of the product origin on the label, olive oils from other areas of the Mediterranean, especially Turkey and Tunisia, are bottled in Italy and resold as Italian extra-virgin olive oil. It is an uphill battle, but one that the Italian government and high-quality producers are ready to fight to protect the image and quality of the Italian extra-virgin olive oil. Nobody wants to be swindled with fake gold.

flair – from the Fiji islands to Southeast Asia – is likely to provide the necessary background for self-discovery and life-changing insights. When it comes to food, however, the focus is often on southern France (preferably Provence), but above all on Italy, with Tuscany featuring large among the possible destinations. The genre has deep roots, dating back to classics like E. M. Forster's *A Room with a View* (1908), in which a young, repressed English woman tries to escape British society by embracing Italian culture. The theme of the foreigner, often a woman, who is frustrated with his or her life and finds the answer to all existential needs in Italy – often by establishing a new relationship with food, pleasure and desire – has become pervasive in memoirs, in magazine articles and in a growing number of movies such as adaptations of books like *Under the Tuscan Sun* and *Eat, Pray, Love,* as well as original scripts like *A Month by the Lake, Letters to Juliet, A Good Year* and *When in Rome,* in which the authors decided to invent a new fountain, as Rome did not have enough . . .

We often find ourselves in the realm of the pastoral fantasy: far away and acceptably foreign, Italy is at times imagined as a backward but charming place where there is no room for the hustle and bustle of modern efficiency; where productivity is not a priority and life is different, sweeter. Visitors expect to get back in touch with nature and with themselves while rediscovering food as enjoyment and partaking, rather than as a source of anxiety and the cause of extra pounds. In this kind of narrative, Italians seem to play the cultural role attributed to the 'noble savage' in eighteenth-century European culture, defined by qualities such as 'health, frugality, liberty, and vigour of body and mind: the love of virtue, the fear of the gods, a natural goodness toward our neighbours, attachment to our friends, fidelity to all the world, moderation in prosperity, fortitude in adversity, courage always bold to speak the truth, and abhorrence of flattery', in the words of the French writer Fénelon.[4] However, as the cultural critic Edward Said emphasized in his famous discussion of Western colonial perceptions of Eastern cultures, the projection of such qualities on a different, exotic population is often wrought with ambivalence: it is easy to detect on one hand the envy for a natural state beyond the modern individual's reach, on the other a pervasive sense of superiority, as transpires for instance from this passage in Mayes's book.

> How Italian will we ever be? Not very, I'm afraid. Too pale. Too unable to gesture as a natural accompaniment to talking . . . We never will master the art of everyone talking at once . . . After a soccer game, we'll never gun through the streets blowing the horn or drive a scooter around and around in circles in the piazza. Politics always will passeth understanding.[5]

Tomatoes, parsley and garlic are among the most popular ingredients that are widely identified as symbols of the Mediterranean diet.

## The Mediterranean Connection

Italian food is not only considered restorative for the soul, but good for you. So much so that widespread appreciation for the benefits of the Mediterranean diet has turned into a mantra.[6] For centuries, populations around the Mediterranean, including Italy, found themselves fighting against food scarcity, wars, invasions and an environment that was often not very favourable to agriculture. With limited access to meat, dairy and fats, they developed eating habits that hinged on grains, pulses and vegetables that varied depending on their location, their cultural background and their sociopolitical situation.[7] Only after the 'economic miracle' that swept the country starting in the late 1950s were most of the Italian population – including the less fortunate – finally able to afford a more diverse and abundant diet, even though that often implied severing ties to traditional ways of life and their culinary habits. As we will see, new packaging and conservation techniques, industrial mass production and more sophisticated systems of transportation and distribution brought profound changes in the way Italians ate and thought of food. As these epochal changes were affecting diet in Italy and elsewhere in southern Europe, the rest of the world seemed to realize that the practices adopted by Mediterranean people to fight hunger actually constituted a healthy eating model. Immediately following the Second World War, the

American epidemiologist Leland Allbaugh, sponsored by the Rockefeller Foundation, conducted in-depth fieldwork on the diet of people on the island of Crete to assess the conflict's impact on local food security. However, the correlation between what people around the Mediterranean ate and their health – despite their poverty – became clear only later, thanks to the work of Ancel Keys. Having spent time in Naples in the early 1950s, he noticed that locals, despite their poverty, showed very low rates of heart disease and relatively long life expectancies, a finding confirmed by further research conducted in seven different countries. Another study, commissioned in the 1960s by the European Atomic Energy Commission (Euratom), emphasized the correlation between dietary patterns and lower incidence of heart disease. It was not until the 1980s that the American and northern European public became aware of these findings, when Ancel Keys and his colleagues published the results of their seven-country survey work. Later, in 1993, after the u.s. Department of Agriculture issued the Food Guide Pyramid as a visual representation of dietary recommendations for Americans, a Mediterranean Diet Pyramid was presented at a conference organized in Boston at the Harvard School of Public Health by the World Health Organization together with the Oldways Preservation & Exchange Trust, an organization connected with the olive oil and wine industries, among others.[8] The media fell in love with the Mediterranean diet, which not only promoted healthy and palatable food, but also supposedly facilitated weight loss, especially if paired with a more active lifestyle.

Beyond the health aspects, it is necessary to look at the Mediterranean diet as a cultural artefact that heavily influences the attitude of many foreigners, including Americans, towards the food of southern Europe, namely Italy. What is the Mediterranean diet after all? The media representation is mixed; it is unclear whether the diet is considered as a cultural and historical construction, as a selection of specific foods or, more scientifically, as a nutrient profile.[9] The three elements all appear in magazines and popular literature, but when the focus is on nutrients and food selections, little space is given to the deep connections between a specific nutritional pattern and the society that created it as a part of its culture.

Defining the Mediterranean diet has become even more complicated after the 2010 unesco decision that placed the Mediterranean diet on the 'List of the Intangible Cultural Heritage of Humanity', following a proposal from Morocco, Italy, Spain and Greece. Despite the acknowledged need to consider 'the millenary qualities and values of an important heritage, transmitted from generation to generation', the document hints that the Mediterranean diet is, in fact, an evolving food tradition. For instance, it points out how 'new ways of transmitting expertise and knowledge as well as of meaning are added to the informal and traditional modes of transmission (participation and imitation within the family, oral communication in the markets, etc.)'.[10] So the declaration recognizes the dynamic element of the uninterrupted process of recreation of a lived experience and the inherent intercultural dialogue that establishes a Mediterranean cultural space.

The document offers no specification as to who is part of the diverse communities of the area: only locals, born and raised, or also immigrants? The question is not an idle one, since large sections of the population in the European countries on the Mediterranean shores are exhibiting growing unease towards what is often perceived as the assault of hordes from southern parts of the world. The presence of Morocco – the country of origin of a great number of immigrants in southern Europe – among the signatories of the UNESCO document suggests that the spirit of the declaration is inclusive and aimed at intercultural dialogue and social integration. However, in most countries that backed the initiative, immigration issues are often framed by conservative parties, focusing on the perceived threat to the local traditional way of life in terms of customs, culture, religion and more material aspects that range from clothing to food. Food-related cultural heritage is considered too weak to survive by itself, besieged by globalizing forces. In this specific case, the equivalence between the constraints of globalization and dietary models based on fast foods, fat- and sugar-rich diets and mass-produced goods is quite immediate.

At any rate, it is not easy to pin down what the Mediterranean diet is in terms of cultural traditions, dishes or even sheer nutrients, since it varies in time and space. A growing attention to food, however, suggests a change of focus from diet to cuisine, which is particularly alluring to those readers who are always looking for authenticity and prone to adopt foreign fare as a sign of distinction. In fact, in many areas around the world – and not only in developing countries – access to affordable, healthy food is a serious issue: not everybody has the financial and cultural means to include the ingredients and dishes of the Mediterranean in their diets. Furthermore, limited availability can be a problem, as anybody who has tried to cook Italian dishes abroad knows well. Tasty

Broad (fava) beans, cultivated in Italy since Roman times,
are among the ingredients of *vignarola* pasta.

tomatoes, fresh herbs and specific produce like Romanesco zucchini and
cauliflower are not easy to find, and can also be quite expensive. As a
Roman, I have struggled to find simple ingredients like tender artichokes
and broad (fava) beans for *vignarola*, a typical spring pasta dish that calls
for fresh peas, artichokes and broad beans, very common and cheap at
that time of the year in the countryside around Rome. Furthermore,
the mystique that surrounds certain products becomes at times dispro-
portionate, allowing for more or less intentional miscommunications
and for the spread of counterfeits. The case of extra-virgin olive oil
provides a perfect example. Indicated in many quarters of the culinary
world/community as a panacea for several ailments, the product is often
described as completely natural, hiding all technology involved in its
manufacturing. The frequent and widespread frauds involving extra-
virgin olive oil have shown how consumers can be duped into buying
foods that do not deliver what they promise.[11] The scientific theories
about the Mediterranean diet only became popular in Italy in the 1970s,
first among nutritionists, and later in the media. The very expression
became current in the common language only in the late 1980s, when
a variety of diets were gaining traction due to growing concerns about
body image and weight loss.

## THE NEW APPRECIATION FOR THE OLD

Italians seem happy to play along with the apparently harmless myths and stereotypes about their food, partly out of sincere pride and attachment to their culinary customs, partly as a way to bask in the whole globe's admiration for this particular aspect of their heritage and partly as good business. These themes appear, for instance, in a Parmigiano Reggiano advertisement that ran in the *New Yorker* in the summer of 2011:

### *Parmigiano Reggiano: Always Naturally Handmade*

Parmigiano Reggiano is a collaboration between Italian master craftsmen and Mother Nature. The air, the soil, the temperature, the humidity have as much of a hand in what makes every morsel of Parmigiano Reggiano a delight to the senses as to the centuries-old production methods used to create it. Aged for 24 months or more (the longest of any cheese) it has a slightly crystalline texture that melts on the tongue into buttery and fruity notes. It is handmade by people with a passion for their craft and enjoyed by people with a passion for the very best man and nature can bring to the table.[12]

*Casu marzu* cheese from Sardinia.

Besides the European Union mark for the Protected Denomination of Origin products that will be discussed in chapter Eight, the advertisment carried the logos of the Italian Ministry of Agriculture and Forestry (Ministero delle Politiche Agricole Alimentari e Forestali) and Buonitalia, the trade institution for food promotion whose motto is 'The Real Taste of Italy'. The entire message is built around the oxymoron of a food 'naturally made', which points to its wholesomeness and its connection with the natural environment where the cheese is produced, and at the same time to the skills involved in its manufacturing. The whole idea highlights the closeness of nature and culture, and portrays quality as the result of a positive interaction between them. The other elements that emerge from the advertisement are the passion and investment Italian producers put into the food they make, and a laid-back approach to time. The period it takes to age the cheese to perfection is just a prolongation of the centuries-old traditions, and their impact is visible in the final results. Time is slower in Italy, providing consumers all over the world with the perfect antidote to the fast lifestyle that many in post-industrial societies both resent and embrace.

Part of Italian food's recent success is due to the increasing importance of buzzwords such as 'authenticity', 'tradition', 'typical', 'local' and 'artisanal' in the culinary world, popular culture and the media. Against the background of fears and anxieties about the provenance and safety of what we eat, these expressions reveal the desire for products whose origin is not only clear and recognizable, but also connected to specific people, their skills and their lives. Although industrial and mass-produced food is affordable, convenient and accessible, growing segments of high-end consumers are ready to pay premium prices for items they perceive to be of higher quality and thus more enjoyable. Many of these delicacies are available in limited quantities, due to the rarity of their ingredients, the length of the production process and the small numbers of artisans involved. Marketers have become aware of this trend, informing food lovers about the personal stories of those who manufacture their purchases, the traditions on which they base their activity and their dedication to excellence. In many ways, Italian products are very well placed to satisfy these kinds of demands. Many specialities now labelled as 'typical' and 'authentic' have survived (albeit barely) the industrialization of the food system that started much earlier and had a much longer history in other parts of the world. Specialities like *colatura di alici*, the sauce obtained by filtering the liquid produced by the fermentation of anchovies and salt, and *casu marzu*, the Sardinian sheep cheese softened by the digestive action of maggots, which breaks down the cheese's fats, are alive and well, their sales thriving due to the renewed interest in traditional foods. Since much of the Italian population was rural, traditions connected with local productions were maintained until the late 1950s, when Italians moved en masse from the countryside to the cities, and from the south to the centre and north. Entire villages were abandoned, and agricultural activities were often identified with poverty and perceived as backward. The post-war generations wanted to be modern, and they embraced the new industrial products with great passion, partly stimulated by the growing influence of the media, in particular television.

Only recently, as a consequence of the new appreciation for traditional and artisanal products, have the jobs of running a small farm or producing high-end wine become respectable, and at times even glamorous (of course, that is not the case for rural labour engaged in large-scale agriculture for industrial uses, often composed of undocumented immigrants). This does not imply that the fabrication, the flavour or even the looks of these newly cherished items are the same as fifty years ago. Many have evolved over time to respond to different needs and unprecedented opportunities. As we will see in chapter Eight, the definition of food's characteristics has been complicated by the establishment of regulations for the geographical indications referring to wine and food. Parameters and standards of production, while ensuring the quality and the survival of traditions, also have the potential to freeze any further development. Are these foods being saved from extinction and protected from globalization and corporate greed, or rather, are they turned into museum pieces? Who decides what the 'original' or 'authentic' standard of the product is, and what political and economic interests go beyond the negotiations behind it? From the cultural point of view, what does it mean to elevate a traditional food item to a higher status? How does it affect its actual usage, and even accessibility to the communities that produce it in the first place?

As scholar Barbara Kirshenblatt-Gimblett observed, heritage can be considered 'a mode of cultural production in the present that has recourse in the past . . . [it] is a value added industry . . . [it] produces the local for export'.[13] This implies that food traditions are not simply objects or practices already existing out there, just needing to be discovered, uncovered or saved. Instead, they are frequently established in the form we know by our very act of observing and defining them. They may fall under what Eric Hobsbawm defined as an 'invented tradition', as a 'response to novel situations which take the form of reference to old situations, or which establish their own past by quasi-obligatory repetition'.[14] The recent rediscovery and revamping of food traditions can be interpreted as a manifestation of contemporary cosmopolitanism, solidly rooted in the global flows of goods, ideas, practices, capital and people. The revitalization (or even resurrection) of a culinary tradition does not only operate on the past, but also tends to solidify the present, guaranteeing a better future for the communities involved in global tourism and consumption. From an economic point of view, international exposure leads to increased demand for, and pricing of, traditional products that would otherwise become extinct. The international organization Slow Food launched local initiatives called *presidia* to 'sustain quality production at risk of extinction, protect unique regions and ecosystems, recover traditional processing methods, safeguard native breeds and local plant varieties', as their website declares.[15] Operating through social actions, media campaigns and political interventions, Slow Food has demonstrated the effectiveness of this approach. The intense and strongly flavoured black celery from Trevi in Umbria, the *radìc di mont* (wild radicchio) from Friuli Venezia Giulia and the *regina* tomato from Torre Canne in Apulia have acquired national visibility thanks to their induction into the *presidia* system. The production of *lardo* (cured pork fat) from the Tuscan

Vineyards in Piedmont, Italy. Producing high-end wine is considered a respectable, and at times even glamorous, activity.

*Lardo di Colonnata.*

village of Colonnata, traditionally aged in marble vats from the nearby quarries, risked being discontinued in 1996 under the new food safety regulation introduced by the EU. However, the intervention of Slow Food and the public involvement that followed led to changes in the regulation, which now allow for traditional products to maintain practices that would otherwise be forbidden.[16] The financial viability of products, skills and daily practices at the centre of culinary revival and promotions also depends on the willingness of consumers and tourists elsewhere to spend money. Recipes featuring *lardo* are now widely appreciated, and the summer festival in Colonnata, dedicated to delicious pork fat, attracts visitors from all over the world, spurring a wide variety of activities connected with the traditional product.

## BACK TO HISTORY

For the professionals who produce and import Italian food, or for authors and journalists who write about it and need to pitch a good story or a book proposal, it may be hard to maintain a critical distance from the hype and the stereotypes. This is particularly the case if consumers and readers are more than ready to embrace them. Born and raised in Rome, and having worked for many years for the popular Italian food and wine magazine *Gambero Rosso*, I have had many opportunities to witness these dynamics, and over time I have realized that as soon as you scratch the surface, there is quite a lot that deserves to be explored. However, I have grown increasingly wary of the concept of unchanging traditions. When it comes to Italian food, it is necessary to re-inject history into culinary romance to put things in perspective. Where did the food grown, produced and consumed in Italy come from? Has it always been there, or did somebody (but who? and when?) introduce it into the Italian rural and urban landscapes? And have Italian culinary traditions always been so diverse, rich and local? How have they changed over time, and how are they still changing? Which factors have caused or accompanied these developments?

These are some of the questions I address in this book. In doing so, I explore different sources, multiple approaches and various fields of research, including agricultural sciences, environmental studies, biology, nutrition, economics, business, law, marketing, politics, postcolonial studies, gender studies, cultural studies, sociology, anthropology, design, architecture, technology and media and communication, among others. Food finds itself at the core of many social, economic and political issues at the global level, while keeping us close to the most concrete and material aspects of culture. After all, what we eat literally becomes part of us and affects the way we think about ourselves. What and how we produce, purchase, cook, consume and dispose of what we eat has always had an enormous influence on who we are as individuals and as members of communities on all scales.

Food culture has a life and a logic of its own, which cannot be exclusively reduced to external factors. As Alberto Capatti and Massimo Montanari contend in *Italian Cuisine: A Cultural History*, it is important to understand the dynamics behind the development of dishes, techniques and cooking styles, or the changes in the use of ingredients, as self-sustaining processes with their own internal logic.

> The history of food cannot be reduced to extraneous dimensions. It is related more closely to the sciences and technologies of every-day material culture, to the rituals and necessities of ordinary life, and to forms of taste than to anything else.[17]

Following their approach, this book will also look at the history of gastronomy, that is to say the way food has been thought about, talked about and represented through history. We will see how the first examples of food criticism emerged in the Greek cities of Sicily, how medieval and Renaissance authors conceptualized the different kinds of food and their impact on the body, and how a merchant from Romagna, Pellegrino Artusi, established a new language to talk about cooking after the unification of Italy. However, this is not enough to assess the complex history of food in Italy. It is also crucial to look at the cultural aspects of economic issues of production, distribution and consumption. Antiquity scholar Peter Garnsey has acutely pointed out:

> Two questions pose themselves under the heading of food and the economy: first, how far conditions were favourable for the production of food, that is to say, the physical environment, the state of agricultural technology, and the way ownership of and access to land and its resources were distributed among the population; and second, how far market mechanisms and institutions promoted the circulation of food between areas of surplus and areas of deficit.[18]

It is impossible to grasp fully how the economics of Italian food have changed over time without some background information on the peculiar political history of the country, including the long succession of populations that settled down in Italy over the centuries, their organizations and their influence on material culture. Throughout the book we will see how the transformations that took place through the centuries have contributed to the diverse culinary mosaic of Italy, where ingredients, products and customs still play a noticeable role in defining local identities.

Information from the past is not enough to make sense of the present and what readers might see when visiting Italy. When we find ourselves in a foreign place, as much as we think we have the tools to understand it, there are always layers and layers of objects, signs and simple gestures that require interpretation. We do not want to risk going through a different reality, trying to understand it through meanings and expectations that we carry with us from the places we come from, unable to use those that the new reality offers to us. We would end up missing a lot. What's the origin and sense of the dishes we see on a restaurant's menu? Why is the menu formatted as it is, with dishes divided into courses that do not fall under the sequence 'appetizer (or starter)', 'entrée (or main course)' and dessert? Have restaurants always

Riomaggiore, Cinque Terre. The five villages in the Cinque Terre area in
Liguria form one of the most popular tourist destinations.

existed? Have they always been the same or have they changed over
time? Who ate there? And where did people buy food? Have the markets
where we shop been there for a long time, and always in the same form?
Has it always been possible to buy the things we now have access to?

Visitors are often struck by Italy's rural landscape, the sense of peace
and beauty it conveys with its variation from the alpine meadows where
cows graze at ease to the flat fields of the Po plain, the small plots
wrapped around hills and mountain slopes in the Apennines and the

24

stunning fruit orchards of the Mediterranean coast. Every time I visit my grandparents' village on the slope of the Gran Sasso mountain I am moved by the jagged profile of the peak, the patchwork patterns of fields and orchards on the hilly terrain, and even the smell of the grass and trees. It is easy to get lost in a pastoral dream of harmony and traditions, where men and environments have adapted to each other over centuries. We can easily rent a countryside villa, or get a nice room in one of the farms that have turned to *agriturismo* (rural tourism) to make ends meet and take advantage of the city people's renewed interest, without asking ourselves how those structures ended up where they are, looking the way they do. Pastures, trees and canals have plenty to tell those who are patient enough to listen about the lives and the traditions of those who shaped them. These are tales of wealth and poverty, delight and survival, of communities and individuals that have left deep – although often veiled and silent – marks on the food Italians grow, make, sell, eat and even throw away. I hope the stories and the information in this book will increase readers' interest in the varied products and cuisines of Italy, their desire to know them better and their enjoyment when they consume them.

Our voyage through history looks at the events that have shaped food – its production, consumption and perceptions – in Italy, from its prehistoric origin to more recent developments. Each chapter focuses on a specific period and the cultural, political, productive and technical

Artichokes (*carciofi*) play an important role in the culinary tradition of Rome.

*Fusilli alla Vignarola*

For 4 people
3 artichokes
squeeze of lemon
2 tbsp extra-virgin olive oil
1 whole, peeled clove garlic
300 g (10 oz) shelled broad (fava) beans
300 g (10 oz) shelled peas
450 g (1 lb) fusilli
2 tbsp chopped fresh parsley
grated Romano cheese
black pepper, salt

Clean the artichokes by removing the internal fluff, cut them into thin slices and place them in water with some lemon squeezed into it. Sauté them in a pan for about fifteen minutes with the extra-virgin olive oil and the garlic. Add the beans and the shelled peas, 2 tbsp of water, salt and pepper. Cover with a lid and cook until the ingredients become soft but not mushy. Remove the garlic clove. Meanwhile, cook the pasta in salted water till al dente, drain and add it to the pan with the vegetables. When serving, sprinkle with grated Romano cheese and the chopped fresh parsley.

*Bruschetta with Lardo di Colonnata and Prawns*

*This is a creative take on the traditional Roman bruschetta, usually simply seasoned with garlic, salt and olive oil.*

For 4 people
4 prawns
4 slices country bread
4 thin slices *lardo di Colonnata*
extra-virgin olive oil, salt

Quickly blanch the prawns in boiling salted water and peel them. Grill the bread and season it with salt and a drizzle of olive oil. Place a *lardo* slice on each bread slice and place a prawn on top.

factors that have determined the introduction of new crops and dishes, shaped diverse landscapes and established distinctive ways to cook, eat and think about what is cooked and eaten. Finally, the last three chapters will assess the current situation and the impact of globalization on what Italians and the new immigrant population consume.

We will end our journey with the exploration of a crucial aspect of food culture in Italy: *campanilismo*, an expression that refers to the love, pride and attachment that the inhabitants of a certain place – those who find themselves under the shadow of the town bell tower – feel for it. What role do these elements play in the development of local culinary identities? How do they affect the ways Italians think of themselves in relation to what they eat? For centuries, towns and cities have boasted about what's unique to their tables, often originating in the surrounding areas. Other customs have their roots in rural cultures that are inexorably changing and, some say, disappearing. Over the years, after the establishment of regions as administrative structures in the 1970s, Italians started thinking of their eating patterns, ingredients and dishes in terms of regional traditions. I must admit I am emotionally connected with the dishes of my Roman upbringing: *pajata*, tiny knots made of the intestines of suckling veal calves and cooked in a tomato sauce; bruschetta, slices of bread grilled and seasoned with various toppings; the crunchy, deep-fried *carciofi alla giudia* of the Roman Jewish tradition; and pasta *alla Vignarola*, reminding Romans of their connections with the surrounding countryside. Dishes that remind me of my family roots in Abruzzo resonate in a special way, particularly the rough texture of spaghetti *alla chitarra*, made with a wooden contraption that looks like a strange harp, and *crespelle*, a savoury version of crêpes served in broth.

As much as I try, when it comes to food in Italy I always feel I am just scratching the surface, and I believe my suspicion is quite legitimate. However, this is precisely what makes Italian cuisines unique and fascinating: we can rest assured that, as much as we expand our knowledge, we never risk getting bored and that surprises are always around the corner.

*Buon appetito!*

# ONE

## A Land in the Mediterranean

The variety found in Italian food is certainly among the reasons for its international appeal: the mosaic of local traditions, industrial and artisanal products, dishes and ingredients, always allows for new excitement and discoveries. It would be easy to assume that crops like wheat, olives and grapes, widely considered the backbone of Italian cuisine, have always been there. Archaeology and historical investigation seem to indicate differently, suggesting that the expansion of agriculture was the result of a lengthy and complicated series of historical events. In fact, despite its rich and long-lasting culinary traditions, the territory that we call Italy today was relatively late in playing a relevant role in the food culture of the ancient world. To understand how this happened, we need to shift our focus to other areas around the Mediterranean.

### THE ORIGINS

Mediterranean agriculture began in what we now call the Middle East, and more precisely in the area that historians often refer to as the Fertile Crescent, from the plains of the rivers Tigris and Euphrates in today's Iraq and from the western mountains of Iran to southeastern Turkey, Syria, Lebanon and Israel. It is in this region that archaeological researchers place the transition from hunting and gathering to agriculture and shepherding at the end of the last glaciation, from 13,000 to 10,000 years ago.[1] The Fertile Crescent was covered in a wide variety of trees, bushes and several wild grains and pulses, hosting many species of small animals that proved apt for domestication, such as aurochs (the ancestors of cows), sheep, goats, pigs and rabbits. Among the first crops in this area were the predecessors of wheat – emmer (*Triticum dicoccum*) and einkorn

(*T. monococcum*), together with rye, barley and pulses such as peas, lentils, bitter vetch and chickpeas. Plants like olive trees and grapevines were domesticated in a later period, as they required sedentary communities that invested work and time into cultivating their fruit trees.[2]

Gradually, the agricultural techniques and many domesticated crops from the Fertile Crescent spread from East to West, around the Mediterranean and beyond. These features were accompanied by the adoption of specialized tools like axes, hoes, grinding stones, mortars and pestles, as well as clay containers, and the development of larger villages. It is still unclear if indigenous inhabitants imitated what they saw their neighbours do, or the diffusion of agriculture followed an actual movement of populations, as the speed of the dispersal (0.6–1.1 km per year, as some scholars have calculated) would seem to suggest.[3] Probably advancing both along the Danube into central and northern Europe and following the north shores of the Mediterranean, the adoption of agriculture led to the domestication of crops like poppy, spelt and oats. While some scholars argue that Neolithic agriculture reached Italy from the north, the farming of wheat, barley and legumes was already present on the coasts of southern Italy starting from the sixth millennium BCE, and in central Italy in the fifth, suggesting instead a maritime acculturation from Turkey via Greece and the coast of the eastern Adriatic.[4]

The Neolithic populations that occupied the territory correspondent to today's Italy were composed of groups that, although still hunting and foraging, also knew how to farm and herd, focusing especially on areas closer to the villages. The limited technical achievement forced them to practise agriculture in temporary clearings, often obtained by burning vegetation and taking advantage of the fertilizing effect of the ashes.[5] These forms of cultivation could only be productive on virgin terrains and for a brief period, driving the farmers to move constantly. This initiated the long and still ongoing social and cultural interaction between humans and their environment that has shaped the landscape of Italy.[6] Raising sheep, goats, cattle and pigs – probably domesticated from wild boars – became important activities.[7] These basic forms of agriculture were shared by new waves of populations, often referred to as Indo-Europeans, semi-sedentary groups that originally inhabited the vast space between Central Asia and Eastern Europe, growing crops such as barley and wheat and raising livestock. Presumably including the ancestors of the Mycenaeans in Greece and the Hittites in Anatolia, Indo-European tribes moved across Europe and the Mediterranean from the 24th century BCE, after domesticating the horse and inventing the two-wheeled chariot.[8]

In the north of the Italian peninsula and in the Po river plain, settlers founded villages that archaeologists suppose were suddenly abandoned in the twelfth century. These hamlets are known as *terramare*, from the dark 'fat earth' (*terra marna*, in the local dialect) found in mounds that local farmers used to fertilize their fields until the nineteenth century CE. This culture, although still largely based on hunting, practised bronze technology, herding and agriculture (mostly cereals), which often required heavy deforestation of the surrounding territory.[9] Many settlements indicate the use of various technologies for the capture of natural streams and the management of water for irrigation by wells, artificial ditches and channels.[10]

The connection between the *terramare* settlers and the new waves of migrant populations of Indo-European origin is not clear. The Indo-Europeans penetrated into Italy absorbing – and at times displacing – the previous inhabitants. The newcomers spoke similar languages and shared common cultural traits, including herding techniques and a limited agriculture. Their tribes settled sparsely in the peninsula, such as the Veneti in northeastern Italy, the Osco-Umbrians in central and southern Italy, the Picens on the coasts of the present-day region of Marche, the Latins in Latium and the Iapygians in today's Apulia.[11] One of these groups, the Ausonians, settled first in Campania and then made their way to Calabria and Sicily, mixing with pre-existing populations and creating an original, egalitarian culture which – judging from the archaeological remnants – appears to have been based on the cultivation of barley, animal shepherding, hunting and the foraging of local varieties of plants, including wild grapes.[12] The Greek colonizers, who penetrated the coasts of southern Italy from the eighth century BCE, would refer to them with the general name of *Italioi*, an expression that might derive from the word *italòs*, young calf.

Archaeologists have found clear indications that by 1500 BCE many areas, especially Sardinia and Sicily, maintained steady contacts with the Greek peninsula and the eastern shores of the Mediterranean.[13] It is unclear whether connections with the eastern Mediterranean influenced the development of the Nuragic civilization, taking its name from the *nuraghi*, the monumental conical stone towers built in Sardinia between 1800 and 900 BCE. These constructions, which appear to have had security functions, also showed a family's wealth and were meant for domestic use, as traces of husbandry as well as grain growing and processing suggest.[14]

Pottery and bronze weapons indicate that Italy was part of the various maritime long-distance networks, relying on village chiefs eager to bolster their power by displaying luxurious, exotic goods. At the time, the most advanced forms of exchange, such as trade, tributes, diplomatic gifts and even religious offerings, relied on water transportation, which was simpler and cheaper than moving goods overland.[15] Many new agricultural techniques and crops that, over time, were adopted in Italy probably arrived as part of these exchanges and of the population movements that at times followed them. In fact, around the twelfth century BCE, Italy was affected by a new wave of migratory peoples collectively known under the name of the 'Peoples of the Sea', some of whom had already spread in the eastern Mediterranean, threatening Egypt and destroying the Hittite and Mycenaean cultures. In Egyptian texts they are indicated as Trsh (maybe the Tyrrhenoi or Tyrsenoi mentioned by the Greeks), Shrdn (Sardinians) and Shkrsh (Shkelesh or Sikels, one of the populations attested in Sicily by Greek sources).[16]

## THE ETRUSCANS

What happened in the four centuries that followed the movements of the Peoples of the Sea is not entirely clear, but Italy established its position as the fulcrum of Mediterranean trade, as suggested by the interactions from the tenth to the third centuries BCE between Etruscans, Phoenicians and Greeks, who vied for control of the maritime commercial routes. They all enjoyed a strong position due to 'the intense activity of the cities, techniques of navigation and metal-working, the practice of trading and the power of the markets', as historian Fernand Braudel aptly put it.[17] In different ways and following distinct patterns, these colonizers from advanced societies slowly grafted themselves onto a landscape that had already been occupied and transformed by wave after wave of migrations, each bringing new elements to the material and culinary cultures of the area. Although it is hard to tell who exactly introduced what in terms of crops, ingredients, agricultural techniques, culinary traditions and social customs surrounding food, it is undeniable that the settlements of these populations and their interactions laid the basis for all future developments. From antiquity, Italy proved to be not a monolithic block, but a fragmented territory that gave birth to a mosaic of civilizations ferociously attached to their own customs, including culinary ones. Italy's *campanilismo* and the persistence of its local traditions seem to echo this primordial diversity.

The Etruscans settled in the territory of today's southern Tuscany and northern Latium, with Caere and Tarquinia their oldest town, not far from the sea. For many years archaeologists could not interpret their language, written in a script derived from the Phoenician alphabet (the base for the modern Western alphabet). Despite many material traces of their presence (tombs, constructions and such), the Etruscans remained shrouded in mystery until linguists succeeded in deciphering inscriptions and documents, noticing the similarities to a language that, as an inscription shows, was used in the Aegean island of Lemnos.[18] Scholars found similarities with the Lydian language, spoken in the western areas of present-day Turkey.[19] Mitochondrial DNA analysis of Etruscan bones confirms traces of genes also found among the elites of the eastern Mediterranean. A similar analysis of the contemporary inhabitants of the town of Murlo, near Siena, has shown analogous results.[20] Genetic similarities of gene pools between Tuscan bovines and Near Eastern ones have also been confirmed.[21] Some researchers suggest that the Etruscans could be identified with the Trsh, one of the Peoples of the Sea that the Egyptian pharaoh Ramses III chased out of his territory in the twelfth century and that might have then settled in Italy, coinciding with the Tyrsenoi or Tyrrhenoi, mentioned in the Greek texts. However, the first signs of the brilliant Etruscan civilization date only from the late eighth century, giving credibility to another theory that argues for its local origins, or at least the assimilation of immigrants from the Near East by a pre-existing Indo-European population known as Villanovans.[22] The arrival of the newcomers would have marked the transition from a culture that cremated its dead to one whose elites buried them in monumental tombs that revealed much about daily life, banquets and food customs. This culture exhibits several Middle Eastern elements, such as the use of the Phoenician alphabet, the reading of the livers of sacrificed animals to interpret the future, the dining couch and certain banqueting habits, the use of filigree in gold jewellery and the overall love of luxury.[23]

Whatever their origin, the Etruscans were highly permeable to the influences that the Phoenicians were introducing into the western Mediterranean. They also embraced elements from Greece, which had become a relevant cultural powerhouse from the eighth century onwards, and relayed them – in their unique interpretation – to the neighbouring populations. The increase of cereal varieties, and the extension of cultivated land around growing towns such as Veio, Tarquinia and Volterra, show that the productive colonization of the Etruscan territory intensified in the seventh century BCE. Following the increase of the population and the consequential agricultural surplus, large tracts of land fell under the control of a small elite that employed farmers whose lives were not so different from those of the serfs.[24] By the sixth century the Etruscans had turned into a true sea and land power, expanding their territory to most of Tuscany and the Apennine mountains, and imposing their authority over an area extending from Campania to the Po river plain, where traces of commerce in metals, slaves and salt with the Celts settled beyond the Alps are evident.[25]

The Etruscan urban elites, apparently attached to the privileges that came with the control over political life and land use, never coalesced into a unified state, but rather operated within a loose federation that guaranteed local independence. Like the Greeks, the Etruscans introduced the 'fallow' system: in order to increase yields and be protected from spontaneous vegetation, after the harvest fields were left uncultivated for a season or more and often open to pasture, which enriched them with manure. This technique, extremely productive compared to the slash-and-burn method used by the other Italic populations, was based on the division of the cultivated lands into defined fields, implying the existence of forms of private ownership that reflected complex social structures. Productivity also increased due to the digging of wells, which in some cases distributed water through a system of artificial tunnels that took advantage of springs and brooks.

Perhaps through jealousy over the prosperity of their territory, the Etruscans were considered decadent and excessive in their consumption habits by neighbouring populations. In the first century BCE, the Sicilian Greek historian Diodorus Siculus described them as lovers of luxury, eating twice a day around tables decorated with silver vessels. According to this author, they had lost their ancestors' prowess in the face of enemies because of their attachment to banquets and feasts.[26] The Latin poet Catullus makes reference to the *obesus Etruscus* and Virgil to the *pinguis Tyrrhenus*, both suggesting a 'fat Etruscan'.[27] The first-known representation of an Etruscan banquet appears on a seventh-century BCE vase found in Montescudaio, where a man sits on a throne behind a round table with three legs, a female attendant standing next to him.[28] Banquet scenes in Etruscan tombs became frequent during the sixth century BCE,

A banquet scene from the Tomb of the Leopards at the
Etruscan necropolis of Tarquinia, in Lazium.

with participants depicted eating and drinking while lying on their sides, either alone or in couples, revealing the influence of Greek culture.[29] Unlike in Greece, however, women were often represented as participating in the banquet, at times wrapped in a blanket with their spouses.[30] Women were in charge of cooking and in aristocratic families, where servants prepared food, women overlooked the organization of meals and banquets.[31]

Based on texts, archaeological findings and pictorial representations, we can gather information about what the Etruscans produced, consumed and traded.[32] However, as is often the case, we lack extensive information about the life and food habits of the lower classes. Barley, together with wheat, *farro* (*Triticum monococcum*), spelt (*T. spelta*) and millet constituted the main staple, usually ground into a rough flour that was cooked as gruel or made into flat breads prepared on hot stones or in the oven, which the Romans would later adopt and call *tracta*. Etruscans also consumed great quantities of vegetables and pulses such as peas, chickpeas, lentils and fava beans, especially in soups. Pork and chicken meat was available, but not often consumed outside festive meals, and the less affluent could rarely afford them. Sheep and cattle were more useful alive, and beef was almost exclusively consumed by the elites. The Etruscans also ate chestnuts, hazelnuts, figs, olives and grapes, and already used medicinal plants that are still widely appreciated in Italy, such as gentian and valerian.[33]

During the sixth century BCE, the Etruscans showed interest in plugging into the trade routes of the Mediterranean, exporting their goods to the western Mediterranean. One of their oldest colonies was Capua, not far from the Greek town of Cumae, in the area of Naples. Rome, positioned around a small island, the Isola Tiberina, on the Tiber, might have developed originally as a passage point for commerce between the southern colony of Capua and the towns in the main Etruscan territory further north. This mercantile expansion caused friction with the other two merchant populations whose ships were riding the sea – the Phoenicians and the Greeks.[34]

## THE PHOENICIANS

The first traces of the Phoenicians in Italy are fragments of inscriptions found in Sardinia, dating from the beginning of the ninth century BCE, which suggest the possibility of previous visits and contacts that might have taken place right after the upheavals connected to the Peoples of the Sea.[35] The Phoenicians developed their culture in towns along a thin strip on the coast of present-day Lebanon. These urban centres included Byblos, Tyre and Sidon, which reached full expansion between the tenth and the seventh centuries BCE. The geographical traits of their territory, with little space available for agriculture, facilitated the development of artisanal skills specializing in glass, jewels and the famed purple fabrics, dyed with a substance extracted from the shells of the marine snails *Murex brandaris* or *M. trunculus*. As seafarers and merchants seeking profitable opportunities and raw materials in new markets, the Phoenicians spread these luxury objects through commercial networks that spanned the Mediterranean. The Phoenicians were not interested in controlling faraway territories, but rather in creating trading bases all along the coasts of the Mediterranean and beyond the Gibraltar Strait, on the Atlantic coast of Spain.

Although they might have been sporadically present from the eleventh century BCE, it is only in the eighth century that the Phoenicians established stable posts in Sardinia, like Nora, Sulci, Bithia and Cagliari, as well as in northwestern Sicily, such as Palermo, Lilybaeum (Marsala) and Motya (near Trapani). These bases were located along the important and fast route that crossed the Mediterranean from east to west and connected the Phoenician towns of origin with Spain, passing by Crete, Cyprus and Malta. Archaeological remains indicate that the traders received food from the hinterland of their posts in exchange for luxury goods coming from all over the Mediterranean, and that they probably adopted local cooking techniques and cooking vessels.[36] Controlling the commerce with North Africa and Spain, the Phoenician trading post of Carthage, in present-day Tunisia, became a settled colony. Later on, when the Assyrians conquered the Phoenician motherland in the seventh century BCE, Carthage grew into an independent sea power with its own trade networks that introduced spices from the Red Sea and, ultimately, the Indian Ocean, to the Mediterranean.[37] As previously mentioned, this new kind of colonization inevitably led to wars with the Greek colonies in southern Italy and the Etruscans.[38] Later on, Carthage would fight against Rome for the control of Sicily and its wheat crops, giving rise to a series of wars that culminated in the destruction of the North African city.

The agricultural techniques developed by the Carthaginians were adopted by the conquering Romans, as indicated in the translation of the agronomist Mago's manual into Greek first and Latin later and the frequent references to it in Roman works.[39] Judging from the remaining fragments of Mago, whom the Roman author Columella calls the 'father of agriculture', Carthage developed methods for oxen breeding as well as vine planting and wine making, with products such as *passum* wine, which was made with grapes dried in the sun.[40] Pliny the Elder marvelled at the capacity of Carthaginian agriculturalists in the oasis of Tecape, in present-day Lybia, to grow all sorts of crops on the same land, despite the fact that water was distributed only at specific times of the day:

> Here, beneath enormous palms, grow olive trees, beneath the olive trees the fig trees, beneath the fig trees, again, the pomegranate, beneath the pomegranate the vine, and beneath the vine first wheat, then leguminous plants, and later on garden herbs are sown, all in the same year, and all growing beneath another plant's shade.[41]

This multi-layered agricultural method is still practised in the Tunisian oases, with irrigation taking place at night to limit water evaporation. The Phoenicians might have brought these fruit trees, and the methods to

Salt evaporation in Mothia, a tradition that was plausibly introduced to western Sicily by the Phoenicians.

grow them, to their trading posts, adapting to the new habitats.[42] It is possible that the shallot onion derived its name from the Phoenician town of Ascalon.

We do not have much information about the daily diet of the Phoenicians or their food customs, but we do know about religious feasts (*mrzh*) during which local clans and merchant associations consumed drinks and made animal sacrifices to a specific god, maybe as a form of remembering the dead.[43] The dietary relevance of the grains is suggested by the presence of small terracotta ovens in private homes. In textual references we read about *puls punica*, boiled cereals or flour with eggs, cheese and honey.[44] The Phoenicians also disseminated techniques to preserve fish. The most advanced factories were located on the coast of Spain, where they launched the production of what the Greeks would call *gáros* and the Romans *garum*: a sauce made by fermenting small fish of little commercial value with salt.[45]

Salt production was an important activity, and saltpans are still found near former Phoenician and Carthaginian colonies in Sicily and Sardinia. The excavations of whale vertebrae from digs in the Phoenician colony of Motya in western Sicily point to the local use of whales, probably as food and oil.[46] The presence of tuna images on coins from Carthaginian colonies suggests the relevance of this fishing activity. It is

Etching of *tonnara* (tuna fishing) in Sicily in the 18th century.

also possible that the Phoenicians introduced or refined methods of catching fish – and tuna in particular – in the western Mediterranean, including harpooning. This requires the cooperation of numerous fishing boats, as well as systems of huge nets (similar to those now called *tonnare*) to trap and move schools of migrating tuna towards closed net chambers. To this day, fishermen in Sicily and Calabria still use a similar technique, called *mattanza*, or 'slaughtering', to capture and kill tuna in great numbers, a disappearing practice that has been harshly criticized both for its perceived cruelty and for its impact on the sustainability of tuna fisheries.[47]

## THE GREEKS

Enjoy organizing your work at the right time,
So that your barns fill up with seasonal goods.
It is thanks to work that men are rich in flocks and wealthy
And when they work they are dearer to the Immortals.
Work is not a disgrace, but shameful is idleness instead:
If you work, the idle will soon grow envious, seeing you get rich,
And wealth is accompanied by honour and glory . . .
As soon as the time for ploughing arrives for the mortals,
Hurry up, you and your slaves alike,
And in the ploughing season plough the soil, wet and dry.
Hasten early in the morning, so that your fields may be full.

Plough in the spring; fallow ploughed up anew in the summer
   will not deceive you.
Sow fallow land when the soil is still light:
Newly ploughed soil keeps off curses and sooths of children . . .
But at that time let me have the shade of a rock and wine
   of Biblis,
A cake made of barley and milk, the milk of goats that have
   gone dry,
The flesh of an heifer fed in the woods that has not calved yet
And the flesh of first-born kids; then also let me drink fiery-
   looking wine,
Sitting in the shade, when my heart is satisfied with food,
Turning my face against the hard-blowing Zephyr wind;
From an ever-flowing and untroubled spring
Pour three parts of water, and add a fourth part of wine . . .
When Orion and Sirius are in the middle of the sky,
And rosy-fingered Dawn sees the middle of September,
Then harvest all the grapes, Perses, and bring them home.
Leave them under the sun ten days and ten nights,
Then leave them in the shade for five, and on the sixth day
   draw off into vessels
The gifts of the ever-rejoicing Dionysus.[48]

This is what the life of farmers in ancient Greece was like, at least according to the poet Hesiod. The author wrote the poem *Works and Days*, from which the extract above is taken, around the seventh century BCE to invite his brother Perses to take care of the land so that it may bear fruit. Perses later seized part of the properties their father had bequeathed to the poet, with the help of corrupt judges. Unlike Homer, who related the magnanimous deeds of heroes and warriors, Hesiod focused on the daily life of those who worked the fields and often suffered injustice by the hand of those who were amassing vast estates to become landed aristocracy. Besides agricultural tips, the poet gave his brother advice on navigation and trade, recommending that he only load the ships with a small part of his goods, leaving most of his wealth on the land. Scarcity and endemic undernourishment were a daily reality, made worse by the occasional food shortages and, in the worst case, by famines.[49] This harsh world of social injustice, back-breaking work, farming, wine-making and navigation constitutes the background of a migration that led to the establishment of Greek colonies in the western Mediterranean, around the Black Sea, and in southern Italy.

The Greeks, both in the motherland and in the Italian colonies, were deeply aware of the cultural divide that set them apart from their neighbouring populations, the so-called *barbaroi*, or barbarians. Based on perceived distance in space and social and political customs, as well as morality, Greeks regarded urban dwellers as more civilized than farmers, who in turn were considered better than nomads.[50] This feeling of superiority penetrated all aspects of social life, including food customs. Wheat, wine and oil, closely connected with sedentary agriculture and its transformative power over the natural landscape, were identified as tangible symbols of civilization. However, this food triad was often more important as an ideological construct than in terms of actual availability. In fact, it was not wheat (in the form of bread or gruel) but barley (consumed as cooked biscuit or as gruel), rye, oats and lentils that ensured the survival of the common people. These staples constituted a central category of food known as *sîtos*, while everything else, considered as mere additions, fell under the category of *ópson*, which included vegetables, eggs, cheese, meat and fish, both fresh and cured (salted, dried or smoked). Despite the supposed simplicity of these accompaniments, Greeks boasted about what they could afford and the delicacies they found in the markets, reflecting the expansion of a monetary economy,

Fresh fish, one of the favourite dishes of the Greeks; red–figure platter, c. 350–325 BCE.

artisanal businesses and wide commercial networks. As game meat and hunting were synonymous with rustic – if not semi-nomadic – life, often attributed to the barbarians, meat consumption was quite limited and connected with religious sacrifices.[51] A hired cook, the *mágeiros*, often butchered large animals. He would also take care of selling the meat, in case it was more than the sacrificing household could consume. In the case of smaller animals or domestic sacrifices, any member of the household could perform the necessary ritual.[52]

The barbarians were commonly accused of consuming food without the refinement and controlled conviviality that distinguished Greek customs – at times even raw. Greek meals, especially the public banquets, played a relevant role in political life by gathering all the free males around food. The private meals of the upper classes were meant to reinforce the social and cultural bonds among adult males, including those who did not reciprocate, the *parásitoi* ('those who feed beside', that is to say parasites).[53] Private banquets were quite elaborate affairs that took place in a dedicated space in the house, called *andrón*, 'the place of the men'. There, the participants ate while reclining on couches placed around the walls. When there were numerous guests, or when the hosts wanted to impress, the *mágeiros* could work with an attendant (*opsopoiós*) and a 'table maker', the *trapezopoiós*, who took care of setting tables and other minor tasks.[54] In this case, food – presented on a first set of tables that was removed once the food was consumed – was abundant and varied, and often included meat and fish. The meal was preceded by tables with appetizers (*propómata*) and followed by tables with fruit and nuts (*tragémata*).

None of these social events included respectable women, who consumed their meals before the men. This remained the case even when sacrifices were involved. On the other hand, slave women, dancers and prostitutes were admitted as a form of entertainment. Lavish meals were often followed by a simple drinking party (*pótos*) or by a more elaborate drinking ceremony called *sympósion* (literally, drinking together). Dinner tables were removed, a religious libation accompanied a prayer addressing the gods, and then wine was mixed with water in proportions determined by the host.[55] Of course not all meals were elaborate or held social relevance, and not everybody could afford them. It is likely that Greeks of lesser status would sit to eat rather than recline, a custom that was still considered the norm in the times of Homer, also for heroes. Greeks usually ate breakfast or *akrátisma*, typically consisting of bread dipped in wine (the word itself comes from *ákratos*, meaning 'unmixed, without water'), a midday meal called *áriston* (a word that in Homer still meant 'breakfast', maybe indicating a different distribution of the meals over the day) and an evening meal, the *deîpnon*, frequently the largest meal of the day.

The habits, beliefs and values expressed through food preparation and consumption were part of the social structure and the material culture that the Greeks carried to the colonies they founded all over southern Italy and in eastern Sicily. The origins of these migrations lie in the demographic dynamics and the geography of the motherland, whose territory is mostly composed of hills and mountains. Starting from the eighth century BCE, the Greek population grew fast and steadily, increasing the pressure over the limited arable land and causing unrest among farmers, who often lived under the control of large landowners.[56] To deal with this problem, the city leaders would send several young males, potentially the most troublesome part of the rural population, to establish a colony elsewhere. They would move under the leadership of a founder, the *oikistes*, who maintained a connection with the home city. The travellers were provided with ships, food for the journey and seeds to start agriculture wherever they decided to land. The oracle that spoke on behalf of the god Apollo at the temple of Delphi helped to determine the destinations of the colonists, as priests in that locality received abundant information from the numerous pilgrims that visited the oracle from all over the Mediterranean.[57]

Pithecusae was the first Greek colony, founded around 770 BCE on the island of Ischia, a short distance from present-day Naples, and the most distant point of the migration. This was followed by a series of cities that over time grew into true Mediterranean powers and centres of refined culture, such as Cumae, Tarentum in Apulia and Sybaris and Crotone in Calabria, as well as Syracuse and Akragas (today's Agrigento) in Sicily. While Pythagoras elaborated his vegetarian theories in Crotone, Tarentum was celebrated for a special variety of sheep that gave high-quality wool and for its abundant wheat crops, part of which could be exported. Sybaris was so rich that the banquets and the excesses of its luxury-loving inhabitants became infamous all over the Mediterranean.[58]

Despite the differences in material culture and the literary sources that deny any miscegenation, it appears from archaeological traces that the Greeks did intermarry with locals and adopt some local customs, such as funerary rites and a more egalitarian social structure, at least at the beginning of the colonization. At the same time, the populations of the

Youth using a wine
jug to draw wine from
a *crater* in order to
fill a shallow cup
(in his left hand) at
a banquet or sympo-
sium. Tondo of an
Attic red-figure cup,
*c.* 490–480 BCE.

interior tended to come together in larger centres and organize themselves, probably to better negotiate with the newcomers. Only later on, when the colonies developed to economic levels that had no rivals in the western Mediterranean, did the Greeks from Italy again embrace cultural forms from the motherland, reaffirming their ethnic identity.[59] The colonists founded their towns in easily defendable places, such as the top of a hill, and according to the availability of arable land in the surround-ing areas. The irregularity in the terrain, legal disputes and heritage customs contributed to an extreme fragmentation of the cultivated plots, surrounded by low walls and ditches, with small constructions. Historian Emilio Sereni defined this model, still visible in today's landscape, as the 'Mediterranean garden': 'closed irregular pieces of land, dominated by the necessity of protecting the trees and shrubs from grazing animals, and their fruits from rural pilferage'.[60]

The Greeks played an important role in the introduction of olives, grapes, capers, asparagus, cabbage, fennel, garlic, onions, oregano, basil and other vegetables originally from the eastern Mediterranean in many areas of southern Italy, and surely spread advanced growing techniques, which put them at an advantage compared to the surrounding populations. For instance, because of high temperatures and the scarcity of precipi-tation during the growing season, the Greeks cultivated vines on dry stakes or low trees close to the ground. Together with specific products, the colonists carried with them culinary principles and cultural concepts, such as the ideological relevance of grains, olive oil and wine, the consumption of which identified the civilized Greek in contrast to the barbarian. As the colonies grew, they attracted merchants and artisans who organized the trade of valuable crops, especially wine and olive oil, not only back to the motherland, but also all along the shores of the Mediterranean.[61] Although the Italian colonies embraced the food culture of the mainland, a few specificities emerged, probably as a consequence of the prolonged cultural exchanges with the neighbouring Italic populations, including desserts like *pyramis*, a conical mound of roasted wheat and sesame bound with honey, *plakús*, a pie made of flour, nuts and dates, and *káundalos*, a confection made of boiled or roasted meat with breadcrumbs, cheese, dill and stock. Mussels from Cumae were so renowned that their image ended up on the local coins.

The most original contribution to Greek cuisine from the Italian cities was probably gastronomy, the literary reflection on food and eating. While references were found in the work of writers from Greece, especially in comedies that used food as a source of social critique and an expedient to make spectators laugh, in Italy, and Sicily in particular, some authors made food the main focus of their reflection, suggesting a greater cultural relevance of cuisine in the Italian colonies (and a technical advancement that required written codification). The first Sicilian author we are aware of is Míthaikos, who might have lived in the fifth century BCE, and is credited with writing the first cookery book. He was mentioned in Plato's dialogue *Gorgias* and in *The Deipnosophists*, written by Athenaeus in the third century CE.[62] From the latter, it would seem that Sicilian gastronomy also developed its own technical vocabulary, with words like 'gutting', 'rinsing' and 'filleting'.[63] Athenaeus mentions a Glaucos from Locri (324a), in Calabria, and a Hegésippos of Tarentum (516c) as cookery authors, and a Philóxenos (probably from Leucas) as the author of a food-focused poem, *Dinner* (685d). Apparently more relevant was Arkhéstratos, either from Syracuse or Gela, whose poem *Hedypatheia*, or 'Life of Luxury', is also quoted in Athenaeus. From the fragments of his text that we have access to, it seems that he travelled extensively, identifying the best places for each ingredient and dish and providing information about their preparation. For the first time, we have a concept that has emerged often in the history of gastronomy: a direct connection between quality and specific places, which guaranteed authenticity.[64]

## THE CELTS

As we mentioned, the Greek colonies got involved in long conflicts with the Etruscans and Phoenicians to ensure control over Mediterranean trade. In these wars, the services of mercenaries from all over the known world were often employed. Some of these came from across the Alps – the Celts. They were probably the descendants of Indo-Europeans who had penetrated into central Europe, originating the so-called Halstatt civilization, which introduced the use of iron and the tradition of cremating the dead instead of burying them. From the eighth century BCE, the Celts occupied a territory that spread from present-day Hungary and southern Poland to eastern France, developing a civilization characterized by the adoption of the horse and the spoked wheel, as well as the presence of powerful elites revealed by elaborate burials.[65] The Romans gave the name 'Gauls' to the tribes in today's France and 'Galatians' to those who attacked present-day Greece and Turkey. The Celtic elites apparently consumed great amounts of wine, bought from the Greek colonies of the Mediterranean and shipped along the Rhone into central Europe. The nobles loved to display their wealth and secure the allegiance of their followers by acquiring Greek drinking sets and other luxury objects that pointed to a steady network of trade contacts with their southern neighbours, including the Etruscan colonies of the Po river plain, which probably offered an interesting alternative to the Greek connections.[66] Greeks and Etruscans often hired Celts as mercenaries, and Celt artisans worked all over Italy.[67] It is likely that information about the wealth that lay south of the Alps reached the tribes beyond the mountains, who, starting in the fifth century BCE, infiltrated the Po river plains all the way to the Adriatic Sea, introducing new forms of vine cultivation. It seems that present-day Lambrusco might derive from a wild variety used by the Celts (which the Romans later referred to as *labrusca*, probably from *labrum*, margin and *ruscum*, spontaneous plant).[68]

In fact, despite the less than flattering descriptions in Greek and Roman literature, the Celts practised advanced forms of cultivation in large areas previously occupied by forests and established farms with underground pits, warehouses for grains and specialized places for husking and winnowing.[69] They employed ploughs to grow a variety of crops that included, depending on the areas of settlement, different types of wheat and barley, oats, rye, millet and legumes like fava beans, peas and vetch. The Celts also raised farm livestock such as cattle, sheep, goats and especially pigs.[70] Specialists now agree that their agriculture was so developed and well adapted to the condition of the northern climate that the Roman occupiers did not bring many innovations.[71] Unlike in Greek culture, hunting was considered a noble activity that trained warriors for combat. Game played a fundamental role in the banquets of the upper classes, which were opportunities to reinforce loyalty ties and settle disputes, as well as occasions for leaders to display their physical prowess and affluence.[72]

The Celts from central Europe also developed techniques for the extraction of mineral salt, which they used to season and preserve pork meat, often stuffed into the intestine or the bladder of the animal. The Romans still appreciated the hams and sausages from beyond the Alps, and they might have learned how to produce their own from the Celts.[73] It might not be coincidence that the Romans founded the colony of Veleia (today's Salsomaggiore, 'the great salt place') near a brine spring in the vicinity of Parma, a Celtic town which centuries later would become famous for its prosciutto and parmigiano, both requiring salt for their production.[74] Despite their agricultural skills, the Celts still took advantage of their environment by hunting, fishing and gathering mushrooms and berries. They also used the forests as grazing spaces for pigs, which were raised widely and provided much of the available meat.[75]

Over time, the Celts launched attacks towards central Italy, often allying themselves to Italic populations. In 390 BCE they reached Rome, only to retreat to their strongholds beyond the Apennines. The clash with the rising power of Rome, however, proved inevitable.

## ROME: A NEW PLAYER IN THE MEDITERRANEAN

Started as a federation of villages on the hills surrounding the Tiber, Rome's economy was based on shepherding and the shared cultivation of the nearby plain, which some authors indicate as the origin of the political concept of *res publica*, the public thing.[76] Under Etruscan control, the first Romans adopted a diet that was quite similar to the neighbouring Italic tribes, based on cereals such as *farro* and spelt, chewed raw but also added to soups or slightly roasted and ground in mortars to make gruels, known as *puls*, in the Etruscan style. The *puls*, to which legumes, wild herbs and other vegetables could be added, was so important that anything added to the staple was considered as *pulmentarium*, or accompaniment to the *puls*. Peas, chickpeas, fava beans, lentils and vetch all played an important role in the diet.[77] Millet and barley were widely consumed. The latter was cooked in a gruel called *polenta*, a word still used in Italian to indicate maize-based gruels. Grain flour was also kneaded into dough and cooked as unleavened focaccia. In the third century BCE, the introduction of free-threshing wheat resulted in an increase in wheat production, providing more grain for trade as well as leavened bread, which was baked in the oven (*furnus*), under the ashes or on the external wall of a hot clay or metal vase.[78] As the techniques for grinding and sifting flour for baking became increasingly complex, breadmaking became the task of specialized bakers called *pistores*, who operated under state control.

In early Rome, homes did not have dedicated rooms for preparing meals, as food was cooked on a fixed hearth or on movable braziers. Kitchens as separate spaces appeared only after the second century BCE, usually located in the rear of the home. In the Roman household storable food, also known as *penus*, included salt-cured pork, cheese, honey and olives. This was so important that it gave its name to the gods that

Pompeii, wheat-grinding stones.

protected the home, the *Penates*. These ancient beliefs were maintained and the *Penates* kept their place in the kitchen even after a new fire goddess, Vesta, became popular and other protective gods acquired importance, such as the Lares or the Genius (representing the father's generative power).[79] Before the Empire, most Romans had little orchards attached to their urban dwellings for the cultivation of vegetables such as radishes, chard, asparagus, artichokes, carrots, leeks, onions, garlic, lettuce and, above all, cabbage, considered particularly nutritious and healthy.

Romans classified their food as *fruges*, the output of agriculture, and *pecudes*, the cattle that grazed on wild land as well as the game provided by hunters. Although the *fruges*, considered the symbol of civilization, were held in higher esteem, the *pecudes* were absolutely necessary as victims for sacrificial ceremonies and banquets, which were paramount to the well-being of social life and to a relationship with the gods.[80] In fact, the early Romans ate very little meat, limiting their consumption to courtyard fowls, pigs and sheep. Cows, mainly used for agriculture, were butchered only on the occasion of sacrifices, religious feasts and important celebrations like weddings and births. Cattle were so precious that they were used as a measure of value in commercial exchanges, and from the Latin name, *pecus*, came the expression *pecunia*, money. Only domestic animals not connected to the wilderness could be used for sacrifices. They were butchered in a special market called a *forum boarium*. Representations of sacrifices point to the importance of butchers and to the widespread appreciation of their skills, despite their low social status relative to meat merchants, who focused mostly on oxen. Reliefs depicting butchers' shops often include pigs.[81]

Since meat from working animals was often tough and lean, beef was mostly boiled, and only then roasted. Sacrificial animals were sprinkled with wine, milk or a mixture of salt and ground wheat, called *mola salsa* (from which the verb 'immolate' derives). The heart, lungs and liver, considered the most precious organs, were offered to the gods, while the intestines were set apart to be used as casing for sausage and other food preparations. The meat was consumed during the banquet that followed the sacrifice. While the *pater familias* presided over domestic offerings, specialized celebrants controlled by a college of high priests called *Pontifices* conducted public sacrifices. Wild animals were *res nullius*, 'nobody's thing', and as such excluded from anybody's private property. In the early period, hunters were often servants and the activity carried the stigma of the underclass. As contacts with the eastern Mediterranean became more frequent, it became common to establish enclosures dedicated to hunting, a leisure activity for the upper classes in the Hellenistic fashion.[82]

Fish was rarely consumed, and only at the end of the Republic did seawater fish and oyster farming become a noticeable economic activity, in particular along the coast near Naples. Villas would feature artificial ponds to provide fish for private banquets.[83] Among the most appreciated fish, enjoying varying popularity according to changing fads, we can mention eel, octopus, red mullet, sturgeon and moray.[84] The *forum piscarium* specialized in fish and was later included in the *macellum*, a single building dedicated to the sale of meat and fowls, whose name can still be recognized in the Italian words for the slaughterhouse, *macello*, and the butcher's shop, *macelleria*.[85] At the *macellum* it was not unusual to find hunted game and other non-sacrificed meats for sale, although some scholars argue that all meat consumed in Rome was sacrificed.[86] Vegetables were sold in the *forum olitorium*.

Sheep's and goat's cheese, eggs, honey and fruits such as apples, pears and figs were part of the Roman diet. Salt played a fundamental role, not only for its nutritional value, but also to cure food. The early development of Rome can partly be attributed to the revenue from the salt produced at the mouth of the Tiber and then stored in a warehouse under the Aventine hill. Techniques to improve pork curing were presumably borrowed from the Celtic populations in the north of the peninsula. Oil, introduced by the Etruscans, was not very relevant in the early diet, but became more common over time, while wine production progressed under Greek influence.

Early Romans had a single main meal, *coena*, which was usually consumed in the early afternoon, consisting of *puls* or a focaccia with vegetables or pulses. They also had a light snack in the morning, called *ientaculum*, and another in the evening, known as *vesperna*. Over time, as living conditions improved and the number of available slaves swelled due to military conquests, food was consumed in larger quantities and the complexity of meals increased. Professional cooks, referred to as *coctor*, *coquus* (the origin of the word 'cook') or *magirus* after their Greek equivalents, became popular among the upper classes, but it was not uncommon for their employers to intervene regarding their decisions for the more significant occasions. The *coena* was pushed towards the evening and the *prandium*, usually fast and often consumed on the go outside the house, became the midday meal. In more affluent families, *coena* was often

## Wine in ancient Italy

Wine was a popular drink all over the Mediterranean and in the Italian peninsula. Etruscan wine production blossomed around the seventh century BCE, sustaining trade networks that reached Rome and the Celtic tribes of the north. The Etruscans conceived of a new method for cultivating vines that allowed them to take full advantage of the rich and humid soils of central and northern Italy. The vines were free to grow around trees with festooning branches that went from plant to plant, high above the ground. This system, which allowed farmers to grow other crops in the same fields, would later be adopted by the Gauls, the Celtic tribe that replaced the Etruscans in the Po river plain and later called *arbustum gallicum* by the Romans.

From their inception, the Greek colonies of southern Italy gave great relevance to wine production. The wine for the city of Cumae, presumably the ancestor of the Roman Falernum and the contemporary Falanghina, was among the most celebrated. Another well-appreciated wine, from the area of Basilicata, might be the ancestor of today's Aglianico, whose name could derive from the expression Hellenikos, simply meaning 'Greek'. Besides its role in formal banquets and symposia, wine was an important part of conviviality.

The Greeks greatly influenced Roman wine production during the Republic and later on in the Empire, through the introduction of new varieties, better winemaking techniques and more advanced ageing methods. To enhance preservation, various substances were added to wine, such as resins, pitch,

shared with friends and guests, its abundance signifying the wealth and power of the host. It was common for notable citizens to have a number of commoners and poor individuals, known as *clientes*, who declared their solidarity and loyalty to them, including their political support, in exchange for protection and material rewards, including food.

Dinners could turn into banquets on civic, religious and family occasions. Public banquets played an important role in the early times of the Republic, not only as a continuation of the sacrifices taking place chalk and even seawater, or the wine was smoked. The most appreciated wines were imported from Greece, but over time some production from the Italian peninsula acquired prestige with wines such as the Falernum, the Trifolinum and the Vesbius (after Mount Vesuvius) from present-day Campania, the Mamertinum from Messina in Sicily and the Pucinum from Veneto. Due to its enormous commercial value and the great demand all around the Mediterranean, wine was produced in large quantities and in a very organized fashion, often in the vast *latifundia* owned by Roman landowners.

The wine god Bacchus and vineyards on the slopes of Vesuvius (before the eruption). Fragment of a Roman fresco.

during holidays dedicated to the numerous gods, but also often in connection with the political and military life of the city. For instance the *collegia* (neighbourhood and trade guilds) organized celebrations that included communal eating.[87] For many urban dwellers, these public events were often occasions to be fed and avoid, at least temporarily, the anxiety caused by endemic scarcity.[88] As the population of Rome grew, access to these public banquets was restricted to the members of the Senate and specific groups of priests. Yet at the same time the affluent elite took to organizing huge banquets to increase their popularity. Many of them took place during Saturnalia, a festival dedicated to Zeus' father Saturn, god of the harvest, in the second half of today's December. During the holiday, which celebrated the fruits of agricultural labour, it was permitted to turn customs upside down so that servants and slaves could be impertinent with their masters, even exchanging roles at the table. We can already recognize the inversion of social roles and the climate of revelry that would later become the core of *Carnevale* (or Mardi Gras), the Christian celebration before the beginning of Lent.[89]

While in early periods Romans consumed their meals seated, under the influence of Greek customs they took to dining while lying on their sides on formal occasions. Due to their social relevance, only men were allowed to participate in those meals. It was only later that women were admitted, but they often sat next to their spouses and did not recline with them in the Etruscan style. The food was placed in front of guests on low tables with three legs. Banquets would start with a service of appetizers, the *gustatio*, with snacks such as eggs, mushrooms, oysters and salads. The main dishes, usually meat and vegetables, constituted the *primae mensae*, the first dinner. The meal would end with refreshments, such as figs, fruits, nuts and sweets, called *secundae mensae*. At times, the main meal was followed by a *comissatio*, modelled after the Greek symposium but without its sacral undertones, when male guests kept on drinking and talking, reaffirming their social and civic ties, including their hierachies.

In the first centuries of their history, Romans often dined in the open room where the fire and the household gods, the *Lares*, were located. This space was called an atrium, from the word *atrum*, indicating the black of soot. Later on, these spaces were enclosed and often placed on the second floor.[90] Private banquets maintained several cultural elements deriving from their religious counterparts, often in the form of superstitions. The dining room was somehow a microcosm reflecting the world. The ceiling was identified with the sky, the table with the soil and its products and the floor with the underworld where the dead reigned, as the presence of skeletons and other symbols of death suggest. When food fell on the floor, it became impure and was fed to the dogs or consumed in the fire dedicated to the *Lares*.[91]

## THE EXPANSION OF ROME

From the third century BCE, Rome extended its control over Italy, expanding first towards the south of the peninsula and then seizing the Etruscan and Celtic territories, where new cities were founded, called *colonia* (pl. *coloniae*), from which the English word colony derives. The relations between the Romans and the conquered populations were not easy, especially because they had to pay taxes and provide soldiers for Rome's wars without acquiring any political role in exchange.[92] Only later, when Rome expanded over the Mediterranean, did the inhabitants of Italy acquire full Roman citizenship. The cadastral maps came to reflect the juridical relationship between the local populations and the conquerors, revealing the penetration of Roman culture. The occupied lands were considered public property and were redistributed to Roman citizens according to a model called *centuriatio*, where the territory was inscribed in orthogonal lines, usually oriented north–south and east–west. This determined the *limites* (the outer limits of the colonies), the roads and the ditches that drained the excess water. To this day, especially in the Po river plain, the placement and the geometrical orientation of fields, the rows of trees that delimit them, the direction of the roads and even the water-management channels still reflect the layout of the ancient Roman colonies.

On their new plots, Roman farmers reproduced the small family-based agricultural enterprise, which employed the household and a limited number of slaves. This ancient model remained the ideological standard throughout the expansion of the Republic. Parts of the newly acquired land, called *compascuo*, were kept open for public usage and for pasturage of animals. These dynamics were less effective in the former Etruscan territories and especially in the south, where under the tyrants of the great Greek cities, the enclosed small parcels similar to today's Mediterranean gardens were disappearing, unified into larger estates for commercial crops. In these areas, moreover, as a consequence of the devastations of the wars against Carthage and the ensuing spread of malaria, the proportion of uncultivated terrains destined to shared utilization was more pronounced. It was through the slow appropriation of these common lands that some individuals established the core of what would later become the *villa rustica*, the extensive agricultural estate whose production was based on the labour provided by a large number of slaves. Its centre was the house of the landowner, the *villa urbana*, a symbol of wealth and aesthetic refinement. Over time, the owners of the smallholdings that constituted the backbone of the Roman economy were often forced to become salaried labour, to move into the city or to join the army.[93]

From its beginning, in case of draughts or bad harvests Rome often bought grains from other parts of Italy, mainly the Greek and Phoenician colonies of Campania, Sicily and Sardinia, but also from their Etruscan neighbours. As the city turned into a metropolis, it became increasingly dependent on imported wheat. Because transporting crops from the newly conquered plain of the Po was more expensive than shipping it from Sicily and Sardinia, farmers north of the Apennines found that feeding grain to pigs and carrying the added-value hams and slabs of bacon to Rome was more profitable than selling the grain itself.[94] A clash was inevitable, first with the Greek colonies of Sicily and then with Carthage, which controlled the wheat trade in the western Mediterranean and its production in northern Africa. Rome waged war against Carthage several times. During the initial conflict, Rome built its first fleet and managed to take over Sicily and Sardinia, which rapidly became the breadbaskets of the growing Republic. Rome eventually took control of Carthage and its maritime empire, making wheat more available.[95]

Bread became more common and affordable, assuming a central role in the cultural identity of the Romans to the point where the populace of the capital considered it an entitlement. Provisioning Rome with food was not an easy task and the political leaders established administrative functionaries, the *aediles*, in charge of ensuring fair prices on the markets. Roman authorities also focused on water distribution within their cities through advanced systems of aqueducts that brought water to public fountains and, more rarely, to the abodes of the elites. Water was usually consumed boiled, warm or cooled, often mixed with vinegar in the so-called *posca*. This beverage was common among the Roman soldiers, who could count on vinegar in their military rations, and for this reason was featured in the Gospel as the drink offered to Christ on the cross. At times, honey was added to water to make *aqua mulsa*, or hydromel, which at times was left to ferment into an alcoholic drink.[96] Feeding the army was a complex undertaking: one of the main components of military rations was wheat, which was ground and usually baked into hard tack called *bucellatum*. The wheat was ground in rotary mills, one for each eight-man squad, which were carried around on mules together with other cooking tools and the squad tents. The ration also included olive oil and an amount of salt (*sal* in Latin), called *salarium*, from which the word 'salary' might derive.[97]

After the conquest of Carthage, Rome became more tightly integrated in the Mediterranean, establishing commercial outposts on its eastern shores. Over the following two centuries it occupied Spain, Greece, the Middle East, France and Egypt. The Romans called the Mediterranean *mare nostrum*, 'our sea'. This expansion increased the cultural permeability of Roman civilization to influences from the courts of the Hellenistic Greek kingdoms that had developed after the fall of Alexander the Great's empire. Scholar Andrew Dalby notices:

> By employing Greek or eastern cooks, by importing and paying high prices for Greek and eastern delicacies, by assiduously transplanting Greek and eastern plant varieties, by adopting Greek names for food and for finished dishes, Romans appear to have displayed in this area, perhaps uncritically, their general ambition to emulate Greek culture and eastern luxury.[98]

An uninterrupted flood of raw materials, crops and luxury goods from the new provinces rapidly increased the standards of life in Italy, making the process of integration of the Italic populations faster and stronger.

However, the availability and the low price of wheat from vast slave estates in the new provinces caused a crisis of traditional agriculture in Italy. Excluded from the best soils, farmers were often pushed towards marginal lands that granted very low yields. This also increased deforestation, along with the growing demand for lumber as fuel and for the construction of buildings and ships. Many small landowners all over

The Roman Empire.

Italy sold their properties to become labourers or to move throughout the Mediterranean in search of a better life. This transformation in the landholding structures stimulated the development of speculative agriculture; wealthy Romans expanded their *latifundia*, the enormous estates where owners found it more convenient and financially rewarding to produce commercial crops with high market value like olives (Apulia and Basilicata) and grapes (Latium, Campania and Tuscany). The availability of land in the *latifundia* did not stimulate innovation to increase yields, as production was ensured by slaves, whose numbers grew with the conquests of new colonies. Following the expansion in the Mediterranean, new exotic fruits like cherries, quinces, peaches and apricots, as well as fowls such as guinea hens and peacocks, were introduced and consumed in the dining halls of wealthy Romans. Luxury dishes increasingly featured spices from lands located to the east of the Empire, along trading routes that connected the Mediterranean and the Red Sea with the Indian Ocean and points beyond.[99]

Despite the growing wealth of the elites and the increase in food consumption across the board, the ideology that underpinned food habits remained mainly the same. Frugality was still considered a virtue, but generosity towards guests was highly valued. Moral or political corruption was often depicted in terms of widespread behaviours that could include gluttony and decadence. Although agriculture relied increasingly on commercial exchanges, independence and self-sufficiency in terms of food were still relevant ideals for the landed aristocracy.[100] The poet Horace expressed these values in his *Satires* with the famous story of the country mouse who lets himself be convinced by a town mouse to move to the city, enticed by abundance and luxury, only to discover that the urban environment is in reality much more dangerous than the rustic life.[101] Nonetheless, the representations of banquets in Roman satire point to a clear contradiction between admiration for the frugality that was attributed to the founders of the city and the social function of dining customs.[102] Despite being denounced, drunkenness (*ebriositas*) was distinguished from inebriation (*ebrietas*) on a continuum that was influenced also by gender and social status.[103] To curb excesses, sumptuary laws were introduced from the second century BCE. In 180 BCE a law was imposed to limit the number of guests one could invite for dinner, while other regulations restricted spending for weddings and festivals. In 78 BCE the consumption of rare species such as the dormouse and exotic animals from the new eastern provinces was drastically limited.[104]

## THE EMPIRE IN THE MEDITERRANEAN

Following the political transition from the Republic to the Empire in the first century CE, the social and political relevance of feasting increased, as Rome found itself at the core of a complex and wide network of commercial exchanges, reaching far to the north into the Baltic region and the Russian steppes, to the south into the sub-Sahara, and to the east into the Persian Gulf, India and beyond. Commerce focused on bulk crops, which were brought to Rome from relatively close areas, such as Spain, North Africa and Syria. However, high-value and low-weight luxury goods, which were embraced as markers of wealth, prestige and status, also constituted important elements of trading. It has been suggested that the orchards in Vespasian's Temple of Peace, near the spice market, or *Horrea Piperataria*, could be considered botanical gardens where exotic plants were grown, as a symbol of the Roman domination over faraway lands.[105]

Archaeological remains from grand houses in Pompeii and many other Roman sites, including paintings, mosaics, reliefs and tableware, as well as bones and other kinds of domestic waste, have confirmed the textual testimony of ancient authors concerning banquets and the culinary practices that surrounded them.[106] The imperial elites took to holding their dinner parties (*convivia*), especially in the evening, in multi functional rooms where guests could be entertained. When used for a formal meal, a room might have been referred to as *triclinium*, taking its name from the three-place bed where guests would recline. Women from the upper classes participated more frequently than those from the lower ones. Visual representations suggest that reclining became a permissible female behaviour.[107] The room would usually hold three beds, for a total of nine guests, but bigger beds for more guests and rooms containing more than three beds were known. Since guests ate using their fingers, food was cut to facilitate handling and bowls of fresh water offered for rinsing. The guest of honour was usually placed on the central bed so that all the other participants could look directly at him.[108] From the early third century CE, however, a single, large semicircular bed, known as *accubitum* or *stibadium*, sometimes replaced the rectangular beds placed along the walls of the *triclinium*. The new layout maintained the relevance of the place for the guest of honour.[109]

One of the best representations of these feasts, although probably exaggerated, is the *Satyricon* by the author Petronius. Petronius described the outrageous party of an imaginary freed slave, Trimalchio, who liked

Reconstruction of a Roman *triclinium* (domestic dining space).

to make his guests admire his wealth by boasting that all the food served came from his property. In one of the most famous food scenes in world literature, turned into a visual masterpiece by the film-maker Federico Fellini in his *Satyricon* (1969), Petronius portrays the extravagance of the dishes, including appetizers in the shape of zodiac signs and a whole roasted pig from which sausages and other pieces of meat fall when cut open.[110] Another important source showing the food consumed in imperial times is *De re coquinaria*, a collection of recipes attributed to Marcus Gavius Apicius, a renowned gourmet who lived under the emperor Tiberius in the first century CE (yet the recipes were likely compiled between the second and fourth centuries). Exotic ingredients like ostrich, camel and pepper are mentioned, as is more common fare such as sausage, *puls* and chestnuts.[111] A striking element in numerous recipes is the incorporation of several expensive condiments and spices, whose presence in dishes must almost have obliterated the original taste of the ingredients. Reasons for this custom might have included the host's desire to show off his wealth, his cooks' skills and his taste and refinement.[112] The recipes in the collection are kept to the bones, without many details about preparation and ingredients, as shown here in two recipes for brains.[113]

Much information about imperial Roman food customs can be deduced from laws and edicts, like the one issued by the emperor

## Book II, Minces. Brain Sausage

Put in the mortar pepper, lovage, and origany, moisten with broth and rub; add cooked brains and mix diligently so that there be no lumps. Incorporate five eggs and continue mixing well to have a good forcemeat that you may thin with broth. Spread this out in a metal pan, cook, and when cold unmould it onto a clean table. Cut into handy size. [Now prepare a sauce] Put in the mortar pepper, lovage and origany, crush, mix with broth, put into a sauce pan, boil, thicken and strain. Heat the pieces of brain pudding in this sauce thoroughly, dish them up, sprinkled with pepper in a mushroom dish.

## Book IV, Miscellanea. Vegetables and Brain Pudding

Take vegetables, clean, wash, shred and cook them. Cool them off and drain them. Take 4 [calf's] brains, remove [the skin and] string and cook them. In the mortar put 6 scruples of pepper, moisten with broth and crush fine; then add the brains, rub again and meanwhile add the vegetables, rubbing all the while, and make a fine paste of it. Thereupon break and add 8 eggs. Now add a glassful of wine, a glassful of raisin wine, taste this preparation. Oil the baking dish thoroughly, [put the mixture in the dish] and place it in the hot plate that is above the ashes and when it is done [unmould it and] sprinkle with pepper and serve.

Diocletian in 301 CE, and from medical treatises. In fact, food also played an important role in the therapeutic theories and practices that Celsus (first century CE) and, above all, Galen (second century CE) codified, based on the work of the Greek Hippocrates of Cos, who lived between the fifth and the fourth centuries BCE.[114] According to the beliefs of Celsus and Galen, a healthy human body was the result of the balance of four fluids, or 'humours': blood, choler (yellow bile), phlegm and melancholy (black bile). Each of these fluids expressed different physical qualities: heat, cold, moisture and dryness. Blood was considered hot and moist, choler hot and dry, phlegm cold and moist, and melancholy cold and dry. The predominance of any one humour determined the health and the character of each individual, and also explained the differences among sexes and ages in terms of sensibilities and constitution. Women were considered particularly prone to excessive consumption, a weakness in apparent contradiction with their social role, which often included the management of stored victuals and their preparation.[115] As sickness was believed to be the result of an excess of certain humours, ingesting and digesting foods that presented opposite qualities could restore a healthy balance. For instance, if a person suffered from melancholy, with weight loss and sunken eyes, the excess of the cold and dry humour was to be counter-balanced by the consumption of hot and moist ingredients. With the fall of the Roman Empire and the arrival of nomadic tribes from northern and Eastern Europe, this medical wisdom was mostly lost, maintained only vaguely in the monasteries, which continued to cultivate the Greek and Roman traditions in the Byzantine Empire. Despite being initially shunned by Roman society, Christians absorbed many elements of the Mediterranean cultures in which they lived. Their early ceremonial common meals were somehow the heir of the archaic Roman banquet and its symbolic meaning. At first they took place in the evening and were based on the sharing of food between all members of the community, regardless of social standing. Over time the Eucharist, which memorialized Christ's Last Supper through the consecration and the sharing of bread and wine, two of the most culturally relevant Mediterranean products, came to be celebrated separately from the common meal, which over time lost ceremonial relevance.[116]

During the Imperial period, the lower classes continued consuming light meals, still consisting mainly of *puls* and vegetables. Bread became more common when, under the emperor Augustus, a special office, the *annona*, was founded to ensure stable prices for grains, even if the best white flour, *siligo*, was meant for the exclusive consumption of the rich. Until the late Republic, Rome had not owned ships to provide food to the cities, but rather relied on private merchants who were obliged to cooperate with the *annona*. Only with the expansion of the Empire did the state begin importing directly from the provinces into Rome, establishing an efficient 'command economy' in the provinces. Functionaries amassed grains obtained as tax or as rent. To avoid social unrest in the capital, the *annona* would distribute grain for free in Rome and later in Constantinople so that the effects of price fluctuations and speculation were limited.[117] However, shipments, usually suspended between March and November, could be delayed or interrupted by logistic failures, bad weather or war.[118] In most cities it was up to members of the elite to avoid the brunt of food scarcity, and as a consequence political instability, by distributions of free staples that ensured the gratitude of the urban masses. At the same time, food donations were used to acquire prestige through their munificence and to ensure a following.[119] As historians Broekaert and Zuiderhoek observed,

> Once the determinants of empire – such as the gradual unification of measures, weights, and currency; Greek and Latin as *linguae francae*; diminution of piracy and war; and more uniform legal systems – reduced trading costs and stimulated economic integration, market exchange was allowed a more substantial role in the Mediterranean food system, without, however, eliminating reciprocity and redistribution.[120]

The living conditions of the urban poor, who were crammed into huge buildings called *insulae*, were often hard, especially outside Rome where they could not count on free food distribution or gifts from the elites. Their living spaces usually did not have kitchens for fear of fires, so they tended to eat out, getting their meals from shops that sold cooked, warm food to take away, known as *thermopolia*. It was not uncommon to have a light lunch on the street: covered stalls called *lixae*, under the control of

Pompeii, street-side *thermopolium*, a kind of shop that sold cooked, ready-to-eat food.

the *aediles* functionaries, sold drinks, sausages and sweets. Those with more money would have slaves follow them with prepared dishes. Meals could also be consumed in establishments called *tabernae*, which seemed to serve both food and wine, and *popinae*, presumably focusing mainly on the food. Although their structures can be easily identified thanks to the presence of counters, storing areas and cooking facilities, at archaeological sites it is difficult to distinguish fully the different types and functions of eating establishments.[121]

Due to less than reputable owners and often even less respectable clientele who engaged in gambling and prostitution, these places tended to have bad reputations and were constantly controlled by the police. Romans who found themselves in cities where they had no connections could stay in inns known as *hospitia*, which offered room, board and stables (*stabulae*) and were often located near the city gates or in close proximity to popular places such as the forum, baths and theatres. When journeying between cities, travellers could count on little countryside eateries known as *cauponae*, and on inns managed by public authorities, called *mansiones*. Travellers did not have to worry about carrying wood for lighting fires or salt to season their meals because they were provided by public functionaries known as *parochi*, placed along the roads.[122]

The seemingly all-powerful Roman Empire was actually fraught with deep internal tensions, partly due to the contradictions inherent in the agricultural production, based on a slave system. As new populations started pressing at the borders, attracted by the riches of the Mediterranean, the Empire was eventually condemned to face its violent demise.

# TWO

# Invaders

After a period of unstoppable growth, the Roman Empire showed increasing signs of crisis in the last two centuries of its existence, partly due to internal dynamics and partly because of the growing pressure at its borders. Coming from the north, east and the Mediterranean, wave after wave of newcomers brought with them instability and destruction. At the same time, they introduced changes in social relations, production and technology that laid the groundwork for the future development of food in Italy. The processes of miscegenation, adaptation and appropriation that accompanied these transformations were not always painless and peaceful. At the same time, they allowed the transition from the Roman civilization to a political and economic environment that, from the twelfth century, saw the take-off of agriculture, the rebirth of markets and urban life in the centre and north of Italy and the innovative elaborations of culinary traditions that led to the splendour of the late Middle Ages and the Renaissance.

## THE END OF THE ROMAN EMPIRE

The Roman Empire's economic structure remained fully functional until the end of the second century CE, with forms of agriculture and trade that established a common food language in the Mediterranean area. Roman emperors ruled over a multi-ethnic world that, despite the apparent wealth, was brewing with internal contradictions that eventually led to its demise. The productive system was based on vast private estates (*latifundia*) belonging to rich families where slavery was prevalent.[1] Some landowners managed only a small part of their estates, known as *pars dominica* (portion of the master), entrusting the rest of their properties to middlemen (*conductores*) who in turn divided the land into plots. These smaller units were rented out to free farmers (*coloni*) or entrusted to slaves who were granted considerable autonomy (*servi quasi coloni*). Later on, when the pressure from the Germanic population became stronger, plots were also assigned to 'barbarians' who were legally free but in fact tied to the soil they tilled, and often sold and transferred with it (*inquilini*). The excavation of small sites usually referred to as 'peasant farms' suggests that the patterns of land use in the late Roman agricultural enterprise were complex, diverse and integrated with other aspects of production and trade.[2] These new forms of rural management allowed nobility and high-ranking military commanders to take control of vast agricultural areas. The old senatorial aristocracy gave way to a new class of landlord connected to the army, often of humble origins, who did not feel invested in the stability of the central state.[3]

It became fashionable for the Roman upper crust to spend more time in their country properties, isolating themselves from the growing political turmoil. Hunting acquired a new meaning, representing the elites' sense of control over the land they owned and the natural world that thrived in it. Vast tracts meant for the exclusive hunting of the landowners, called *vivaria*, were frequently surrounded by walls and overseen by guards. The emperor Hadrian (117–138 CE) hunted the most dangerous beasts in the territories he conquered as an expression of his military and political power, while Marcus Aurelius (161–180 CE) considered hunting as both training for war and physical exercise for health purposes.[4]

Rich merchants often invested their profits in land acquisitions, considering agriculture to be a more secure form of wealth than commerce, which became a less relevant source of taxation and revenue for the state. When the territorial expansion of the Empire came to an end and the military stopped providing conquest booties, the central government found itself in financial quagmires and had to increase levies, turning tax agents into targets of fear and hatred. The most powerful owners of *latifundia*, who frequently had close connections with the local and central administration, were able to strike deals to pay taxes directly to the state, bypassing the tax agents. Working as independent entrepreneurs, these functionaries were forced to make up for the lost revenue by increasing the fiscal pressure on small landowners, who at times were forced to relinquish their property to larger landowners in exchange for protection.

Permanent armies were gathered to defend the Empire, giving greater power to generals who fought amongst themselves and strived to enthrone their allies as emperors. Heavy taxes had to be levied to pay the soldiers, who would otherwise plunder resources from the territories they occupied if they did not get their salary on time. By the end of the third century CE, the Roman emperors, pressured by the need to pay their troops, took to decreasing the content of silver and gold in the coinage. As inflation skyrocketed, commerce shrank ever more and rural properties turned into the last safe haven for wealth. As a result, many landowners ended up abandoning the cities to take refuge in their country dwellings. Over time, large estates became virtually independent and self-sufficient, at times reverting to forms of exchange based on barter and payment in kind. With the monetary economy floundering, landowners found it beneficial to make groups of farmers from the same area collectively responsible for the payment of rent, while allowing them access to uncultivated lands.

The internal crisis of the Empire allowed the neighbouring populations, especially the Germanic tribes beyond the northern and eastern borders, to slowly penetrate Roman territories and settle as *hospites*, or 'guests'. Whole tribes were absorbed into the folds of the Empire with 'federate' status (*foederati*) to repopulate lands whose inhabitants had been decimated by wars, famines or epidemics, and to defend the frontier from new and less 'civilized' waves of Germanic populations. These tribes were often offered either a third of the houses and lands of their area of settlement, or the right to collect the crops grown in said lands by Roman farmers, who found themselves in a state of quasi-servitude.[5] Agriculture's productivity continued to decrease, while populations shrank both in the countryside and in urban centres. Cities lost their cultural primacy, while the market economy, based on monetary exchanges, entered a crisis that would continue for several centuries. Once the cultural and trade networks that connected the Mediterranean urban elites began to wane and the upper classes settled in the countryside, living off the products of their own estates, culinary customs inevitably lost much of their cosmopolitanism and focused on local crops and manufactures.

In 395 CE the emperor Theodosius divided the Roman territories between his two sons, Arcadius and Honorius. The eastern part, with Constantinople – present-day Istanbul – as capital, would enjoy a much longer life than the Western one and develop its own culture based on its Greek heritage. The western part, which moved its capital to Ravenna, on the Adriatic coast on the Italian peninsula, became increasingly weak, allowing the penetration of Germanic tribes. The Visigoths, led by their leader Alaric, marched into Rome in 410 while trying to reach northern Africa, Rome's breadbasket. When in 476, Odoacer, king of the German tribe of the Goths, deposed Romulus Augustulus, the last Roman emperor, and sent the imperial insignia to Constantinople, acknowledging the pre-eminence of the Emperor of the East, the end of the Empire of the West was accepted as inevitable.

## THE GERMANIC MIGRATIONS

Long before the end of the Western empire, the Germanic populations that had settled at the margins of the Roman territories had been absorbing elements of Roman culture. The newcomers, although attracted to the refinement of the Mediterranean environment, were also proud of their own traditions. When Germanic populations such as the Ostrogoths and their leader Theodoric occupied Italy, they maintained tribal traditions based on their personal loyalty for their ruler, yet his closest followers relied on Roman administrative structures. The elites also adopted some of the Roman customs, especially when it came to official occasions. Cassiodorus, the Roman statesman who served under Theodoric, observed:

> The splendid abundance of the royal table is considered an important ornament for the State, because most consider that the lord of the house owns all the unusual foods that are offered at his banquets. It is appropriate for a simple citizen to have access to what the surrounding territory can offer. When a prince is inviting, it is proper that he offers more of the things that provoke wonder.[6]

*Latifundia*, the sprawling agricultural estates that constituted the most important productive units in the peninsula, became mostly independent from any form of central control. Their core was the villa, the sumptuous dwelling of the landowner, surrounded by vast extensions of land tended by slaves and *coloni*. Roman proprietors accepted the presence of Germanic soldiers as a form of protection. In many cases, tribal nobles took direct possession of large landholdings, known as *curtes* or *massae*, increasingly assimilating with their Roman peers. Moreover, their strongholds and central buildings were frequently fortified to resist external attacks. In this case, they were referred to as *castra* (singular *castrum*), the old name for the Roman permanent military encampments.

These forms of ownership were slowly adopted in many areas of Italy, building on legal institutions still in place during the final period of the Empire. The Roman property laws known as *quiritian*, which were only applied to Roman citizens, defined a specific possessor (*dominus*) for each tract of land and required complex civil procedures for sales and transfers. A new kind of tenure called *bonitarian*, which was not exclusively based on Roman civil law and allowed for easier land transfers, acquired increasing relevance. With the penetration of Germanic farmers, used to communal forms of agriculture, Roman legal customs were gradually sidelined by the expansion of open fields that could be temporarily occupied by other users after the legitimate owner had harvested whatever he had planted. These legal developments went side by side with a degradation of the agricultural system. Animal husbandry, which played an important role in the peasants' subsistence, took place in uncultivated areas and in open fields once the harvest was completed. Forests and woods acquired relevance not only as hunting grounds and sources of wood and various edible products, but also as places for rearing free-ranging swine, which ensured protein for the winter months. Since most fields were open, the large numbers of roaming pigs were considered a scourge for agriculture.[7]

The Germanic tribes that settled in the countryside introduced semi-nomadic herding habits together with foraging, hunting and forms of subsistence agriculture based on what the Romans had considered to be lesser cereals, like millet, spelt, rye and barley, which required less care than wheat due to their shorter growing cycle.[8] These grains could also be used to make beer, the most common alcoholic drink among the newcomers, at the time still produced without hops. In areas with larger Germanic populations, Mediterranean crops like pulses, olives, wine grapes and orchard vegetables were supplemented but never entirely replaced by products that enjoyed popularity in the Nordic traditions, such as butter, lard, game and wild berries. Many of these culinary elements were already common in imperial times, but were ideologically excluded from the triad of wine-oil-bread that embodied the Roman conception of agriculture, shaped by the preferences of urban consumers. For the Romans, working the land to grow crops was the mark of civilization, expressing the domination of man over nature. The newcomers had a different approach to the natural environment. They tended to use what they needed from the land without trying to modify or tame it.

Despite being an activity that anybody could practise, hunting enjoyed higher status and performed more relevant social functions among the Germanic newcomers. An important part of the warring lifestyle, it was considered a form of training that allowed the transmission of cultural values and fighting techniques to the young. It also had a political valence, since by publicly displaying prowess in hunting, tribal leaders reaffirmed their primacy over the other warriors in their clan. For young free men, the first hunting expedition had the value of an initiation; on that occasion, they had to show their abilities, embodying the strength and courage of the prey they were meant to kill.[9] Following this connection between hunting, the warrior ethos and tribal social structures, consuming great quantities of meat during banquets was considered necessary to acquire physical strength and fighting stamina. Moreover, offering food to the other members of the social group was perceived as an expression of wealth and power.

## Byzantines, Longobards and Franks

The Germanic tribes that determined the crisis and eventually the dissolution of the western part of the Roman Empire never reached its eastern regions, home of what was eventually known as the Byzantine Empire. Byzantium, the ancient name of its capital Constantinople, was a settlement strategically located on the straits that connected the Mediterranean to the Black Sea. For centuries, the political leaders of this territory, which at the end of the fifth century CE included Greece, the Balkans, Turkey, Egypt and parts of present-day Syria, Israel and Lebanon, considered themselves the heirs of the Roman and Greek culture. This identification was so strong that citizens of the Eastern Empire referred to themselves as *Romaioi*, 'Romans' in Greek. In the first half of the sixth century CE, after conquering North Africa from the Germanic Vandals and securing its wheat production, the Byzantine emperor Justinian took control of the maritime routes of the central Mediterranean and launched a war to take the whole Italian peninsula from the Ostrogoths.[10] In a bold public-relations move, the Ostrogoth king Totila promised to expropriate the estates occupied by the Byzantines and to redistribute them among the population, while setting slaves and serfs free. The manoeuvre did not achieve the expected results and many

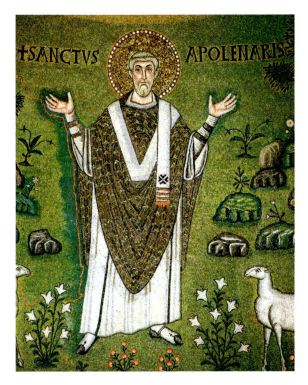

St Apollinaris, first bishop of Ravenna (6th century). Byzantine mosaic in the basilica of Sant'Apollinare in Classe, Ravenna.

farmers of Roman origin did not give their allegiance to the Ostrogoths, allowing the Byzantines to conquer the Italian peninsula. Still attached to the remnants of legal order of the old institutions, the descendants of the Romans were not attuned to the tribal relationships of loyalty, central to the Germanic cultures, which had acquired greater relevance than legal structures.[11] However, the inhabitants of Italy, who had suffered the brunt of the long war and the ensuing food scarcity, also considered the Byzantines foreign conquerors. The newcomers came from different parts of the Empire and included Armenians, Slavs and even Persians. They spoke Greek and had an exotic appearance, as alien as the previous Germanic occupants.[12] From the examination of a register from the papacy of Gregory I (590–604), it appears that in the sixth century CE, large estates in Sicily still belonged to the Latin-speaking population, while the Byzantines mostly settled on the east coast of the island, around cities of Greek origin like Catania and Syracuse. Only later did larger groups of Greek-speaking Byzantines – including monks – settle in the interior of the island and in southern Italy, in an attempt to leave behind the political and religious turmoil of the eastern Mediterranean.[13] At first, Byzantine monks lived either as hermits or in small groups, without holding large properties, and maintained activities like salt pits or grain mills.[14] In the following centuries they would receive vast tracts of land from local authorities including the pope, as in the case of the St Nilus abbey in Grottaferrata, near Rome.

During the twenty-year conflict between Byzantine and Germanic armies, a new form of religious piety flourished, providing respite from the surrounding mayhem: the monastic life whose rule was written by Benedict in the first half of the sixth century CE. Monastic traditions that stressed the relevance of community life and curbed the excesses of ascetic dedication, isolation and fasting practised by hermits had risen first in the eastern Mediterranean and Egypt. Benedict's rule adapted their customs to the new Italian situation and allowed monks, who worked in the fields, to build their daily schedule around productive activities. The motto of the religious order, which made a point of offering hospitality to pilgrims and the vagrant poor, was *ora et labora*, 'pray and work'. In the following centuries, the monks following Benedict's spirituality were often involved in the reclamation of marshy lands, canalization and the construction of drainage systems, establishing closed plots from Lombardy to Tuscany and offering an example that was followed by the popes in the area around Rome.[15]

In the Benedictine monasteries, monks took turns to cook and serve, but in the case of a large community, the cellarer, responsible for the storage and preparation of food, was excused from these duties.[16] While meat was excluded from the monks' diet, two different items of food were to be provided at the meal, with a third item added when vegetables or fruit were included; however, monks engaged in heavy work could be given extra food with the abbot's permission.[17] Abstinence from wine was valued, but the rules acknowledged that monks could drink, allowing them to imbibe with measure and without excess of drunkenness.[18] The customs practised echoed the dietary traditions of Rome: pre-eminence was given to the bread-oil-wine triad, crucial also for Christianity. Wine and bread were used in the Holy Communion, while oil was employed as a symbol of strength and endurance in many sacraments. However, as abbeys grew in wealth and splendour and their properties expanded, monks increasingly relied on the labour of serfs and lay brothers and were allowed greater and more varied amounts of food.[19] In the same period, the Byzantine monks in central and southern Italy lived according to rules established in Constantinople. They embraced the Eastern traditions of abstinence from meat on Wednesdays,

Fridays, Lent and many other holidays, stimulating the creativity of the monastery cooks in their use of vegetables.[20]

In 569, a few years after the Byzantines won the war against the Ostrogoths and secured their control over most of the peninsula, the Longobards, a Germanic tribe that had never been exposed to Roman culture before, crossed the Alps. They established their capital in Pavia and occupied the northern areas of Italy, including most of the Po river plain, part of which is still called Lombardy after them. The conquered territories were divided among the chiefs that had distinguished themselves in battle (known as dukes from the Latin word *dux*, leader) and headed the military and social units that constituted the Longobards' organization during their migration.

Despite their decision to settle mostly in cities, when the Longobards first arrived they remained distinct from the natives, whom they did not consider to be peers. Individuals of Roman descent did not have recourse to Germanic tribal laws and were prohibited to carry weapons. In the countryside, the Longobard warriors, whose social relationships were based on kinship ties and oaths of military loyalty, founded small settlements called *farae*, to separate themselves from the heavily exploited peasant population of Roman and Germanic-Roman descent. The Longobard presence has left traces seen in the names of many towns in Italy, such as Fara in Sabina near Rome, renowned for its olive oil, and Fara San Martino in Abruzzo, where the industrial pasta makers Cocco, Delverde and De Cecco are located. During the first years of the Longobard rule, since the landowners of Roman descent were forced to transfer a good portion of their harvest to the occupants, agricultural output decreased to an all-time low, while hunting and foraging secured the survival of the local farmers. Over time, when it became clear to the Longobards that they were in Italy to stay, they embraced the Christian religion and codified their ancient customs in Roman-style written laws, in an edict issued in 643 by the king Rothari. Segments of the former Roman elites began to cooperate with the Longobard dukes, who in turn placed native functionaries in important positions.

The Longobards penetrated into Tuscany and moved south along the Apennines, establishing dukedoms also in Umbria (Spoleto) and Campania (Benevento). As a result, for almost two centuries, Italy was divided between the Longobards and the Byzantines, a situation that amplified the contrasts between the Roman-Greek and the Germanic cultures. The province of Liguria, whose capital Genoa would play an important role in Mediterranean trade starting in the tenth century, fell to the Longobards in 643.[21] The Byzantines were left with Venice, founded by refugees running from the Longobard invasion, the Exarchate (Ravenna and neighbouring territory) and the Pentapolis (the word means five cities, located on the Adriatic coast) in today's Romagna and Marche areas, Latium, around Rome, and Apulia, Calabria, Sicily and Sardinia in the south, which the uninterrupted presence of tax collectors indicates was among the richest territories of the Byzantine Empire. In fact, documents attest the travels of Byzantine emperors to their Italian possessions, indicating their relevance to the Mediterranean economy.[22] To underscore the continuity with Rome, the Greek-Byzantines called their provinces in Italy 'Romania', a word from which the modern region of Romagna derives its name. In these areas archaeologists have noticed an early presence of the fortified towns, referred to as *castrum* in Latin or *kastron* in Greek, which indicated deliberate military policy. When faced with invasion, other towns followed their example, establishing the phenomenon known in Italy as *incastellamento*, from the word *castello*, 'castle'. The multiplication of fortified urban centres in defendable places, often on top of hills, tended to attract the surrounding peasant population, changing the demographic layout of the Byzantine territories.[23]

Venice achieved its de facto independence from the Byzantines in the ninth century. Its location was favourable to the production of salt – a precious commodity in Mediterranean trade during the medieval period because it was used to preserve food and so fend off periods of scarcity.[24] The enterprising population of Venice also thrived on the commerce of slaves, spices and other products from Byzantium. The city experimented with original legal tools, such as the *commenda*, a sort of joint-stock company that connected an investor with available capital and a junior trader, who travelled with the merchandise bought with the investor's money. This arrangement established paths for upward mobility, allowing new families to acquire wealth and join the political elite while expanding the Venetian trade networks, which would play an important role later in providing foods and other goods from the eastern Mediterranean.[25] From the mid-ninth century, involvement in maritime trade allowed the expansion of Amalfi, another Byzantine colony located on the stretch of coast south of Naples that is now known as *costiera amalfitana*. The small town thrived on the commerce of wheat, wines and fruit from nearby areas of Campania. These products were sold all over

Terraces on the Amalfi Coast, built to make the most of the rugged slopes
overlooking the sea.

the Byzantine Empire in exchange for gold and luxury objects that found
an easy market in Italy.[26]

The Byzantine elites in the colonies maintained close ties with
the imperial government, and most of the functionaries and military
commanders rotated frequently, which limited blending with the natives.
In turn, local landlords were frequently close allies of the administrative
and military representatives from Constantinople, who levied heavy
taxes that weighed mainly on the peasants. In the Byzantine-controlled
areas, large estates survived and the legal organization of land ownership was based around the *fundus*, clearly identified parcels used as
units of management.[27] Over time, these traditional production structures
became less efficient and large tracts of land were left uncultivated,
allowing the expansion of herding activities. The introduction of water
buffalo into southern Italy has been attributed by some scholars to the
Byzantines, while ANASB, the National Association of Buffalo Breeders,
points to the possibility that the Longobards might have played some
role.[28] The expansion of herding does not necessarily indicate that the
large estates in the Italian colonies were isolated from the monetary
economy of the Byzantine Empire. Grapevines and olive trees were
partially reintroduced in the areas devastated by the passage of the

Germanic tribes, originating a surplus for trade. Mulberries were also planted in southern Italy to promote silk production (the Byzantines had managed to break the Chinese secret of sericulture in the sixth century).[29] Sicily maintained its relevance in wheat production: the portions that were not commandeered for tax payments were consumed locally or directed to other markets in Italy, since shipments to Greece became increasingly difficult due to the Muslim expansion in the eastern Mediterranean.[30]

The Byzantines maintained the upper-class Roman use of exotic spices, including sugar, and of aromatics like aniseed, which was added to wines and was perhaps the originator of the anise-flavoured liquors now common across the Mediterranean.[31] It is hard to decipher the actual influence of Byzantine cuisine, with its Greek and Roman roots, on the colonies in the Italian peninsula. Two popular wines, *moskhâtos* and *monembasiós*, are reflected in the name of contemporary *moscato* and *malvasia* wines. Although the upper classes displayed a certain preference for red meat, which indicated the ownership of large estates and herds, most Byzantines, like their Greek ancestors, were particularly fond of salt fish and seafood. It is in the eastern Mediterranean that we find the first written reference to caviar, *kabiári*, and salt-cured roe, *oiotárikhon*, a word that might have given origin to the Italian *bottarga* (the salt-cured roe pouch of tuna or grey mullet). Peasants and monks consumed black bread, vegetables, dairy products and probably pork.[32]

When the Byzantine authorities started to exert fiscal pressure on their possessions in order to finance their war against the Muslims, who began their rapid expansion in the eastern Mediterranean, they also proceeded systematically to destroy all religious icons for theological reasons, prompting the colonies of Italy to rebel against Constantinople. Amalfi and Venice elected local leaders, taking steps towards a de facto independence. The Longobards took advantage of the situation, and conquered the Byzantine territories of the Exarchate and the Pentapolis in today's Romagna and Marche areas. In an attempt to solidify their local alliances, in 728 the Longobard king Liutprand gave the newly conquered town of Sutri to Pope Gregory II. It was the first time that the Roman Church had secured formal secular control over a territory. After a few years, Pope Stephen II, who was afraid that the Longobards would try to attack Latium, still formally part of the Byzantine Empire but understood to be under papal control, invited the Franks, a Germanic tribe who had settled in present-day France and converted to Christianity, to join in his defence.

In 754 the Franks invaded northern Italy and conquered most of the Longobard possessions, formally bequeathing the Exarchate, the Pentapolis, Umbria and Latium to the pope and establishing the basis for the future State of the Church. To show appreciation for the Franks' help and to strengthen his alliance with them, in 800 CE Pope Leo III crowned their new king, Charlemagne, and bestowed on him the title of Holy Roman Emperor, acknowledging him as the heir of the glory of Rome and, at the same time, the defender of Christianity. In southern Italy, the Longobards were left with only the dukedom of Benevento, which included parts of present-day Abruzzo, as well as parts of Apulia and Campania. The Byzantines maintained control over Sardinia and Sicily (which would soon be lost to the Muslims), as well as eastern Apulia, Basilicata and Calabria, until the Normans conquered them in the eleventh century. In these southern areas, the vast Roman-style estates continued to constitute the core of agricultural activities that still focused on ideologically indispensable (and commercially profitable) crops such as wheat, wine and olive oil, whose production had decreased in the north of the peninsula.

## THE MANORIAL SYSTEM OF PRODUCTION

After the Byzantines acknowledged the existence of the Holy Roman Empire in exchange for the promise that their territories would be safe, the Franks were able to reinforce their presence in northern and central Italy, where massive movements of populations, wars and violent changes of political leadership had caused the inevitable decline of the old urban centres, the settlement of the nobility in the countryside and the virtual disappearance of commerce. Without markets, cities lost their appeal for artisans and tradesmen, who instead found employment in the manors of the lords. The only vestige of past glory in the cities was the presence of ecclesiastic authorities, as bishops frequently chose to stay close to the cathedrals that reflected their role of spiritual (but also often civic) guidance. However, remnants of more organized agricultural activities, such as orchards, groves of fruit trees and closed fields, often survived in the areas of the countryside nearer to the urban centres.[33] For these reasons, despite their state of decadence, Italian cities maintained a cultural, economic and political role that was unknown in other parts of Europe in this period.

The Franks introduced a social, political and economic system based both on their tribal traditions and customs inherited from the

Germano-Roman civilizations, such as the lifetime concession of land, called *beneficium*, and the *commendatio*, the protection of another person in exchange for services.[34] Kings and great lords assigned sections of the territories under their control to their closest followers, who came to be known as 'counts', from *comites*. The Latin word, originally indicating companions, had been used during the Roman Empire for those who enjoyed the emperor's trust, obtaining formal positions in the administration or the army. Border areas (or *marcae* in Latin) were usually entrusted to a military general, in this case called *marquis*. At first, the relations of vassalage were based on military and economic obligations towards the king and were revocable. The king sent representatives known as *missi dominici*, which means 'sent by the master', to the periphery in order to control the local lords, who were expected to serve him in case of war. However, over time the sovereign's lieges turned the territories they controlled into hereditary fiefs where rural workers did not legally belong to the lords but were tied to the lieges through various forms of servile dependence.

From an economic point of view, this system, known as feudalism, was based on a regime of rural lordship organized around the *curtis* or manor, an institution that was already common in the Frankish territories of northern Europe and adapted to the territories conquered in Italy through customs and social functions inherited from the Roman legal traditions. Estates were divided into two parts: the lord directly exploited the lands around his dwelling, known as the *pars dominica* or demesne, feeding and taking care of the peasants (called *servi dominici*, or master's servants) who lived there. These were neither free to leave the land they worked on, nor to change occupation. The *pars dominica* often included structures necessary to manufacture food products, such as wheat mills, bread ovens, oil presses, vats for wine fermentations and cellars. Artisans lived in quarters located close to the residence of the lord, providing him with their services. The rest of the lord's estate, or *pars massaricia*, was divided into little plots (*mansi*) toiled by peasants known as *servi casati* (servants living in huts), who lived in a state of greater independence than the *servi dominici*. Nevertheless, being obliged to work the lord's fields for a certain number of days every year and to give him part of their meagre agricultural surplus, they were also more prone to food scarcity. Peasants had few incentives to expand cultivation or to improve yields and land quality, because much of what they produced was taken away from them.

Europe in the 9th century.

Over time the Frankish domains in Europe broke down into three parts. The Italian territories first fell under the jurisdiction of the portion that included the Low Countries, Lorraine, Alsace, Burgundy and Provence, and were later incorporated into Germany, whose king also assumed the title of Holy Roman Emperor. Taking advantage of these developments, the Church tried to affirm its autonomy from the imperial authority, causing a rift that would last for centuries. The feudal system introduced by the Franks maintained its prevalence in northern and central Italy until the eleventh century CE, while the south of the peninsula remained under Byzantine control.

## THE RICH AND THE POOR

Almost no surplus resources were available for investment or commerce as most food was produced for consumption in the largely self-contained and self-sufficient rural units controlled by feudal lords and in the agricultural plots inside and around cities. Long-distance exchange based on monetary economy virtually disappeared, being limited to luxury items like spices for the most affluent strata of society.

The rich and the nobility practised diets and table behaviours that reflected distinctions of wealth and social status. To celebrate successions, weddings, victories and other relevant events, feudal lords organized social gatherings where abundant meals were used as instruments to reinforce solidarity among the members of the nobility and to define their cultural identity. Nevertheless, banquets were not too frequent. The ordinary food of the nobility was not that different from what their humbler counterparts consumed. In his biography of Charlemagne, the courtier Einhard describes the Frankish emperor as a restrained eater.

> He rarely ate at banquets, and only for special occasions, but in that case with many guests. Everyday dinner only had four courses, besides the roast meat that hunters were used to put on a skewer for him and that he enjoyed more than any other food . . . He was so moderate in drinking wine or anything else that during dinner he rarely drank more than three times. In summer, after the midday meal, he used to eat some fruit and drank only once, after which he disrobed and rested for two or three hours.[35]

During their feasts, guests consumed alcoholic beverages and large amounts of grilled or roasted meat. Hunting and game continued to play an important role in the diets of the upper classes, as the nobility enclosed increasingly larger tracts of land for their own private use. During Frankish domination, counts, marquises and even lesser vassals affirmed their prerogative to reserve wooded areas without the express permission of the king. These enclosures became much more frequent starting from the thirteenth century, with the exception of Sicily where, as we will see, the Norman kings maintained strict control over the natural resources in their territories.[36] The exclusive control over hunting grounds was not only an expression of power, but also ensured access to products that could be used in a network of gift exchange that reinforced social connections within the upper classes. This transformation of property rights paralleled what has been defined as the 'aristocratization of violence', that is to say the exclusive right for nobles to bear weapons.

Wine regained pre-eminence, not only in the feudal courts but also among all those who could afford to buy it. The beverage, which played an important part in the medical practices of the time, was considered conducive to good health. Mostly popularized by calendars, dietetic advice was also presented in more systematic ways in treatises like *De Observation Ciborum*, written in the sixth century by the doctor Antimus.[37]

Often very strong and not very well made, various sources suggest that wine was usually consumed with water to soften its taste and moderate its alcohol content. At the same time, the wine was supposed to make the water it was mixed with safer to drink. The cultivation of vines in the early Middle Ages cannot compare to the organized and trade-oriented production of Roman times. It was mostly concentrated in monasteries and in the closed fields around the cities, with dry stakes and low-down growth as technologies of choice.[38]

When it comes to the eating habits of peasants and lower-class city dwellers, the lack of visual and textual documents is mitigated by archaeology findings, which in the past decades have allowed historians to form a much clearer picture of what most of the population ate. Peasants based their diets on cereals and pulses, often ground and made into bread or mixed with water for porridges. As ovens were, in most cases, located in the manors and controlled by the lords, bread was relatively expensive even when made of grains such as rye and oats. Cabbage, beetroot, carrots, fennel, leeks and onions were used in soups that cooked all day long on pots hanging in the hearth, to which pieces of dried or salted meat, especially pork, could be added, as fresh cuts were considered a luxury. From the available iconography, it appears that pigs were smaller and hairier than today's, probably more closely connected to wild varieties. All over Italy goats and sheep (also smaller than contemporary ones) maintained their relevance as sources of wool, milk, cheese and meat. Oxen were employed for fieldwork and cows were milked to produce cheese, a very important source of proteins. In fact, archaeological findings indicate that peasants also consumed beef meat, and not only from animals that were too old to work. Furthermore, peasants were allowed to hunt and fish. This availability changed from the ninth century, when the elites started enclosing hunting areas dedicated to their exclusive use.[39] These discoveries complicate the widespread perception of the Middle Ages as plagued by frequent and prolonged famines, as texts like this, penned by a monk around the year 1000, seem to confirm:

> When there were no more animals or birds left to eat, people, forced by the pain of hunger, resolved to feed on any kind of carrion and other things that disgust even if you only talk about them. To avoid death others had recourse to tree roots and river grass, but to no avail, because there is no escape from God's wrath, except than in God himself.[40]

# Hunger in the Middle Ages

Was hunger really endemic in the Middle Ages? After the fall of the Roman Empire, peasants — both Roman and Germanic — developed strategies to employ diverse sources of food in times of scarcity. They regularly practised agriculture and foraging, blurring the cultural distinctions between what in Roman times had been known as *ager* (cultivated land) and *saltus* (wilderness). Despite war, social turmoil and the loss of arable land, the demographic contraction and the lack of administrative structures allowed the lowest strata of the population to have easier access to food, even if only in terms of mere subsistence. Once rural techniques reverted to a level that did not require stable investments, improvements or efficient organization, landowners did not feel the need to enclose their properties, and peasants were allowed temporary access to land to establish clearings for the cultivation of their crops, to feed their animals or simply to hunt.

With the advent of the manorial system from the ninth century, landlords were able to exert stricter control on food production and transformation, frequently depriving farmers of any available surplus. In situations marked by low rural productivity, lack of stored food, the slightest change in weather, a bad harvest or any turmoil would cause scarcity among the exploited peasantry. Even in the absence of catastrophic famines, hunger became an endemic phenomenon and a structural presence in everyday life, playing an important role not only in art, religion and legends, but in terms of political ideology and strategies of production. Of course, the cultural perception of what was considered food scarcity or famine changed over time, with relevant political consequences. While it is true that food riots always derive from food insecurity and high prices of staples, food scarcity does not necessarily lead to turmoil if it is framed in socially acceptable terms. Conversely, times when food is available can be marked by social instability connected to perceived scarcity or, more often, to a sense of unjust distribution determined by cultural categories and political power struggles.

Hunger played an important role in art, religion, legends and literature, especially represented as lack of bread.[41]

Monasteries continued the tradition of fasting and abstinence from meat on Fridays, at Lent and in preparation for other religious holidays. Nevertheless, in many monastic communities a more refined cuisine emerged, based on fish, eggs and wheat bread. As monasteries expanded their control over larger tracts of land, which often included rivers and ponds, freshwater fish became more readily available for the monks. Fish, which had already been used in Roman funerary ceremonies, had played an important cultural role in Christianity since its inception. As well as being the protagonist of many relevant episodes in the Gospels, from fishing events involving the apostles to the multiplication of loaves and fishes, the animal had been adopted by the first Christians as their symbol because the Greek word for fish, *ichthys*, was an acronym for Jesus Christ son of God and Saviour (Iēsous Christos, Theou Yios, Sōtēr).[42]

As literacy plummeted after the fall of the Roman Empire, including among the upper classes, we do not have recipes dating from the early Middle Ages. However, it is possible to access documents that deal with food and eating in unexpected fields, for instance diplomacy and religious life. Anthimus, who worked at the court of the Byzantine emperor Zeno and then in Ravenna under the Ostrogoth king Theodoric, wrote a letter – *De Observatione Ciborum* (Observations about Food) – to another Theodotic, the king of the Franks in Metz. His observations reveal the cultural contrasts between the Greek-Roman food customs and the practices of other less 'civilized' people, who ate raw meat and acted like wolves:

Therefore, as we said above, first and foremost health comes from well-cooked and properly digested food. If somebody asked: 'How can a man on a war campaign or during a long journey observe these precepts?' I would answer: whether a fire is available or not, the above mentioned things must be done. When circumstances require one to eat meat or anything else raw, these should be eaten more sparingly, not to one's satiety. But what else could I add to this, as since antiquity it has been said that 'everything hurts in excess'? When it comes to drinking, if one is riding a horse or is busy toiling, that person will be troubled by the stirring of the horse, and in the stomach worse things may happen than when eating food.

81

But if somebody asked me: 'Why are the nations that eat raw and bloody meat still healthy?' Although they may not be healthy at all, since they make remedies for themselves – when they feel sick, they burn themselves on the stomach and the belly and the other places, just like horses burn themselves when they are mad – I want to provide an explanation. They eat one kind of food only, just like wolves. In fact they do not eat many kinds of food, because they only have meat and milk. They eat whatever they have and one could think they are in good health because of scarcity of food. As for beverages, sometimes they have them, sometimes they have none for a long time, and that scarcity seems to ensure their health. In fact we, who enjoy different foods, different delights, and different cups with delight, need to govern ourselves in such a manner so as not to by overcharged with abundance. Eating more sparingly may maintain our health.[43]

Chapter 39 of the Holy Rule of St Benedict, entitled 'Of the Quantity of Food', gives directions about the quantity of food that monks should consume, and allows us to peek into the daily lives of these men who dedicated themselves to work and prayer:

Making allowance for the infirmities of different persons, we believe that for the daily meal, both at the sixth and the ninth hour, two kinds of cooked food are sufficient at all meals; so that he who perchance cannot eat of one, may make his meal of the other. Let two kinds of cooked food, therefore, be sufficient for all the brethren. And if there be fruit or fresh vegetables, a third may be added. Let a pound of bread be sufficient for the day, whether there be only one meal or both dinner and supper. If they are to eat supper, let a third part of the pound be reserved by the Cellarer and be given at supper.

If, however, the work hath been especially hard, it is left to the discretion and power of the Abbot to add something, if he think fit, barring above all things every excess, that a monk be not overtaken by indigestion. For nothing is so contrary to Christians as excess, as our Lord sayeth: 'See that your hearts be not overcharged with surfeiting.'

Let the same quantity of food, however, not be served out to young children but less than to older ones, observing measure in all things.

But let all except the very weak and the sick abstain altogether from eating the flesh of four-footed animals.[44]

The lack of recipes in Western Europe contrasted greatly with the diffusion of culinary texts in the eastern Mediterranean, where starting from the ninth century CE a new power developed that would have a dramatic and sudden impact on the political balances in the Italian peninsula: the Islamic Empire.

### The Muslim Expansion: A Wave from the East

After the death of the prophet Muhammad, who had founded the first Muslim community in 622 when he moved from Mecca to Medina in the Arabic Peninsula, the followers of the new religion expanded their domains with amazing speed. Within a few decades, northern Africa as well as large parts of the Byzantine Empire and Central Asia had fallen under their control. Their seemingly inexorable expansion was stopped only in the middle of the eighth century by the Franks in the West and by the Chinese in the East. Having secured most of Spain and the southern coast of the Mediterranean, in 827 the Islamic state based in modern-day Tunisia attacked Sicily and several Mediterranean towns. Over time, the Muslims occupied Corsica, Sardinia and the small island of Pantelleria. In 846 they sacked Rome, then Apulia, where they founded the emirate of Bari, and organized raids as far as southern France. In 902 they completed the conquest of Sicily with the defeat of the city of Taormina, on the eastern coast of the island.

From the technological point of view, the Muslim civilization adopted and diffused agricultural practices based on intensive cultivation, irrigation, canalization and drainage that increased outputs, while facilitating the adoption of plants with far-flung origins. Recent debates have questioned the actual role Islam played in reviving Western European agriculture through the introduction of new crops and technologies, some of which were in fact already known in the area, although fallen into disuse.[45] At any rate there is little doubt that a territory that stretched from Central Asia to the Atlantic facilitated the movement and adoption of diverse agricultural techniques, ingredients, dishes and cooking styles. For instance, aubergines, spinach, pomegranates,

Terraces built by Muslim settlers in Tricarico, near Matera in Basilicata,
adapting to the steep slopes and the scarcity of water.

almonds, rice, saffron and indigo were introduced into Sicily, together with
the cultivation of sugar cane, which stimulated the production of sugar.[46]
Lemons, sour oranges (the sweet ones would be introduced later, in the
sixteenth century) and limes – known as *lumie* – also became an important
part of the Sicilian landscape. Many of these crops did not expand to
the rest of the Italian peninsula. Because they required advanced agricultural skills and technologies they were not easily adaptable to the manorial
production system, and were often perceived as too closely connected
with the 'infidels'. The Muslim newcomers managed to reintroduce – at
least in Sicily – the ancient tradition of the Mediterranean garden that they
had adopted in the Byzantine territories they occupied in the Middle
East. Agricultural technologies, crops and products circulated easily across
the Islamic world. For instance, we have traces of the use of Sicilian
cheese in Arabic recipe books.[47]

Original cooking styles and food practices emerged in the urban
centres of the Muslim empires, so refined that they greatly impressed
the uncouth Christian knights during the Crusades in the eleventh and
twelfth centuries. Meals were served on large trays placed on small trestles,
and customarily consumed with the hands; spoons and knives were used
by the upper classes who dedicated great care to food presentation,
especially decorations and colours. Gold, white and green were among
the favourites.[48] Probably out of concern for purity and cleanliness, also

recognizable in other features of Islamic culture, scents and perfumes were very important not only in food preparations but also as a requirement for those who shared meals, who were always expected to be perfectly clean and fresh (an aspect which baffled Westerners). As for the recipes, Islamic cuisines are the result of encounters between various culinary cultures, such as the Arab, the Byzantine, recognizable in the consumption of Mediterranean products, and the Persian, with its penchant for fried meats, the presence of fruit and nuts (including almonds) in meat dishes, and rice.[49] Due to the availability of sugar, sweet-making and pastry reached high levels: sherbets – non-fermented, sweetened fruit juices – were often added to ice, marking the origin of sorbets. Sugar was mixed with ground almonds to make marzipan. Techniques to candy fruit and to model sugar for decoration slowly spread in the Mediterranean, and through Italy they would reach all of Europe.

Despite the ethnic fragmentation, the Islamic world maintained a strong cultural identity and became an integrated economic space where commerce flourished along the trade routes connecting the Mediterranean to the Indian Ocean, Southeast Asia and East Africa.[50] Thanks to Muslim merchants, spices from India (pepper), Sri Lanka (cinnamon) and as far as the Moluccas (clove and nutmeg) reached the Christian kingdoms of Western Europe, where they were considered luxuries with a notable role in medical and dietary theories. Under its Islamic rulers, Sicily became part of this lively commercial network. Considered *dhimmi*

*Frutta di Martorana*, fruit-shaped confectionery made from marzipan, a technique probably introduced during the Muslim presence in Sicily.

(protected subjects), Christians and Jews were allowed to profess their own faith, and many kept their occupations as merchants and artisans in major urban centres in the Mediterranean under Islamic rulers. Jewish communities, whose food traditions gave birth to what later became known as Sephardi cuisine, were very influenced in terms of technique, ingredients and sensual appreciation of flavours by the Muslim environment. Palermo became one of the most important cultural and economic hubs in the western Mediterranean. Numerous Islamic elements were absorbed into local culinary traditions. As well as the success of candied fruits, marzipan and sorbets, dried nuts and fruits such as almonds, raisins, pistachios and dates were also incorporated into the local pastry industry. To this day, sweet-and-sour recipes, the addition of pine nuts and raisins to savoury dishes and the overall love of sugar and honey are still recognizable in Sicilian dishes such as the aubergine relish *caponata*, *sarde in beccafico* (baked sardines rolled around pine nuts, raisins and lemon zest) and fried *sfinci* drenched in honey for the St Joseph holidays.

## THE NORMANS: A NEW WAVE FROM THE NORTH

The culinary traditions and crops introduced in Muslim Sicily managed to survive – at least temporarily – the arrival of the Normans, who at the beginning of the eleventh century invaded the island. The new-comers were descended from the Viking tribes of warriors and seafarers who, around the year 900, had settled in the French region of Normandy, still named after them. Converted to Christianity, they occupied Britain by defeating the English army at Hastings in 1066. From their bases in northern France, Norman warriors sold their services as mercenaries all over Europe, including southern Italy, where they became aware of the riches of the Mediterranean lands

The Normans were not the only population that swept through Europe after the Muslims. The Hungarians, who had settled in Pannonia (present-day Hungary) in their movement from the steppes of Eastern Europe, organized destructive incursions into the Po river plain and the Tuscan Apennines. Their attacks shook the remnants of the Frankish power structures and allowed individuals, known as *boni homines*, or men of good will, to assert themselves and assume leadership against the invaders. At times these men coincided with the local counts, and the agricultural land they controlled came to be known as *contado*, or 'land of the count', from which the Italian word for farmer, *contadino*, derives. Later on, the word *contado* would slowly take the meaning of 'countryside' as urban areas in the centre and the north of Italy gained various degrees of autonomy from feudal lords, thanks to special immunities.

The actions of these *boni homines* focused on building fortifications, walls, ramparts and towers, which became the core of the towns perched on hilltops that still charm visitors to this day. Homes were built next to each other to allow better defence in case of attack. Many of the farmers who had been living in isolated houses in the surrounding countryside moved into these fortified centres, introducing changes in agricultural practices as workers then had to go back and forth between their residences and the fields.[51] Furthermore, in many areas where the abandoned plains had turned into malaria-infested marshes, the hilltops offered a healthier environment.

While the political landscape was changing radically in the north of the peninsula, some Norman families in Salerno were hired as mercenaries to protect the city against the Muslim incursions, and later received feudal rights over the towns of Aversa, Melfi and Capua in exchange for their services. They quickly assumed the role of defenders of the pope against Islam and the Byzantines. In 1091 one of these nobles, Robert of Hauteville, defeated the Muslims and expelled them from Sicily. His son Roger later extended his dominions to include the former Byzantine colonies of Apulia, Basilicata, Calabria, the Longobard territory of Benevento and the cities of Salerno, Amalfi and Naples, which up to that point had maintained varying degrees of autonomy.

The Norman kings, who ruled over a mixed population of Greeks, Arabs and subjects of Germanic and Roman-Germanic descent, absorbed many Byzantine elements in their practices related to ceremonial matters, politics and bureaucracy.[52] They introduced a very centralized political structure, employing Greek and Arabic functionaries, but they also applied elements of the feudal regimes whose principles and workings the Normans had embraced in northern Europe. The Normans' rulers had direct control over vast possessions and were particularly preoccupied with the taxation of trade and agriculture. Overall production decreased, affected by the conquest wars, lack of maintenance of the irrigation systems and the deportation of Muslim farmers from Sicily.[53] At times wheat, one of the most important crops in the area, was not made available to the local inhabitants but rather sold elsewhere to take advantage of the higher prices connected with the increase of the European population (we will discuss this in the next chapter). The Hauteville kings granted tax reductions to foreign

Castel del Monte, fortress built by the Norman king and German emperor Frederick II near Andria, in Apulia, a standing symbol of the Norman military power over southern Italy.

Illustration from a copy of Frederick II's hawk-hunting manual, 13th century.

merchants, maintaining the relevance of southern Italy and especially Sicily in Mediterranean trade.[54] In case of scarcity, however, the king would embargo all exports and ensure that wheat was moved to where it was needed, a system inherited and expanded by the Anjou rulers who replaced the Normans in southern Italy in 1268. Furthermore, the Norman crown reserved monopolistic control on important activities such as salt production and tuna fishing. Monasteries and churches often received important tax-exempted land donations and even free pasturage in the royal territories, despite the problems caused by the transhumance of sheep.[55]

The south and north of Italy had fallen under two completely different kinds of political rules, developing divergent economic structures with relevant consequences in the following centuries. The long period between the penetration of the Germanic tribes into the Roman Empire and the arrival of the last wave from northern Europe with the Norman conquests marked a pivotal transition in the history of food in Italy. The presence of populations coming from remote lands and living according to very diverse customs had a profound impact on Mediterranean agriculture and its products. The demographic decline caused by migrations, wars, famines and epidemics determined a decrease of cultivated areas, with large tracts of land reverting to the wild and often turning into woods. The relationship with nature embraced by the Germanic newcomers increased the cultural appreciation of hunting, fishing and foraging, largely absent in the Greek-Roman civilization that focused instead on agriculture as the highest expression of human control over the environment. Eating habits also changed, with every new wave of migrants bringing new products, customs and techniques. The resulting mosaic would fully express itself from the twelfth century, when innovations in agriculture, a substantial demographic increase, the rebirth of a market economy and new political and social structures laid the foundation for one of the most refined, creative and original periods in Italian history: the Renaissance.

# THREE

# Rebirth

S tarting in the twelfth century, for the first time since the splendours
and excesses of the Roman Empire, the Italian peninsula became once
again one of the cultural engines of the world. Despite the increasingly fragmented political landscape, marked by frequent wars, foreign invasions,
civil unrest and intrigues, Italian cities experienced intense growth in terms
of production, trade and social mobility. These rapid changes were reflected in their arts and culture, which flourished in what came to be known
as the Renaissance.

## THE AGRICULTURAL TAKE-OFF

Enjoying de facto independence from their Byzantine rulers, coastal cities
such as Genoa, Pisa, Amalfi and Venice, also referred to as seafaring
republics, had reacted to the lack of productivity of their agricultural
hinterland by focusing instead on commerce in valuable goods such as wine
and olive oil. During the Crusades, the expeditions that the Christian
kingdoms organized against the Muslims in the Holy Land, these trading
hubs on the Italian coast assumed the role of mediators between Europe and
the territories around the Mediterranean under Islamic control.

The most radical changes took place in northern and central Italy, in
areas still nominally under the control of the German emperors, who had
succeeded the Franks as leaders of the Holy Roman Empire. After centuries
of decadence, Italian cities gradually moved towards self-governance,
establishing political structures based on voluntary associations of citizens,
known as *comuni* (communes). Not only merchants and artisans but
also lesser feudal lords who moved their residences from the countryside to
the cities dominated civic life. Monetary circulation took off, motivating

Arezzo, Piazza Grande. Squares became the centre for cultural and political life
in the Italian cities that adopted self-government under the *comuni*.

landowners to invest in commercial and financial ventures managed by
the urban elites. These activities led in turn to the development of banking and credit instruments, such as credit letters, that facilitated
long-distance movement of capital. The bustling markets became once
again the centre of urban life, absorbing surplus production from the
countryside, boosted by technical innovations in agriculture. Commerce
turned into a fundamental source of tax revenue for the cities. It became
a priority to establish more efficient controls on food quality and consistent
forms of measurement for all sorts of products and merchandise.

With the limitations imposed by the conservation techniques
available at the time, a few food products from the countryside –
especially wines and cheese – acquired renown well beyond their place
of origin, thanks to far-reaching trading networks. Parmigiano Reggiano
is mentioned in the *Decameron*, the famous collection of novellas written
in Italian by Giovanni Boccaccio in the 1350s.[1] Boccaccio describes
mountains of grated parmigiano with plenty of macaroni and ravioli
rolling down their slopes in the country of Bengodi, an imaginary land of
never-ending abundance.[2]

Andrea Mantegna, *Jesus Praying at the Mount of Olives*, 1459, San Zeno, Verona. The painting
reflects the careful landscaping and agricultural work on the hillsides close to large towns.

These fantasies on one hand channelled the desire for a life without
any worries about lack of food, which indicates that food scarcity was
a widespread issue; on the other it reflected new products and customs
that were the result of the epochal changes that were taking place in the
centre and north of Italy. There, peasants deforested, reclaimed, drained
and toiled large expanses of previously abandoned lands in the areas
around the cities. Far from the customary control of local lords, the
increase in arable land would prove fundamental to feeding the growing
population. At times, the intense process of deforestation and the enclosure
of previously open fields limited pasturage and the production of forage,
with the consequence that cattle could be raised only in low numbers,
causing scarcity of dung for fertilization.[3] Some feudal lords improved the
productivity of their lands by inviting monks to found abbeys in their
domains, especially where draining of marshes was necessary. The monks
also contributed to the reorganization of large-scale pasturage, including transhumance: the seasonal movement of sheep between the plains
in the south, where flocks spent the winter, and the hills of central Italy,
which provided cooler climates and more grass in summer.[4] Inevitably,
monasteries increased in size and power, thanks to the frequent donations

from landowners and rural lords. Their lands were worked by hired labour, with monks managing the production and the commercialization of their crops. Over time, monastic diets became more abundant and varied, even if monks still observed the fasting periods and consumed more vegetables and fruit than the upper classes.

Urban centres organized the reclamation and management of nearby territories, especially in the case of hills whose soil conditions deteriorated due to excessive deforestation.[5] Responding to the growing need for timber for construction and firewood, hillsides were subject to clearings, while trees like chestnuts and olives were often planted in open fields. Around the Apennines, especially in times of scarcity, chestnuts were ground into a versatile and filling flour. While fields were usually ploughed straight down hill slopes, increasing soil erosion in some areas of Tuscany, the coast of Liguria, the Amalfi coast and Sicily, where the mountains were closer to the sea and the dangers of erosion and running waters were more urgent, farmers built banks (*ciglioni*) and terraces (*terrazze*) planted with olive trees, grapevines and citrus fruits.

Cities undertook projects to regulate water supply, build irrigation canals and maintain riverbanks. Around the river Po, these interventions increased the use of waterways for transportation and trade and fostered the diffusion of efficient water-powered mills. Technological innovations played a fundamental role in improving agricultural productivity. The introduction of the three-field crop-rotation system replaced the old method of two-year rotation (cereals and fallowing), allowing farmers to

Around the Apennines, especially in times of scarcity, chestnuts were ground into a versatile and filling flour.

plant fields with autumn crops (wheat), spring crops (pulses, barley, rye) and fallow herbs. As metal technologies advanced and iron became more accessible, blacksmiths forged innovative tools such as the heavy mouldboard plough. At the same time, the introduction of the front yoke allowed oxen to breathe better and to pull the ploughs with full force, increasing productivity. Planted by landowners and monasteries, vineyards constituted a common feature of both urban and rural landscapes. However, the productive improvements in the countryside did not always mean better life conditions for the peasants, freed from the traditional powers of feudal lords but increasingly subjected to the control of the urban elites. Contractual relationships were now based on economic and juridical obligations, rather than on tradition, and were designed to intensify efficiency and trade. Rural populations removed from urban centres continued to produce and consume lower-yielding cereals such as rye, oats and barley.

Reclaimed lands closer to cities were frequently planted with wheat, allowing the increase of bread consumption in urban centres. City authorities frequently regulated wheat trade and its taxation to secure supplies.[6] Venice established a flour warehouse as soon as 1228, and in 1284 Florence instituted the *Sei del Biado*, an office charged with grain provisioning and sales.[7] Following the growing availability of wheat, fresh and dried pasta consumption increased in the cities. Fresh pasta, customarily made with soft wheat, was frequently rolled into thin sheets referred to as lasagna, a word already present in ancient Greek texts as *laganon*, testifying to the long history of this product in the Mediterranean. Fresh pasta was produced either domestically by the cooks of the elite families or in specialized shops that sold locally. Dried pasta was called *tri* or *tria*, a corruption of the word *itriyya* that appeared around the ninth century in Syrian and Arabic medical texts and that in turn probably came from the Greek *itrion*, used by Galen in his medical work. Later on, *tria* came to be known as *vermicelli* (little worms). The expressions *fideos* in Sardinia and *fidelli* in Liguria, both deriving from the Arabic *fidaws*, were also employed for vermicelli-like or rice-shaped pasta products.

Dried pasta was instead produced for long-distance commerce. With vast durum wheat cultivation and its location at the heart of the Mediterranean, Sicily was the perfect place for this activity. In twelfth-century Sicily, *itriyya* pasta was manufactured not far from Palermo and traded by the shipload to Calabria and other Christian lands. This activity was mentioned in the work of al-Idrisi, the Muslim geographer at the court of the Norman king Roger II. Genoa and the area of Naples would later emerge as relevant centres for this commerce but until the fourteenth century the only competition was Sardinia, which under the control of the Aragon king produced great quantities of durum wheat and traded in *obra de pasta*, as pasta merchandise was defined by the local customs officials. Dried pasta was rarely mentioned in the recipe collections of the time, reflecting its contested place in the diet of the nobility. The upper classes preferred fresh and perishable products, perceived as more desirable and consonant with their status than dried or cured ones, as employing cooks who made fresh pasta whenever needed was plausibly considered a sign of distinction and wealth. However, dried pasta did appear among the products provisioned for the court of Aragon and it was consumed by well-off urban dwellers.[8]

## Urban Culture and Culinary Refinement

In the burgeoning cities, professions connected with food became increasingly specialized and regulated. To elevate their status, artisans established guilds (*arti* or *corporazioni* in Italian), which, under strict control from the local authorities, imposed standards and procedures on production. Accessible only after long apprenticeships, guilds ensured employment to their members and assistance in case of accidents. At the same time, by limiting access to the profession, they kept the prices for their services high. Among the most respected categories were flour millers, breadmakers, who prepared breads and cakes with the flour provided by their clients, and oven owners, who eventually baked the final products. The breadmakers from Piacenza were so highly regarded that they were allowed to pay for one of the pillars of the local cathedral, with images of their activities sculpted on its capital. Even tavern keepers and butchers, who in the past had almost been considered sinners, were allowed to organize themselves in guilds. Foodstuff was often produced and processed in the outskirts to keep bad odours and filth out of the cities, as in the case of butchers, cold cut curers, and cheesemakers.[9] Butchers left the messier aspects of their activities to other artisans, such as tripe vendors, *lardaroli* and *salaroli* (lard and salami makers). Tavern keepers thrived on the intensification of market activities, selling wine, bread and cheese (less often cooked meals) to travellers.

The expansion of trade and artisanal production, together with a wider availability of food due to the increased output of agriculture,

## Spices and explorations

Spices, considered luxury items, featured prominently in Italian culinary texts from the end of the Middle Ages. Coming from India (pepper), Sri Lanka (cinnamon) and places such as the faraway Moluccas or Spice Islands (clove and nutmeg), they reached the Mediterranean and the Christian kingdoms of Western Europe through the trade routes controlled by Islamic rulers. In the fifteenth century, the Portuguese were stimulated by the expulsion of the Moors from Spain and Portugal and were also determined to break the monopoly held by the Egyptian Mamluks and the Ottomans over the trade in gold, slaves and the precious spices that trickled into Europe through Venice and a few other ports. They thus embarked in a programme of explorations under the guidance of Henry the Navigator (1394–1460), brother of the Portuguese king Edward.

The colonization of Madeira (1420s), the Canaries (1430s) and the Azores (1440s) became stepping stones for the introduction of Old World crops such as sugar and bananas into the Atlantic world. After establishing trading bases in Senegal and in the Cape Verde islands off the western coast of Africa, the Portuguese passed the Cape of Good Hope in 1487, imposing their presence along the Indian Ocean trade routes. They did not establish colonies but opted for the

Nutmeg was among the most priced spices in the Renaissance.

occupation of crucial ports, such as Hormuz in the Persian Gulf, coastal towns in Mozambique, Aden at the entrance of the Red Sea and Malacca in today's Malaysia. Furthermore, the Portuguese established bases in Macao, to trade directly with China, and Nagasaki, opening the first commercial gateway to Japan.

These developments temporarily limited Venice's spice trade at the beginning of the sixteenth century, but it seems that later on the flow of spices found its way back to the Mediterranean, partly as a result of the inefficient control over the Red Sea and the Persian Gulf by the Portuguese functionaries in India. The Venetians focused on Alexandria in Egypt and Aleppo in Syria, located on the caravan routes from Basra and Baghdad. As a consequence of the greater availability of spices, and in particular pepper, their consumption increased greatly in Europe.

transformed diets and culinary habits all over Italy. The nobility and the urban upper classes were able to afford frequent banquets that shone with refinement, elegance and the choice of prestigious ingredients. The ideal of the noble warrior who displayed his physical prowess, wealth and social capital through the ingestion of enormous quantities food was outmoded. Instead, diets and table manners became markers of social distinction. On formal occasions guests shared bowls, goblets and trenchers, usually slices of bread or pieces of wood on which solid foods were placed. Spoons were available to serve soups and food with sauces. Guests used their fingers to eat, cleaning them on the tablecloth, a new addition to the decoration of the table. It was considered impolite to suck one's fingers clean, to put back the food taken from the serving dish or to spit close to the table. Wine was likely to be found on all kinds of tables, with price, quality, origin and prestige determining its status and its use among different classes. According to medical and dietary practices, wine was nutritious for everybody, regardless of age, season or location. It prevented and cured illness and was considered 'hot' in humoral theories. As such it was believed to favour digestion and the production of blood.

Refined dishes tended to incorporate expensive spices such as cinnamon, ginger and pepper. During the Crusades, the growing connections with the eastern Mediterranean had rekindled interest in exotic styles and ingredients. Saffron gave golden hues to food, while sugar – at the time considered a spice – decorated and enriched many recipes.

On well-off tables, game was side by side with poultry, pork and mutton. Meat was often poached before roasting in the pan or on skewers. Medical theories often indicated that vegetables and pulses were too heavy for the delicate stomachs of the nobles, due to their cold and humid nature. However, as we will see, the Italian upper classes seemed to have fewer qualms about their consumption. Growing close to the earth, they were more suitable for the lower classes. Instead fowls were considered proper nourishment for the sophisticated palates of the upper classes. Noble natures were to consume lighter and more refined food, while workers and countryside dwellers could digest heavier fare like black bread or wild grass. Individual bodies were supposed to reflect the make-up of the universe, determined by God in his infinite wisdom, and diets followed the alleged divine order of the world, which included the organization of society and its different classes. Dietary habits were not interpreted as a consequence of economics, but rather as the expression of innate instincts that reflected spiritual natures.[10] Flavours, reflecting the humoral traits of foods, were considered important not only for the enjoyment of a meal, but also for the health of the eater, since when one ate with pleasure, one digested more easily. Beside the categories of sweet, bitter, salty, sour and acid, traits like astringent, unctuous, spicy and the mysterious *ponticus* were employed to describe flavours.[11]

It is not by chance that the first appearance of cookbooks in Italy of the late Middle Ages coincided with the agricultural take-off, the expansion of urban life and the profound changes in the way the upper classes thought of and performed food consumption. The first cookbook we know of, the *Liber de coquina*, was written in Latin at the end of the thirteenth century, probably at the Anjou court of Naples. As very few people were able to read and write, and books were rare and precious objects, the recipe collection reflected the culinary style of the higher classes. It was meant for well-educated readers, probably nobles who could use it to choose dishes and give orders to their staff, or who were interested in the topic. The *Liber de coquina* refers to recognizable local traditions within Italy, like the *tria* from Genoa or cabbage in the Roman style. It also mentions more exotic fare from other countries, revealing European circuits of recipes and cooks that moved from court to court. The book includes recipes for vegetables, disdained by nobles in other parts of

Europe. Made luxurious by expensive spices and refined preparations, vegetable dishes suggest permeability between the practices of different social strata, as many cooks came from the lower class and cooked for the high. Towards the end of the fourteenth century, various collections in local dialects and in Italian appeared, such as the anonymous *Libro per cuoco* (Book for the Cook) in Venetian dialect. Books written in the vernacular, where recipes included practical directions on ingredients, cost, preparation time or necessary tools, were probably directed at professional cooks who were able to read, indicating their upward status.

Tuscany emerged as a centre for cookbook production in vulgar Italian – the forefather of the modern standard Italian language – with the *XII gentili homini giotissimi* (The Twelve Very Gluttonous Noblemen), a collection probably meant for the upper bourgeoisie, and the *Libro della cocina*, heavily indebted to the *Liber de coquina* in Latin but with a larger section dedicated to vegetables and written between the end of the fourteenth century and the beginning of the fifteenth. The two recipes I have translated here suggest a collection targeted towards well-to-do households who could afford the services of professional cooks. Both dishes display a certain flair for spectacle, which assumes their use in formal banquets.

---

*How to Stuff a Peacock*

Skin the peacock, leaving the feathers on its head. Take some pork meat, not too fat, and grind and pound it together with some of the peacock meat. Also pound cinnamon, nutmeg and the spices that you prefer. Mix them carefully with egg whites and the meat, and beat them with energy. Put the yolks aside. Stuff the peacock with the ground meat mixed with spices, then wrap it with pork caul fat [the lacy white 'net' around a pig's intestines] and secure it with wood skewers. Place it like this in a pot of warm water and let it simmer gently. When it has lost some of its volume, roast it on a skewer or grill it, and brush it with some of the eggs yolks you had set aside. Don't use them all, but save some to make meatballs. To do so, finely chop a raw pork loin with a knife and beat it hard; mix the meat with the yolks and the spices, then make small balls

---

with the palms of your hands. Roll them in yolks to give them colour and boil them in water. After boiling them, you can roast them and decorate them with egg yolks, using a feather. You can place these balls inside the peacock or underneath the caul fat. When you are done, dress the peacock back inside its skin, with all its feathers, and bring it to the table.

*Trout Pie*

Make some hard dough [with flour and warm water] and mould it in the trout's shape or in a round shape. Gut, scale, wash and salt the trout, place it in the dough mould and put ground spices, oil and saffron on it. Close the mould following the shape of the trout, and make horns at each end, like a boat. Make two small holes in the dough, at each end, or make just one in the middle. Cook it in the oven, or in between testi [hot stones]. When it's well cooked, pour rose water or the juices of oranges or citrangole [a variety of orange with a stronger taste that was appreciated for its medical qualities]. During the times of the year when meat is allowed, put some melted lard in it instead of oil. You can make similar pies with other fish: sardines, anchovies, red mullet and others.

## CRISIS AND RECOVERY

The economic and social ferment did not extend to all of Italy. In the south, still under Norman rule, political autonomy and economic entrepreneurship were not allowed to flourish and commercial agriculture lost some of its relevance for lack of specialized labour. In the thirteenth century, King Frederick II of Hohenstaufen, who happened to be both king of Sicily and the Holy Roman Emperor, because of dynastic intricacies, tried to revamp the cultivation of indigo and sugar, together with more common products such as oranges, aubergines and almonds. He employed members of the dwindling local Muslim communities and hired specialized farmers from Muslim countries. However, after Frederick's death these attempts at reviving cash crops were abandoned, and only revived at the end of the fourteenth century, thanks to the investments of foreign merchants.[12]

Frederick II enforced strict controls over trade. The chronicler Riccardo from San Germano informs us that in 1232 the king issued an edict against offences that included exchanging sows for pigs, selling the meat of dead animals or tainted food, keeping perishable goods for long periods and watering down wine. The merchants who were caught infringing the edict were condemned to the payment of an ounce of gold, or two if the transgression was committed against pilgrims. If they did it again, a hand was cut off, while for the third offence the punishment was death by hanging.[13] The edict demonstrates the widespread mistrust of merchants and the market and the king's will to assert his rights against local traditions and prerogatives, extending his direct control over city life and commercial activities.

The Norman rule over southern Italy ended in 1268 when Charles of Anjou, a son of Louis VIII of France, seized power with the help of the pope, who felt threatened by the union of the crown of Sicily with the Holy Roman Empire. Although Jews in southern Italy were forced to convert en masse, some maintained their cultural and religious identity in secret, while others migrated to the eastern Mediterranean communities.[14] The Anjou presence in Naples lasted until the mid-fifteenth century, but their power did not survive in Sicily, where in 1282 they were ousted by local nobles who chose the king of Aragon, in Spain, as their lord.

After the end of the thirteenth century the economic and demographic expansion that had stimulated Europe and Italy for two centuries slowed down. The climate got colder and wetter, causing frequent famine. The Black Death killed millions, striking Italy in 1347 after sweeping across the eastern Mediterranean. Arable lands and whole villages were abandoned. High demographic density and unhygienic conditions inside cities made urban dwellers particularly vulnerable. The shrinking population caused food demand to drop, which in turn depressed the price of wheat. With the exception of Lombardy, where agricultural activities remained stable, at the end of the epidemics landowners had a hard time finding cheap labour. Many survivors occupied the plots left available by the deceased, bargaining for higher salaries and developing forms of sharecropping, or *mezzadria*, particularly in Tuscany and central Italy, where farmers owned cattle and tools.

In the south, however, where feudal property was still prevalent, French and Spaniard lords colluded with the local nobles to circumvent royal controls, enclosing common agricultural lands and expanding theirs 'preserves' for sheep pasturing in response to the growing demand for wool.[15] While in the north cattle breeding developed around stable farms, the centre and the south of the peninsula saw the expansion of the transhumance system. Revenues from flocks that spent winter in Apulia were collected by the *Dogana delle pecore* (literally the Customs of Sheep) established in 1447 by King Alfonso 1 of Aragon, first in Lucera and then in Foggia. The popes created a similar institution in the Agro Romano. Southern peasants lived in dramatically poor conditions, as the nobility had little incentive to embrace agricultural innovations. Additionally, there were only limited attempts by the kings of Naples and the popes to reclaim marshy lands and to adopt new technologies.

The general state of uncertainty and unrest led *comuni* from central and northern Italy to hire professional leaders, called *potestà*, whose task was to find a balance among divergent interests and factions within the cities. When this kind of solution did not work, various forms of autocracy became common, such as *signorie* (when an individual seized power and the *comune* recognized his position) and *principati* (when the new leaders were, at least at first, representatives of higher powers, such as the emperor or the pope). This turn towards oligarchic and aristocratic systems had already taken place in Venice, where in 1297 access to the

Venice merchants built their wealth — and the splendid palaces that reflected it — on the spice trade with the eastern Mediterranean.

governing Great Council was barred to those individuals who had not been members in the previous years. The ruling elite abolished the *commenda* contract, actively eliminating upward mobility for new merchants, and limited access to international trade only to the nobility – especially in the lucrative routes to the eastern Mediterranean.[16]

The aristocratic turn in politics, however, had positive consequences for land management in many parts of Italy, increasing yields and rural production. Especially in the Po plain, the concentration of power around Milan and Venice allowed a better coordination of public works, particularly in terms of sanitary improvements, canalizations and irrigation systems. Each court financed projects to increase agricultural revenues and to showcase power and wealth, recruiting technicians and scientists from all over the peninsula. Canals in the Po plains divided the land into fields with quadrangular shapes, with banks planted with trees, shrubs and grapevines festooned from trunk to trunk.[17] The diffusion of this landscape, known as *piantata*, corresponded to the diffusion of mulberry trees from southern Italy, where they had been introduced by the Byzantines.[18] Mulberries stimulated the growth of the silk industry, which is still relevant in the area. In the fifteenth century, improved water control allowed the expansion of rice cultivation, which thrived in northern Italy thanks to the involvement of the local political powers. Modern farms were established where crop rotation was practised together with well-organized cattle breeding, cheesemaking and dung collection, which in turn ensured manure for the soil. Alfalfa, sainfoin and clover were planted to ensure the fertility of the fields and provide forage for cattle.

## POLITICAL INSTABILITY AND THE RENAISSANCE

With the establishment of *principati* and *signorie*, each using diplomacy and intrigue to expand at the expense of its neighbours, Italian cities and kingdoms were frequently involved in wars. Foreign powers such as France and Spain took advantage of this situation by extending their influence over the peninsula, often descending on their enemies with massive armies that brought chaos and destruction. Despite the long-lasting political instability, fourteenth-century Italy saw a deep cultural transformation marked by the rediscovery of classic Roman and Greek arts, the increased relevance of lay literature and philosophy over the traditional teaching of the Church, and an overall re-evaluation of the

Italy, 1635.

role of people in history and nature. The arts flourished thanks to the patronage of the Italian courts (including the pope's), each displaying their magnificence by competing to hire the best artists.

Each state had its own legal and commercial system, its own currency and even its own weights and measures. If this situation hindered the circulation of goods, still subject to scarcity, drought and war, it also made the possibility of accessing products from elsewhere more attractive, in some cases turning certain goods into novelties and markers of social status.[19] Cities in northern and central Italy became engines of conspicuous consumption. Marketplaces were important public spaces where customs, taste and social relationships were negotiated. They were politically crucial, since the disruption of the provisioning channels was likely to incite social unrest, and morally problematic, if not dangerous, partly because of the presence of taverns and brothels. It was not considered proper for respectable women to shop unaccompanied or to look lingeringly at goods in various establishments.[20]

The physical environment of the market facilitated the surveillance of trade by functionaries and passers-by, with customers milling in the open space of the street or the square and sellers behind the counters of shops. Porticos and other permanent structures were built, although food was also sold in temporary markets that took place regularly in locations established by tradition and sanctioned by local authorities. Farmers coming into town from the countryside were allowed to sell their goods from stalls, tables and even just cloth on the ground, after paying a fee to the market functionaries. Cooked food was available from street vendors selling from carts, shops with permanent kitchens and counters, taverns and inns that also offered lodging to travellers. To avoid fraud, states and cities organized forms of control with the collaboration of ecclesiastic institutions and trade guilds, which maintained their medieval functions and structure to dominate many sectors of food sales, production and transformation. Male cooks belonging to organized guilds were hired by the elites to coordinate kitchen servants, often women, who were also in charge of food preparation in common households.

## COURTLY SPECTACLES

The variety and abundance that consumers could enjoy in the marketplace was reflected in the domestic environment. The renewed interest in the sensual aspects of human life, often neglected in previous centuries, influenced the social and aesthetic appreciation of food.[21] During the Renaissance banquets remained an important form of socialization for the upper classes, where excitement, entertainment and visual dazzle were as significant as the quality of food and the cooks' skills.[22] The relevance of these occasions is revealed by their frequent representation in many paintings of the period, as artists focused on an activity that was likely to entice viewers, while paying homage to the wealth and refinement of their patrons.[23] Banquets were so spectacular that public authorities all over Italy attempted to pass sumptuary laws meant to curb excesses in the quantity and the quality of the food consumed, as well as the number of guests.[24] The extreme display of wealth was considered not only morally reprehensible, but also dangerous in terms of public order, especially during periods of food scarcity. Even in fasting periods (Wednesdays, Fridays, many holiday eves) great care was given to copious and sophisticated menus. However, sumptuary laws had to be reissued frequently, revealing the low level of respect held for these provisions by the upper classes.

Banquets were structured in a number of successive 'services', composed of several dishes placed on the table at the same time. Guests could taste what they wanted or, more often, what they were closer to. Presentation was paramount: fowls would be served dressed in their own feathers, and rams in their own skins. In the Italian courts, meals frequently included an alternation of 'kitchen services', or warm dishes, and 'sideboard [*credenza*] services', consisting of lighter or cold dishes. The meal usually began with a sideboard service and included at least two kitchen services. At the beginning of the meal, it was not unusual to offer a 'service' of fresh fruits or salads seasoned with oil and vinegar, which were thought to prepare the stomach to receive more substantial dishes. Grand banquets required specialized servants such as the *trinciante*, who spectacularly carved meats tableside, off skewers and serving forks. All the staff were coordinated by the *scalco*, who also supervised the cooks and established the sequence of the services with the host. He was also helped by the *credenziere*, in charge of the *credenza*, and the *spenditore*, who scouted the markets to secure the provisions.[25] Wine was highly appreciated in all social classes, but during banquets only the best quality was offered: the *bottigliere* (bottler) was in charge of choosing, buying and pairing wines with the dishes, while a *coppiere* (cup bearer) served them.

Great attention was paid to etiquette, reflected as early as the late thirteenth century in *De quinquaginta curialitatibus ad mensam* (Fifty Courtesies at the Table), written by the lay friar Bonvesin da la Riva. The short poem, with a Latin title but written in Italian, describes 50 forms of courtesy around the table, including washing one's hands, waiting politely before sitting down and keeping one's elbows off the table:

> The eighth courtesy, God will, is to avoid stuffing your mouth excessively and eating too fast; the glutton who eats quickly and with his mouth full would have problems responding when talked to . . .
> The sixteenth courtesy is to be careful about how you behave when you sneeze or have a cough; be courteous and turn in another direction, so that saliva does not fall on the table.
> Another courtesy is not to put your fingers in your mouth to clean your teeth, while you are eating with educated men.[26]

Manuals on good manners developed into their own literary genre, peaking with the *Cortegiano*, published in 1528 by the diplomat Baldassarre Castiglione, and the 1558 *Galateo* by the archbishop Giovanni della Casa. Guests were expected to restrain from excessive gluttony and from

Limonaia, Villa La Pietra, Florence. Renaissance villas had large gardens that were often used for entertaining and outdoor dinners.

conversing openly about the dishes they were consuming (with the exception of wine). Rinsing bowls, napkins and tablecloths helped improve hygienic conditions. In the case of formal banquets, several tablecloths were placed on the tables to be removed after each course. Dinner tables were not permanent yet; food was still served on planks placed on portable trestles, which allowed meals to take place not only in formal rooms, but also on terraces, under loggias and in gardens. The fork was adopted as a sign of personal refinement. Although the two-pronged fork was a common serving and carving implement, its use for individual eaters spread among the upper classes of Italy only in the fifteenth century. We already see it in the painting *The Wedding of Nastagio degli Onesti* (1483) by Sandro Botticelli. By the sixteenth century the tool was widely employed for consuming fruit and sweetmeats.[27]

While wooden eating vessels were still prevalent among the lower classes, ceramics were appreciated among more affluent diners, who showed preference for individual dinner plates. Since the late Middle Ages, pharmacists had used ceramic vessels for storage with the name of the content clearly painted on, to keep herbs and spices in good condition.[28] During the Renaissance, beautiful ceramics, tin-glazed and brightly hand-painted over an opaque white background, were manufactured in specialized centres such as Faenza in Romagna, Castelli in Abruzzo,

Early 15th-century jar from Faenza, one of the main Renaissance centres of ceramic production.

Deruta in Umbria, Ariano in Campania and Laterza in Apulia.[29] Technical improvements were probably connected with the diffusion of methods and procedures from the Islamic world.[30] Similar dynamics also took place in glass production, with the appearance of thinner materials, clearer hues and original shapes that fitted well with the demands of the elites.[31] Venice, and in particular the tiny island of Murano, became famous centres of glass production.[32] From the sixteenth century, serving vessels made of metal became fashionable, allowing artists like sculptor Benvenuto Cellini to show off their skills and originality. The production of table objects such as salt cellars reflected the sensibilities of the new and intellectually sophisticated style known as Mannerism, which aimed to surprise with inventiveness, wit and recourse to compositional complexity.[33]

In the sixteenth century, Italy was the epicentre of innovation and fashion in high-end food, a role later taken on by Spain in the first half of the seventeenth century.[34] Elements from lower-class food customs were introduced into courtly cuisine, such as wider use of cheese (cookbooks mention pecorino, *provatura*, parmigiano, *caciocavallo*, mozzarella and Sardinian cheese), offal (brain, ears, even eyes) and vegetables such as fennel and artichoke. Beef and veal appeared on refined tables as did fish like cod, sturgeon and caviar, especially during 'lean' days of liturgical fast. Bartolomeo Scappi mentions goose foie gras, which Jewish communities produced in Ferrara, Piedmont and Veneto.[35] It was still impossible to identify what we now refer to as 'national cuisines' – a set of ingredients, techniques and dishes that characterize the food customs of a specific nation state. All over Europe, elites shared a wide canon of dishes and a similar style that maintained medieval traits, such as the lack of clear distinction between sweet and savoury courses, the abundant use of spices, sour sauces bound with breadcrumbs or ground almonds, and visually stunning dishes meant to impress diners. However, cookbooks identified dishes with specific foreign origins, exhibiting the circulation of techniques and ideas among professional cooks working in the courts of Europe.

It is difficult to establish the precise sway of one cuisine over another. Scholars contest the theory that in 1533 the arrival of Caterina de' Medici in France as wife of the future king Henry II, together with a cohort of cooks from Florence, established the Italian influence over French culinary arts starting from the sixteenth century. This initial introduction was probably limited to the incorporation of Italian table manners, including the fork, the taste for fresh vegetables and the techniques for the use of sugar in confectionery, jams and candied fruit.[36] Triumphs and decorative sculptures made of sugar were also in fashion, as Venice and Genoa imported the sweet substance from the new Portuguese colonies of Brazil and Madeira and exported it all over Europe.[37]

## Health, Diet and Cooking Manuals

During the Renaissance, as intellectuals emphasized the centrality of man in the universe and in culture, cuisine became a field of learned reflection built on moral principles and health theories. This approach was ushered in by the rediscovery of the ancient Greek and Roman medical texts that had been lost in Western Europe during the Middle Ages. The Islamic world played a fundamental role in the transmission of the medical sciences and the dietary principles codified by Galen and other authors from antiquity, based on the humoral theories discussed

*Homo signorum*, or the Man of the Zodiac Signs, from an almanac of 1580. In the late Middle Ages, the human being was considered a reflection of the universe and its rules.

previously. This corpus of knowledge, transmitted throughout the Byzantine Empire, had been translated by Nestorian refugees into Syrian and later brought to Persia, where it was made available to the local scholars and eventually integrated into the scientific discourse of Islamic intellectuals. Humoral theories were further enriched by authors such as Averroes and Ibn Sinna, also known as Avicenna. Avicenna, who lived between the tenth and eleventh centuries, reorganized the humoral theories in his canon of medicine (*Qanun*), an encyclopaedia in five volumes that became the authority in the field. Much of this information was later arranged in tables that took the name of *taqwim al sihha*, meaning 'summary' or 'organization of health' in Arabic, which in turn gave birth to the genre of the *Tacuinum Sanitatis*, propagating medical information about diet.[38] Starting from the eleventh century, the ancient texts were translated back into Latin, as the work by Costantitus Africanus in the Benedictine abbey of Montecassino (near Rome) indicates. In the twelfth century, the school of medicine founded in Salerno, near Naples, compiled the *Regimen Sanitati Salernitanum*, a dietary manual in the form of a poem that embraced the humoral theories and popularized them all over Italy. Here are some excerpts:

The best wines are white and sweet.
If you drank so much at night that you feel sick, drink again the
    morning after: it will be your medicine.
With sage, salt, pepper, garlic, wine and parsley, you can prepare a
    great sauce, as long as you do not corrupt with other ingredients.
Drinking only water during the meal provokes great disturbance

Page of a *Tacuinum Sanitatis* from the 14th century, explaining the
medicinal qualities of wine.

to the stomach and blocks digestion.

After a peach, eat a walnut, and after meat, cheese.[39]

In the heart of Salerno, the Silvatico family built a garden filled with officinal plants used for therapeutic purposes, organized according to the humours they represented. A doctor from the Silvatico family, Matteo, used it to teach the students of the medical school, showing them the plants, their names and their characteristics. Only recently was the garden rediscovered and restored to its original plan.[40]

In the second half of the fourteenth century, intellectuals such as the poet Frances Petrarch fought against the influence of religion and Church-approved philosophy over medicine and other sciences. The terrors of the plague of 1348 convinced many of the powerlessness of current medicine. After the fall of Constantinople in 1453, numerous Greek scholars came to Italy, boosting the cultural overhaul that was sweeping the country. From the 1470s to the first half of the seventeenth century, a great number of dietary volumes were published, stimulated by the invention of the printing press. The first works, still deeply influenced by the Muslim teachings, were destined for the courts. As Greek original sources became available, scholars embraced the moderation they extolled to critique the lifestyle of royal and noble households – including the papal court in Rome – for their excess, often labelled as gluttony. At the same time, the spreading Reformation undermined traditions connected with Catholicism such as Lent fasting and abstinence. Although Leonardo da Vinci had already gained an understanding of digestion in terms of mechanical forces, it was only at the end of the sixteenth century that independent investigation flourished, often revising the received wisdom derived from ancient sources.[41] Scholars such as Andreas Vesalius and Gabriele Falloppio demonstrated the weakness of the anatomical concepts in the Galenic theory by dissecting corpses. Numerous authors, including Gerolamo Cardano, Alessandro Petronio and Giovanni Domenico Sala, opposed widespread nutritional concepts, basing their critique on personal observations.[42]

Considering the growing cultural and political relevance of banquets and the influence of learned reflections on health and diet, it is not surprising that cookbooks flourished. The most famous recipe collection from the early Renaissance, Maestro Martino's *Liber de arte coquinaria* (Book on the Art of Cooking), was probably written between 1464 and 1465.[43] We have little information about the life of the author, whose work is available in five manuscripts. Providing few references to specific local traditions, Maestro Martino's work was groundbreaking in many ways. For the first time, recipes were placed in coherent chapters and provided precise information about the necessary ingredients, procedures and even the required tools, unlike previous works that tended to hide this kind of information, which was likely perceived as trade secrets. The recipes testify to the slow transformation of courtly food in the Renaissance, when refinement and sophistication were embraced not only by nobles, but also by the bourgeois notables that actively participated in the civil and economic life of the Italian cities. While still focusing on the spectacular aspect of the dishes and reflecting the popularity of Catalan cuisine at the beginning of the fourteenth century, Maestro Martino's recipes also reveal the influence of Muslim culinary traditions, probably filtered through Sicily, in the use of rice, dates, bitter oranges, raisins and prunes. The distinction between sweet and savoury dishes became more noticeable.

Vegetables and legumes are conspicuous in Maestro Martino's collection, showing how fresh produce was reaching the table of the elites. He offers recipes for peas, fava beans, turnips, fennel, mushrooms and cabbage 'Roman style,' seasoned with pork fat and stewed in meat broth. Garlic, parsley, elder, thyme (*sarpillo*), mint and other aromatic herbs are widely included. The presence of urban orchards and markets dedicated to the sale of herbs and vegetables in many Italian cities proves that their consumption was much more common than contemporary dietary treatises suggest.[44] The elites appreciated the fruit of their own properties, as suggested by Maestro Martino's inclusion of recipes for cherries, quinces and even prunes. Noble households often used fruits as gifts, but since self-sufficiency was impossible they bought provisions from merchants, preferably from those they knew and trusted. Of course, for the elites, raw and cooked vegetables were just a small part of a meal, prepared in dishes ennobled by the presence of spices such as pepper, saffron, ginger and cinnamon, intended to entertain and impress guests as an aspect of what historian David Gentilcore defines as 'reverse snobbery'.[45] Later on, as the Counter-Reformation led to a more controlled and orthodox cultural climate, especially in the pope's territories, painters and writers employed fruits and vegetables as sexual metaphors and sources of humour, reflecting the cultural relevance and the ubiquity of these foods on the upper classes' tables.[46]

The influence of Maestro Martino is confirmed by the incorporation of his recipes in the book *De honesta voluptate et valetudine* (Honest

Pleasure and Health, 1474) by Bartolomeo Sacchi, also known as Platina, a food connoisseur and a librarian at the Vatican, who wrote in Latin and acquired fame all over Europe. Platina, trained in the study of classic literature, stressed the cultural aspects of dishes and products, giving cuisine a higher status while renewing its association with the medical and philosophical theories of the time. He gave a new interpretation to the concept of culinary pleasure, far from the excesses of gluttony: 'Who is so removed from the life of the senses out of sanctity or severity of customs, who is so silly that he does not want to provide pleasure to body and soul, eating with measure to ensure good health?'[47] He frequently referenced local dishes and ingredients, especially from the areas he was most familiar with – Rome, central Italy and the Po river plain – connecting their specific qualities with their places of origin. Platina acknowledges that most of his recipes came from Maestro Martino, whom he knew well and admired to the point of defining him as a 'prince of the cooks' who taught him all he knew about cooking.[48] Platina's Latin work was translated into many vernacular languages all over Europe, helping to make Italian courtly cooking the culinary standard of the time and the centre of all gastronomic innovation.

In the following decades, Italian banquets became more complex in terms of dishes, service and vessels involved, reflecting the taste for complexity, originality and inventiveness that Mannerism was expressing in the arts. Most cookbooks were written by *scalchi*, the professional in charge of the choreography of the meal, the composition of the menu and the order of the services. At the same time, the expansion of the printing industry made these works available in unprecedented numbers, spreading the technical information and the aesthetics they contained. Cristoforo Messisbugo, with his *Banchetti, compositioni di vivande, et apparecchio generale* (Banquets, Course Composition and General Preparation, 1549), and Domenico Romoli, author of *La singolar dottrina* (The Unique Doctrine, 1560), exemplify the prestige of banquets where the variety and the inventiveness of the services was meant to dazzle diners and emphasize the taste and the wealth of the host. While sugar and spices were still very much in evidence, a leftover of the medieval style, Romoli highlighted vegetables in many recipes, dedicating a whole section to ordinary meals.

Messisbugo provides a detailed description of a few banquets that he organized. For instance, on 8 September 1531, the day celebrating the birth of the Holy Virgin, Bonifacio Bevilaqua had him 'prepare the table with two tablecloths, napkins, knives and saltcellars, and place a twisted

Cristoforo Messisbugo, in *Banchetti, compositioni di vivande, et apparecchio generale*
(Banquets, Course Composition and General Preparation, 1549).

bread and a small marzipan biscuit for each guest'. The menu includes a first
course comprising figs, eel pies, small puff pastries filled with *farro* in the
'Turkish style' and stuffed eggs, among other dishes, followed by little tarts
'Italian style', fried sea bream, pike tails, stuffed veal in broth 'Lombardy
style' with yellow mortadella, bread tarts, pork loins, small quince pies and
a sweet green sauce. Of course, other courses would follow, highlighting the
skills of cooks and *scalco*, and the munificence of the host.[49]

Bartolomeo Scappi's *Opera* (Works, 1570) constitutes the epitome
of the late Renaissance cooking style. In Rome, Scappi worked for
cardinals and two popes (Pius IV and V), becoming one of the great
innovators in Italian cuisine by providing precise instructions, guidance
regarding table arrangements – often inspired by architecture – and the
use of ingredients from America, such as turkey.[50]

Kitchen scene from
Bartolomeo Scappi's
*Opera* (Venice, 1574
edition).

It is necessary, as I understood in my long experience, that a wise
and careful cook who wants to have a good start, a better middle
and the best end, always honours his work as a judicious archi-
tect would do. After a good design, he lays good foundations
and building on that he gives the world the gift of useful and
wonderful edifices. The cook's design has to show beautiful and
secure order, based on experience that needs to be so extensive
that it is easier for him to work as a *scalco*, than for a *scalco* to
work as a cook.[51]

Structuring his monumental book as an encyclopaedic treatise,
Scappi reveals his interest in the ingredients that were available in the
markets of Rome, both local and imported from other Italian states. In
fact, he includes culinary elements from the Po river plain and from
southern Italy, commenting on the difference between the east and the

west side of the peninsula, especially when it comes to fish.[52] This allows us to explore the regional cuisines of the time, highlighting the most renowned products for each area and explaining methods and recipes to prepare each dish.[53] The same interest for local customs and ingredients emerges in Ortensio Lando's *Commentario delle più notabili e mostruose cose d'Italia e d'altri luoghi* (Commentary on the Most Notable and Surprising Things in Italy and Other Places, 1548). The book, describing the travels and discoveries of an imaginary 'Aramaic' foreigner in Italy, includes descriptions of foods from different parts of the peninsula.

## Mainstream and Minorities

Despite the lack of the advanced and sometimes extravagant equipment that adorned the grand kitchens of the elites, like copper pots and kettles, griddles, iron skillets, long revolving spits and grills, the basic cooking procedures employed in households from every walk of life were similar, designed to respond to fuel scarcity. The deforestation and expansion of arable land that had transformed Italy starting from the twelfth century had made wood hard to come by, especially in the cities. Roasting and baking were rare among commoners, and people brought foods and breads to ovens in specialized shops. Braising in closed metal or earthenware vessels on embers was popular. Boiling and stewing remained common cooking methods, as liquid ensured that no substance was lost during cooking.[54] The fire was moved from the centre of the main room of the house to a fireplace located along a wall and connected to a chimney.[55]

Grains still constituted the bulk of the diet of the lower classes, both in the cities and in the countryside. While wheat remained prevalent in the south, in the countryside of the north other grains were common, such as buckwheat, often ground and mixed with corn flour, and rice. At times the latter was acquired by local authorities as food for the poor to be distributed in case of scarcity or famine. The availability of wheat made cooking with dough more common. *Pasticci*, two layers of hard dough filled with all kinds of ingredients, were popular as a cooking implement, placed on the embers in the hearth and then frequently discarded. *Torte* and *crostate* were similar to *pasticci*, but the dough was thinner and had butter or lard kneaded into it, which made it edible and tasty. Scappi mentions *torte* in Naples which, less than half an inch thick and without a dough lid, were the likely progenitors of pizza. The consumption of fresh and dried pasta increased thanks to technical innovations such as the manual break to knead greater quantities of dough and the extruder to shape it. Commercial production became more efficient, more affordable and of better quality. As the control by city authorities over pasta production intensified between the end of the sixteenth and the first half of the seventeenth century, fresh pasta artisans, known as *lasagnari* or *vermicellari*, became autonomous from bread-makers and established their own professional associations.[56] The use of butter spread among all classes as its consumption was allowed on 'lean' days to replace lard, but olive oil was only available to the most affluent strata of society. Most protein for the lower classes came from sheep, goats and, above all, pigs, with cured cuts prevalent in the cities, where direct access to fresh meat was more expensive.

The Italian population was far from uniform and this diversity was reflected in culinary customs. However, no minority stood out as much as the Jews, whose culture set them apart from all Christians, whatever ethnicity or nationality they belonged to. Jewish culinary customs were largely influenced by frequent contact with fellow communities in the Middle East who still lived in Muslim environments. Among the more characteristic traits were sweet and sour seasoning, the incorporation of pine nuts and raisins in savoury dishes, little pieces of various foods covered in batter and deep-fried, and the use of exotic ingredients such as aubergine, considered dangerous by other Italians (the Italian word for aubergine, *melanzana*, derives from *mela insana*, unhealthy apple).[57] Of course, it is not possible to generalize: upper-class Jews showed a strong resistance to aubergines right into the nineteenth century.[58] Many of the Jews who were expelled from Spain in 1492, as well as from Sicily and Sardinia under Spanish control, moved to the Italian peninsula.[59] These arrivals were soon followed by an influx of German Jews escaping the persecutions that took place during the Reformation. The newcomers settled in Ancona, in the Marche regions, Rome and Venice, which in 1516 established a policy forcing Jews – who previously were not allowed to reside in the city – to live together in the same area, grouped according to their origins: *Tedeschi* from Northern Europe, *Levantini* from Egypt, Syria and Turkey and *Ponentini* from Spain and Portugal, each with their own culinary traditions.[60] The area where they lived came to be known as the ghetto, from the Venetian word *getar*, 'to smelt', because it used to have a foundry. In 1555, Pope Paul IV adopted the same policy in

A kosher baker's in the former ghetto in Venice.

Rome, obliging Jews to stay in the ghetto at night and to wear a yellow hat. Jews expelled from Avignon in 1570 moved to the Piedmontese town of Cuneo, preserving some of their French habits. In Trieste, a major port with strong ties to the Habsburg Empire, central European influences shaped the local Jewish traditions.

During the Renaissance Jews were not persecuted in all parts of Italy: many sovereigns welcomed them to attract their economic activities. Lively communities flourished in Verona, Ferrara, Mantua (its famous pumpkin *tortelli* may be connected with the Jewish presence), Florence and, above all, Livorno, a port town founded by the Grand Duke of Tuscany at the end of the sixteenth century. Here the Jews found themselves at the centre of trade networks that connected them to North Africa, Greece and the Middle East.[61] Couscous with meat and eggs as well as a fried cod and tomato stew are among the recipes of Jewish origin that are still popular. Some smaller towns in Tuscany allowed the presence of Jews. Among the most interesting is Pitigliano in the area of Maremma, where the Jewish community thrived until the Fascist persecutions. The *sfratto*, a staff-shaped dessert filled with

The small Tuscan town of Pitigliano.

nuts and honey, is a reminder of the stick used to knock on doors and announce the forced eviction (*sfratto* in Italian) of the Jews who then found refuge in Pitigliano.

The difficulty of keeping kosher dietary rules in Italy led rabbinic authorities to grant a small number of women permission to practise ritual slaughtering, although it does not seem this exception implied any change in female public roles.[62] Specialist shops and trades responded to the dietary needs of the Jewish population, as the numerous food-related words in the Italian–Hebrew dictionary *Dabber Tov* (Speaking Well), published in Venice in 1579, indicate. The dictionary's vocabulary does not include New World products such as tomatoes, potatoes or maize, which the Jews had probably not yet adopted. More surprisingly, the volume does not mention vegetables often identified with Jewish customs, including aubergines, artichokes and spinach.[63]

## THE NEW WORLD REVOLUTION

The Portuguese exploration of Africa and the Indian Ocean, followed by the arrival of the Spaniards in the Americas, led to the opening of new markets all over the world. Even if the Italian principalities and kingdoms were not directly engaged in colonization, many merchants from the peninsula were heavily involved in moneylending to princes and lords. Italian navigators such as Cristoforo Colombo (Christopher Columbus), Giovanni Caboto (John Cabot), Antonio Pigafetta, Giovanni da Verrazzano and Amerigo Vespucci made a name for themselves in the explorations financed by Portugal and Spain, later followed by France and England. These events laid the groundwork for the biggest ecological revolution in history, commonly referred to as the Columbian Exchange (after Columbus).[64] A large number of crops and animals were taken from Europe to the western hemisphere, where the Spaniards and Portuguese introduced wheat, olives, grapes and many vegetables like onions and cabbage, together with domestic animals such as chickens, pigs, cows and horses. The same phenomenon happened in the opposite direction. Unknown plants and animals from the Americas became the object of scientific interest, since they did not fit the traditional categories and classifications. The necessity to understand and find a use for the new crops relied on an approach founded upon direct observation that radically shook received wisdom, limited by the adherence to ancient texts, and contributed to the scientific revolution of the seventeenth century.

Some of the American novelties were successfully adopted in Italy as early as the sixteenth century. That was certainly the case for turkey, known as Indian chicken, one of the few animals that had been domesticated in the Americas.[65] However, due to the sense of cultural and moral superiority that the European settlers felt towards the populations they were in contact with, the practices connected with the preparation and consumption of new foods often did not cross the Atlantic. For instance, in Europe, maize was consumed without the process of nixtamalization, commonly applied by the American natives. 'Nixtamalization' derives from the words *nextli*, 'ashes', and *tamalli*, 'corn dough', in the Aztec language Nahuatl and indicates that the grain is hulled only after being soaked and cooked in an alkaline solution, usually limewater, as we will see in the next chapter. The lack of this culinary knowledge would lead to devastating health problems such as pellagra in northern and northeastern Italy, where maize replaced wheat as the main staple as peasants were allowed to grow it without having to pay taxes on it or give it to landowners as rent. Already in 1544 the geographer Giambattista Ramusio documented the diffusion of maize in Venice, and in the following decades its cultivation expanded in Lombardy and Emilia. Its high yields and capacity to grow on unfavourable soils determined its popularity, and in many areas it was planted in continuous rotation with wheat.

American beans quickly supplanted the older local types, among which only one, the black-eyed bean, survives to this day. The same happened with pumpkins: the new, bigger American varieties almost replaced the local long and thin *lagenaria*. Other plants, like tomatoes and potatoes, went through a much longer process of adaptation.[66] Tomatoes, whose presence is documented at the Medici court in Tuscany as early as the mid-1500s, were at first considered toxic and only good for decoration. In Italian they took the name of *pomidoro*, 'apples of gold', due either to the bright yellow hue of the varieties available at the time, or their addition to a category that included all sorts of soft fresh fruits.[67] Potatoes were not integrated into Italian eating patterns until the eighteenth century. On the other hand, sweet and hot chilli peppers were quickly and widely embraced, and spiciness became a feature of many southern dishes.

New crops were not all that came from the Americas to change the way Europeans ate. In the last decade of the sixteenth century, the price revolution ignited by the flood of gold and silver from the American colonies of Spain and Portugal unleashed its effect on European economies. Coins, made of precious metals, became less valuable and as a consequence prices increased much faster than the salaries of farmers and workers. Landed nobles, whose fixed rents were tied by customary relations with the peasants living on their estates, were at times forced to sell portions of their land to the upcoming bourgeois class, whose growing wealth often allowed them to join the ranks of nobility. The flight of capital towards rural properties would accelerate at the end of the sixteenth century, following the relative decline of artisan and mercantile activities in the cities. The crisis led many banking houses to redirect capital and investments towards agriculture. Towards the end of the sixteenth century the rise of prices, the population growth and the slowdown of technological innovation in agriculture caused social unrest and widespread food crises. As historian Eric Dursteler states:

> During the last decades of the fifteenth century, one in every six harvests failed in the Mediterranean. Between 1375 and 1791, Florence experienced 111 years of famine, and only sixteen harvests that could be classed as very good. The toll of famine

Peppers and squashes were among the crops introduced to Italy after the
arrival of Europeans in the Americas.

could be harsh: for example, recurring shortfalls between 1587
and 1595 contributed to Bologna's population plummeting
from 72,000 to 59,000.[68]

The anxiety caused by food scarcity was reflected in the work of
the writer Giulio Cesare Croce, from Bologna. Croce, better known for
his 1606 novel about the comical adventures of the peasant Bertoldo at
the court of the Longobard king Alboin, addressed the famine of 1590
in the *Banchetto de'mal cibati* (Banquet of the Underfed, 1608), sketch-
ing a parody of the excessive customs of the upper classes and describing
the sufferance of the commoners. An anonymous poem from the same
period, *Mala cosa e' carestia* (Famine is a Bad Thing) also laments the
consequence of lack of food:

> Often I use the stump of cabbages
> Instead of bread,
> In the dirt I make holes
> Looking for different and strange roots,
> And we use that to grease our faces.
> Wish we had that every day,
> It would not be so bad . . .[69]

In many European states, food scarcity was paired with tensions connected to the expansion of Protestant movements. The reaction of the Catholic Church, the Counter-Reformation, would have far-reaching consequences on Italian culture, starting from the seventeenth century.

# FOUR

# Fragmentation and Unification

The Italian Renaissance – including its culinary aspects – was marked by unprecedented brilliance and originality, with lords and kings competing with one another as patrons of the arts, literature and refinement. Banking on its financial and commercial power, the burgeoning bourgeois class strived to reach comparable levels of conspicuous consumption. However, the lingering social contradictions and the political fragmentation of the Italian peninsula eventually resulted in long-lasting economic stagnation. During the seventeenth century foreign occupants left a strong imprint on local eating patterns, while Italian cuisine lost its role as a powerhouse of culinary novelty and sophistication at the European level.

### ITALY UNDER FOREIGN INFLUENCE

During the seventeenth century, Italy remained politically divided, allowing Spain to extend its direct control over Lombardy and Milan, Sicily, Sardinia and the whole south. The efforts of the Catholic Church to limit the expansion of religious Protestantism against their temporal power, known as the Counter-Reformation, imposed a cultural climate that snuffed out the creative spirit of the Renaissance all over Italy. War, famine and epidemics decimated the population. The resulting decrease in demand for food made staples more affordable for city dwellers, despite the concurrent slump in agricultural production caused by lack of innovation and a temporary cooling of the climate. (A period of cold winters and humid summers, sometimes referred to as the Little Ice Age, had started at the end of the Middle Ages but worsened around 1650.)[1] As grain prices dropped, partly due to imports from Ukraine and

Eastern Europe, landowners – especially in the centre and the south of Italy – shifted their focus to cash crops such as grapes and rice, the latter spreading to Piedmont, Lombardy, Veneto and to the lower plains of the Po River. In those areas, the introduction of rice was facilitated in large expanses of land that had been reclaimed during the Renaissance and had turned back into swamps due to lack of hydraulic control. A similar abandonment of cultivated land took place in Tuscany (Maremma and Arno valley) and south of Rome in the Agro Pontino. As malaria became endemic, hunting and fishing were frequently the only viable productive activities as farmers could not settle down to grow crops.[2]

While depopulation heavily affected agriculture, Italian traditional luxury industries such as silk and wool manufacturing were facing competition from cheaper foreign goods. In northern Europe, textile production had moved out of the cities and into the countryside, far from the control of guilds, allowing for greater efficiency and lower prices. Unable to keep up with technological advances, Italian manufacturers also suffered from the shifting focus of Western trade from the Mediterranean to the Atlantic Ocean. The crisis of Italian commerce caused the stagnation of banking and finance. The *patriziato*, grand families who had made their fortune lending money to the rulers of the Italian states, took to buying land, hoping to be accepted among the upper ranks of society. These dynamics, which historian Emilio Sereni defined as the 'commercialization of the fief', were reflected in the multiplication of luxurious villas surrounded by glorious gardens that maintained no connection with productive activities but reflected their owners' wealth and social status.[3] The famous villas of Veneto, where artists like Palladio were able to express their creativity, continued to proliferate well into the eighteenth century.

Under the influence of Spanish culture, a growing distaste for mercantile and financial occupations shaped the nobility's sense of identity, expressed in the cult of lineage, the practice of duelling and the extreme value of honour. These practices were reflected in juridical institutions such as primogeniture, which ensured that all possessions of a noble were to be inherited by his first male heir, and *federcommesso*, which prevented an heir from dividing or fragmenting the estates he received. The noble landowners in the south of Italy, the *baroni*, suffering from Spanish fiscal pressure, had no interest in investing to increase agricultural yields and focused instead on husbandry activities, especially sheep for wool production. More intensive cultivations were visible only

Bernardo Strozzi, *The Cook, c.* 1625, oil on canvas.

around towns and villages, in small plots and temporary clearings that did not contribute much in productivity.

The deterioration of agricultural production in central and southern Italy was intensified by ecclesiastic organizations owning vast estates that were exempt from taxes and grew constantly through donations from nobility who died without heirs. These lands, on which no investment and little management were applied, could not be sold without explicit permission from the pope, according to a custom known as *manomorta*. The cultural and political influence of the Church of Rome, reinforced by ties with noble families whose cadet sons and daughters often joined its ranks, grew in the years of Counter-Reformation. The Italian Protestant movement was virtually suppressed, with the exception of the Waldensians, a community established in the thirteenth century that took refuge in the valleys of the Alps in Piedmont. In their relative isolation, the Waldensians developed culinary traditions that included buckwheat-based gruels, cheese-and-bread soups (called *barbet* from the local name for preachers), as well as meat-and-potato dumplings (*calhetta*), still found today in some villages in the area.

Motivated by the decreasing value of their agricultural production, nobles and landowners – both lay and religious – increased the pressure on peasants and farmers in terms of rent, services and other kinds of feudal encumbrances that had largely gone unreinforced in the fifteenth century. This trend towards 'refeudalization' limited the peasants' traditional rights of access to common lands that allowed them to practise subsistence agriculture, pasturage and wood gathering. Countryside dwellers moved to cities, increasing the numbers of urban poor and creating conditions for social unrest and full-on riots, especially in southern Italy. Naples, with its 300,000 inhabitants, had become one of the largest European cities, together with Paris and London. Most nobles in the kingdom of Naples lived in the capital, which attracted products from all provinces. At the time, Neapolitans were known as 'leaf-eaters' due to the prevalence of vegetables in their diet and their alleged passion for cabbage and broccoli. In 1647 the populace of Naples reacted to a new levy on fruit by taking to the streets. Their leader, the fishmonger Tommaso Aniello, known as Masaniello, was assassinated right after the riots. The movement, coordinated by the local bourgeoisie in search of greater influence over the politics of the kingdom, spread to the countryside, where peasants revolted against the barons. The Neapolitan rebels proclaimed a republic and asked France for help, but to no avail – the barons tightened their relationship with the Spanish representatives to avoid future reoccurrences of similar events.

Social tensions resulted in episodes of mass hysteria; in Milan individuals accused of spreading the plague were executed. Jews, who in many Italian cities were forced to live in closed ghettos, also became an object of suspicion. They were banned from selling macaroni and lasagne to Christians, and some local authorities issued sumptuary laws to limit food consumption in their communities. Little did they know that these laws were setting the building blocks for the creation of classic Jewish–Italian dishes. For instance, when in 1661 the Jews of Rome were prohibited from eating any fish but anchovies and sardines, they took to baking anchovies and endives arranged in layers, giving rise to the Jewish–Roman speciality, *aliciotti con l'indivia*.[4] Under heavy financial constraints, Jews in major cities were applying kashrut laws with

Representation of Neapolitan fishermen in an illustration for the opera *Masaniello*, by John William Gear, 1829–33.

flexibility, to the horror of the rabbis. Eels and sturgeon were widely appreciated. Roman Jews routinely ate mozzarella from the nearby countryside, while those in Emilia did not refrain from using parmigiano.[5] On the other hand, desserts, biscuits and marzipans produced by the Jews were highly appreciated outside the ghettos, even reaching the tables of nobles and lords.

## DECADENCE AND PRESTIGE

Italian courtly culinary styles lost some of their originality and inventiveness compared to the work of the sixteenth-century *scalchi*, the masters of the banquet that had marked Renaissance splendour. Bartolomeo Stefani in Mantua, in his *L'arte di ben cucinare et instruire i men periti in questa lodevole professione* (The Art of Cooking Well and of Educating the Less Expert in this Praiseworthy Profession, 1662), upholds Renaissance tradition but reveals less creativity, all the while making

## Changing medical theories

From the sixteenth century, authors such as Gerolamo Cardano, Alessandro Petronio and Giovanni Domenico Sala opposed traditional nutritional theories, basing their critique on personal observations. A German travelling doctor, Theophrastus Bombastus of Hohenheim, famous as Paracelsus, introduced chemical factors to explain the causes of diseases, indicating specific remedies for each. Building on the theories put forth by Paracelsus, chemists and alchemists postulated that many natural substances, when heated, separated into a volatile fluid that they equated to mercury; an oily substance, or sulphur; and a solid residue, or salt. While mercury determined smells, sulphur induced sweetness and moistness, and salt controlled the taste and texture of foods.

As the humoral theories were attacked by chemistry, the idea that digestion was similar to cooking slowly became obsolete and the process was interpreted instead as fermentation. Some physicians, referred to as iatrophysicists, tried to explain all physiological processes according to the laws of physics and mechanics. The Croatian Santorio Santorio (1561–1636), the son of a nobleman from Friuli in the

recipes and banquets more complex and overdone, reflecting the prevalent Baroque aesthetics that often highlighted exaggerated grandeur, exuberance, motion and drama over refinement and restraint. In the description of the banquet he organized for the visit of Queen Christina of Sweden in Rome in 1655, Stefani describes dishes from the first service of *credenza* thus:

Strawberries, washed in wine served with white sugar on top, and all around the dish seashells made of sugar and filled with those same strawberries, interspersed with small birds made of marzipan that look like [they are] pecking at strawberries. A soup of large pigeons cooked in milk and malvasia wine and, taken out of the cooking liquid, cooled off, stuffed with angel cake soaked in malvasia and sprinkled with sugar and cinnamon. The pigeons service of the Venetian republic, had studied the human body by weighing its solid and liquid intakes and excretions. Other doctors, known as ierochemists, maintained that chemistry was sufficient to account for all medical facts. Among these, the Belgian Jan Baptista van Helmont (1577–1644) argued that many physiological processes, including digestion and nutrition, are caused by fermentation converting food, a dead substance, into living matter. Franz Sylvius (1614–1672) also sought to explain physiological processes by suggesting fermentation (molecular motion of matter) and 'vital spirits' as moving forces.

Medicine gradually separated itself from dietetics and doctors focused more on identifying and healing diseases than on maintaining a healthy body. Scientific research and the theory of digestion as fermentation presumably had some impact – albeit indirect – on the way food was perceived and prepared; sauces rich in butter and oil were considered useful to bind salts and solid ingredients to substances with a high content of mercury, or volatile fluids, such as wine and spirits. Ingredients that fermented easily, like fresh vegetables and fruit, grew in acceptance and popularity.

were arranged in the shape of a rose, covered in pistachio milk, sprinkled with pine nuts soaked in rose water. On the rim of the dish there was a floral decoration made of sugar-glazed marzipan and outlined in gold.[6]

The pasta dishes and the vegetables conspicuously featured in works from the previous two centuries are almost entirely absent in Stefani's work, probably because they had become too common and accessible to deserve a place on the elite's tables.[7] Despite the stagnating economic situation, made worse by plague, war and social instability, a few high-end products from specific places remained popular among the elites of the Italian states. For instance, in 1661 Bologna had to issue a proclamation against the counterfeiting of mortadella, the famous pork product, still the pride of the city.[8] Some cookbooks displayed a stronger influence of local traditions, like Francesco Vaselli's *L'Apicio ovvero il maestro de' conviti* (Apicius, the Master of Banquets, 1647). However, the clearest examples of this trend were *La lucerna de corteggiani* (The Oil Lamp of Courtiers, 1634) by Giovan Battista Crisci and *Lo scalco alla moderna* (Modern Banquet Directions, 1692) by Antonio Latini, both Neapolitans. Crisci provides us with a broad and detailed list of delicacies and ingredients from the south, including areas like Abruzzo, Basilicata and Calabria. Tellingly, Crisci's references do not focus on cities, but rather on villages and rural areas, revealing the limited relevance of urban cultures in a political system dominated by nobles and landowners with sources of revenue located in the countryside.[9] In his book's preface, Latini declares his affection for Naples:

> Since I wrote in Naples, I decided to use the words that are common in this land, and not the foreign ones that are not understood here; moreover I declare myself particularly fond of it not only because of the advantages I obtained from it but also because of its rare privileges that everybody admires and that nobody can deny Nature has made a particular effort to endow it with.[10]

In his recipes, Latini paid particular attention to the local products of the southern peninsula, including the newly arrived tomato. We know from John Ray, a British naturalist who travelled in Italy in the 1660s, that tomatoes had already entered the culinary customs.[11] Among the recipes that included this ingredient, Latini presented a sauce for boiled dishes, quite similar to contemporary Mexican salsa, an aubergine, squash and tomato soup and a casserole including eggs, veal, pigeon and chicken necks.

Latini moved towards a clearer distinction between savoury and sweet dishes, embracing the culinary renewal spreading from France.[12] Those changes in culinary practices and cultural preferences took place along the lines of innovative medical and dietary theories that marked the end of the humoral interpretation of nutrition, shifting towards ideas and practices based on experimental sciences.

The treatise *Brieve racconto di tutte le radici, di tutte l'erbe e di tutti i frutti che crudi o cotti in Italia si mangiano* (Short Account of All the Raw and Cooked Roots, Herbs and Fruits Eaten in Italy), written in 1614 in London by Giacomo Castelvetro, highlights how Italians ate more vegetables than their northern neighbours. He wrote:

Felice Fortunato Biggi, *Putto with Fruit Festoon*, oil on canvas, *c.* 1750. Italians consumed greater quantities of vegetables than northern European populations, as writer Giacomo Castelvetro observed while living in London in the 17th century.

I am amazed that so few of these delicious and health-giving plants are being grown to be eaten. Through ignorance and indifference, it seems to me they are cultivated less for the table than for show by those who want to boast of their exotic plants and well-stocked gardens.'[13]

Later on, he revealed his dismay at how foreigners handled salads:

It is important to know how to wash your herbs, and then how to season them. Too many housewives and foreign cooks get their greenstuff all ready to wash and put it in a bucket of water, or some other pot, and slosh it about a little, and then, instead of taking it out with their hands, as they ought to do, they tip the leaves and water out together, so that all the sand and grit is poured out with them. Distinctly unpleasant to chew on.[14]

## The Grand Tour

Despite its lag in economic development, between the end of the seventeenth century and the mid-1840s, with the onset of rail transportation, Italy became an important travel destination for upper-class males from northern European countries. The main goal of what became known as the 'Grand Tour' was supposed to be educational, exposing young men to the sources of classic culture through visiting archaeological remains and works of art in cities like Venice, Florence and Rome. In many ways, however, the tour was perceived also as a rite of passage, during which the future members of the upper classes could experience exotic and at times dangerous environments. As only the richest families were able to send their scions to Italy for a long period of time, the tour also became a marker of social distinction.

Johann Wolfgang von Goethe, the famous German poet and intellectual, was one of those who embarked on the tour between 1786 and 1787. He left written memoirs of these travels in his *Italian Journey*, published in 1816–17. After visiting northeastern cities like Trento, Verona and – of course – Bologna, Florence and Rome, he continued south to Naples, even crossing by sea to Sicily to explore Palermo and other towns on the island. Although food was clearly not among his main interests, he provides interesting observations about the culinary customs of Italy, especially among the upper classes with whom he interacted. In 1787, for instance, he dined with the Filangieri family in Naples. Here are some excerpts from the description of the event, where one of the female hosts kept on teasing the monks at the table, a reflection of the changing intellectual climate at the time:

'The meal will be excellent,' she told me, 'all without meat, but all good; I will show you what's best, the choicest morsels. But beforehand, I need to torment the monks a little bit. I cannot stand this kind of people: every day they take something from our house. All we have, we should eat it with our friends.'

Meanwhile, soup was served and the Benedictine was eating with a modest attitude. 'Please, no ceremonies, reverend,' she said. 'If the spoon is too little I will have somebody bring you a larger one. You are used to eating in larger mouthfuls.' . . . During our conversations the good fathers were not left alone a second by the petulant insolence of my neighbour. In particular fish, which – respecting Lent – had been prepared to look like meat, became the never-ending source of irreligious and immoral comments.[15]

Goethe's description of Naples during the Christmas holidays is lively and rich with interesting details.

The stores where they sell herbs and show cantaloupes, raisins and figs, really cheer you up. Edibles are hung in wreaths along the street: you can see large crowns of golden sausage, tied with red ribbons, and turkeys all have a red banderole on their butt. They assured me that 30,000 had been sold, excluding those fattened in private homes. A great number of donkeys loaded with vegetables, capons and goat kids roam the city and the markets, and the mounds of eggs that you see here and there form a mass that you would not imagine this large. It is not enough that all this is devoured. Every year, an officer rides through the city, together with a bugler, and announces in every square and crossroads how many thousands of cows, veal, goat kids, lambs and pigs Neapolitans consumed. The populace pays great attention and rejoices for those numbers: everybody remembers, with satisfaction, the part they had in that delight.[16]

Goethe also left a lively account of the landscape and the inhabitants of Sicily. Nevertheless, the writer seemed to be more interested in the environment from a scientific point of view than in tasting the fruits of nature. For instance, describing Segesta, he mentions the intensely cultivated fields, the farmers at work, the cardoon and the wild fennel, but he does not provide any description of the aromas or flavours of those products. This is not surprising, as it was common for noble travellers to avoid local foods, especially when served by lower-class establishments, for fear of contamination and diseases.

## THE ENLIGHTENMENT

In the eighteenth century, just as in the previous one, the political destiny of the Italian states was determined elsewhere. Tuscany was given to the dukes of Lorraine, related to the Habsburg family. Spain transferred Lombardy to Austria, the Savoy of Piedmont extended their control over Sardinia and the kingdom of Naples passed to the son of the king of Spain, Charles of Bourbon, establishing a local dynasty, independent from Madrid, which ruled over southern Italy and Sicily until 1861. This period of intense diplomacy and widespread conflict also saw tensions grow between the Church and the rulers of various Italian states, who were trying to assert state authority over the nobility and to centralize bureaucracy, the economy and the military. In 1728 King Vittorio Amedeo II introduced the *catasto*, a register of all land estates for fiscal purposes, in Piedmont and Sardinia. The Austrian authorities in Lombardy did the same between 1749 and 1759, reducing fiscal pressure on farmers and peasants and applying taxation to ecclesiastic properties. In many Italian states convents and monasteries were closed, and their estates were expropriated, while it was forbidden to add land to *manomorta* properties. Under the pressure of the European monarchs, in 1773 the pope abolished the order of the Jesuits, and their patrimony passed to lay authorities.

Despite the political upheavals, the eighteenth century was marked by two major developments: a noticeable growth in population all over Europe, sustained by the diffusion of American crops, and the introduction of new technologies and production systems in agriculture. Foods such as tomatoes and potatoes, previously viewed with suspicion, met growing acceptance. Agronomists and politicians promoted the diffusion of potatoes in the countryside and among the lower classes to limit the

The Savoy king
Vittorio Amedeo II
and his family, 1697,
French print.

La Famille de S.A.R.Duc de Sauoye Prince de Piemont Roy de Cypre

effects of famine. The elites did not seem to have any qualms about them. In 1801, Vincenzo Corrado, the kitchen steward of the king of Naples, wrote a treaty on potatoes in which he offered the first known recipe for potato gnocchi, testifying to their acceptance at the royal court.[17] Corn was grown all over Italy, frequently replacing other cereals like sorghum and millets. The grain was easily integrated into local diets in the form of polenta, made with cereals in the past. Rural workers cultivated it in marginal lands and consumed it as a cheap source of energy while growing cash crops to sell in the market. Despite its identification with poverty and the unhealthy conditions in which it was grown, rice was the remedy to food scarcity in many areas. Among the upper classes it was incorporated into refined dishes like the Neapolitan *sartù* and risotto in the north, thanks to the introduction of varieties that were better suited for those specific preparations.

Landowners in the most advanced areas of the country invested in their estates to introduce modern technology and new labour relations with the peasants, shaking traditional rural societies to their cores. In Lombardy, under the 'enlightened' reign of Maria Theresa of Austria, sharecropping slowly disappeared, replaced by rent contracts. Irrigation and better management of the land allowed the increase of rice production, as well as the success of farms where intensive agriculture and livestock herding sustained one another. This kind of management required considerable units, favouring rural entrepreneurs who had the financial means to rent large estates, invest in cattle, organize crop sales and pay for salaried labour. Furthermore, the Austrian empress centralized all traditional levies, taking the right away from nobility. In 1776 she also introduced reforms that facilitated free trade. The reforms continued in Lombardy under her son Joseph II. Following the Austrian example, the duke of Tuscany introduced laws to ease the sale and acquisition of land, allowed the free trade of crops and initiated the reclamation of large marshy tracts in Valdichiana and Maremma. However, sharecropping remained the prevalent form of rural contract in Tuscany, as well as in Romagna, Marche and Umbria.

In regions where large estates were owned by the Church or by nobles who could not divide them or sell them to raise capital, innovation was virtually impossible, allowing customary arrangements to survive.[18] The attempts by the Bourbons to introduce the *catasto* failed thanks to the resistance of the *baroni*, who appropriated the best tracts of land to plant wheat as its price kept on rising. Poor farmers and salaried rural labour bore the brunt of the inflationary trend as their salaries did not grow at the same pace as food prices. However, the increased availability of wheat laid the basis for a dietary shift in the urban populace of Naples, from vegetables to pasta. Neapolitans came to be known as *mangiamaccheroni*, macaroni eaters, a sobriquet that replaced the old one of *mangiafoglie*, leaf eaters. The introduction of the extrusion press and other manually operated machinery allowed an increase in pasta output and in its quality, while reducing its cost. Taking advantage of the local milling industry, the towns of Torre Annunziata and Gragnano, south of Naples, emerged as major production hubs. Manufacturers perfected a drying system in three phases: *incartamento*, in the natural heat of the sun, which produced a thin crust on the surface of pasta, called *carta* (paper); a period in a cool location that allowed the *carta* to absorb the remaining moisture from inside the pasta; and another exposure to the open air, usually away from

Giorgio Sommer, *Mangiamaccheroni*, or macaroni eaters, *c.* 1865, albumen print.

direct sunlight, for the final drying. Spaghetti and other long shapes often needed to undergo the second and the third phases more than once.[19] Other important areas for dry-pasta production were located in Liguria, particularly in Savona and Portomaurizio (today's Imperia), and in Apulia, where artisans in the Bari area took advantage of the long-standing trading relationship with Venice to export their goods.

Not all kinds of food production enjoyed such efficiency. The overall stagnation in the agricultural sector was a target for those who sustained

139

free entrepreneurship and private property, embraced and promoted by intellectuals and businessmen alike. The intellectual movement known as the Enlightenment had a strong influence on how these economic debates unfolded, creating the political climate that eventually led to the French Revolution. Economists known as physiocrats argued that the creation of wealth is based on the land, and the income it creates can be reinvested in other activities. By promoting the privatization of large open fields previously available for traditional uses, the abolition of pasturage rights and the abolition of all constraints that limited the free trade of agricultural products, the physiocrats embraced private enterprise and capital as a crucial factor in economic activities.

The main centres of diffusion of newfangled economic theories were Milan, Florence and Naples. Antonio Genovesi's *Lessons on Commerce and Civil Economy* (1754) solidified political economics as an academic field, while *The New Historical and Geographical Description of the Two Sicilies*, published between 1786 and 1794 by Giuseppe Maria Galanti, painted a harsh critique of the remnants of feudalism in southern Italy. In Florence the main intellectual association was the Accademia dei Georgofili (Academy of the Friends of Agriculture), founded in 1753, which focused on issues of agronomy. Its influence was visible on the work of Giovanni Fabbroni, a Tuscan living in France whose *Reflections on the Present State of Agriculture* (1780) introduced physiocratic principles among Italian thinkers. The Milan circles focused instead on politics and found a public voice in the journal *Il Caffè*, published between 1764 and 1766 by the brothers Alessandro and Pietro Verri, the latter also author of the influential *Meditations of Political Economy* (1771) that explored the notions of demand and supply.

These intellectuals not only made their own unique contribution to the political and technical aspects of food production, but also embodied models of consumption that were considered more attuned to modern and progressive individuals. Their point of reference was, of course, France, where salons and cafés provided new forms of socialization and an environment that was supposed to stimulate free and vigorous discussions based on reasoning and clarity of ideas. Many members of the Italian bourgeoisie embraced the political and intellectual approach of the Enlightenment, with its appreciation of human rationality, the power of scientific research and the ideal of progress. These values were particularly relevant for a class that was trying to assert its role – at the expense of the nobility's prerogatives – in politics, economics and the management of the state. The light of knowledge offered necessary tools to fight superstition, ignorance and prejudice, until then ascribed to the influence of religion and, more specifically, the Catholic Church.

The bourgeoisie was developing its own culinary taste. Food and its consumption was becoming an arena where cultural identity could be shaped and performed. The exotic and excitant substances from the European colonies generated trends and fashions that played an important role in the definition of bourgeois taste. Sugar loafs from the Americas made sugar consumption more affordable. Coffee was supposed to increase intellectual sharpness and alertness, allowing witty conversations at dinners and parties to last late into the night. Its consumption was so fashionable that specialist establishments started catering to a growing and demanding clientele. The coffee shop originated in the Ottoman Empire as a public space for men to gather, relax and discuss current issues outside the structured environments of the home, the work place and the mosque. The first coffee house in Italy opened in Venice in 1683. It was followed closely by ones belonging to Jews in the port cities of

A café in St Mark's Square, Venice. Venice was the first Italian city where cafés opened in the 17th century.

Livorno and Venice, who kept close connections with their peers in the Ottoman trading centres of the eastern Mediterranean.[20] In fact, the Islamic origin of coffee had been problematic until Pope Clement VIII approved its consumption for Christians.[21]

Chocolate and cocoa drinks had been introduced to the Spanish court in the sixteenth century, where their preparation was kept secret. Approved at the end of the century by Pope Gregory XIII as a drink that did not break liturgical fast, chocolate was embraced and promoted by the Jesuits, although other religious orders were not in favour of it. Only in 1606 was the Florentine Francesco d'Antonio Carletti able to get hold of the recipe, bringing it to the Medici court in Florence.[22] Here, in the second half of the seventeenth century, the scientist Francesco Redi developed a chocolate formula that included jasmine, so appreciated by Duke Cosimo Medici that it was proclaimed a secret of state. By the eighteenth century hot cocoa drinks had become fashionable all over Italy. These new trends provoked a backlash from some intellectuals, as we can see in *Il risveglio del Giovin Signore* (The Awakening of the Young Lord, 1765) by the poet Giuseppe Parini:

> I already see your well-coiffed servant enter again; he asks you what drink, among the most popular, you would like to sip today from a precious cup. Cups and drinks are goods from India, choose the one that you prefer. If today you want to give your stomach a sweet fomentation, so that natural heat burns moderately and helps your digestion, choose brown chocolate, given to you as a tribute by the Guatemalan or the Caribbean whose hair is wrapped in barbarian feathers. If you feel oppressed by hypochondria, or too much fat is growing around your pretty limbs, honour your lips with the drink in which the grain from Aleppo and Moca – never exalted by its thousand ships – smokes and burns.[23]

Suspicious of the complicated and expensive dishes of the old nobility, considered heavy and overdone, bourgeois eaters were more in synch with the simple flavours of popular traditions. These new tastes, however, went through their own process of refinement and elaboration in order to satisfy more sophisticated palates. Vulgar and excessive flavours and aromas, including garlic, onion, cabbage and cheese, were to be avoided. Great efforts were dedicated to the study and selection of new varieties of fruits and herbs, stimulated by the accessibility of exotic products like pineapples and the diffusion of glasshouses (*stufe*) to grow tropical plants. Orangeade and lemonade, sorbets and ice creams enriched the menus, and raw oysters and truffles made their appearance. As the great food scholar Piero Camporesi poetically remarked:

> It is striking that the decline of sumptuous Renaissance and baroque cuisine marked an end to the great hunts and the downfall of everything that darted through the air or dashed across the ground, everything that moved, flexed, leaped, expended energy or lived in close animal familiarity with the rain, the wind and the sun. Striking indeed that the century of intellectual light, the enemy of darkness and shadows, should prefer to seek nourishment from gelid, inert, corpse-like organisms, ripped from water, or from sterile bulbs that hated light, fed on the dank lunar dankness of great autumnal forest subsoil.[24]

When entertaining, hosts preferred to impress their guests not so much by sheer quantity, but rather with variety, lightness and harmony among the dishes. Great attention was paid to the visual aspects of the meal such as colour, layout of the dishes and tableware. Chinese porcelain, together with silks and wood objects, were all the rage. Measured sobriety in the menu and on the table was considered a reflection of the *esprit de finesse* of the eater. Sauces, one of the distinctive traits of French culinary technique, allowed eaters to enjoy concentrated flavours without too much heavy matter to weigh on the stomach.

Culinary fashions from France exerted an unprecedented influence over well-to-do tables. The French preference for fresh ingredients, distinct flavours, subdued use of spices and clear separation between sweet and savoury dishes slowly spread throughout Italy. Appreciation for English and French merchandise grew among consumers with disposable income, while Italian traditional products were considered more provincial and of lesser quality. Author Pietro Verri wrote to his brother Alessandro that he preferred mediocre Austrian wine – probably referring to Hungarian Tokaj – to the best product of Lombardy, because the former kept one merry, while the other was just consumed to get drunk.[25] Nevertheless, not everybody shared the admiration of French cuisine. The abbot Giovambattista Roberti took an ironic tone in his *Lettera sopra il lusso del secolo XVIII* (Letter on the Luxury of the Eighteenth Century, 1772):

The people of Paris are more malnourished than any other European people. But the fastidiousness of some French is so arrogant that, when they arrive in Italy and taste some dish cooked in a different way from what they are used to beyond the Alps, they condemn it as detestable, even if they are poor men like dancing instructors or language teachers . . . The glory of this famous nation seems ridiculous to me; we could remind them that at the time of Caterina de' Medici our professors from the fireplaces and the *credenze* of Italy went to teach them the art of eating well.[26]

Kitchen professionals were particularly sensitive to the French culinary influence. Families of means preferred to hire chefs from France who enjoyed higher status than their local counterparts and were more familiar with the customs and fads of their compatriots. The chefs working for aristocratic families in Naples and Palermo were addressed as *monzù*, a local distortion of the French word *monsieur*, used to underline the prestige of French cuisine among the southern nobility. The so-called French-style service, where a first course of soups and appetizers was followed by a second course composed of several main dishes and finally by desserts, became popular. In 1693 La Varenne's seminal *Le Cuisinier françois* (The French Cook, originally published in 1651) and in 1741 Massialot's *Le Cuisinier royal et bourgeois* (The Court and Country Cook, 1691), two masterpieces of the French culinary canon, were translated into Italian, followed by cookbooks that mediated local recipes and ingredients with the French model. Among them, *Il cuoco piemontese perfezionato a Parigi* (The Piedmontese Cook Perfected in Paris, 1766) and *La cuciniera piemontese* (The Piedmontese [female] Cook, 1771) showed how Piedmont had taken on the role of mediator between Italian and French traditions. Outside Piedmont, the Roman Francesco Leonardi explored cold cuts, pork products and all sorts of local specialties in the six volumes of the encyclopaedic and monumental *Apicio moderno* (Modern Apicius, 1790). The author offered recipes for a tomato sauce that includes onions, garlic, celery and basil, and for stuffed tomatoes that are basically the same as recipes found today. In fact, tomatoes had already found their way to refined tables, as suggested by the presence of a tomato-sauce recipe as early as 1705 in a collection by Francesco Gaudenzio, a cook at the Jesuits' college in Rome.[27]

Illustration from the 1721 edition of La Varenne's seminal *Le Cuisinier françois* (The French Cook), originally published in 1651, which had a huge influence on Italian cuisine in the 18th century.

CUISINIER FRANCOIS

Vincenzo Corrado, at the court of Naples, applied French techniques to southern ingredients in *Il credenziere di buon gusto* (The Tasteful *Credenza* Manager, 1778) and above all in his masterpiece *Il cuoco galante* (The Gallant Cook, 1786). Polenta, herbs, capers, swordfish, anchovies, parmigiano, prosciutto, *castrato* (castrated ram), tomatoes and other typical products are featured in several recipes.[28] Corrado's attention to local foodstuffs also shines in *Notiziario delle produzioni particolari del regno di Napoli e delle cacce riserbate al real divertimento* (News about the Particular Productions of the Kingdom of Naples and the Hunting Exclusively Reserved for the King's Amusement, 1792). If on one hand the author wants to give homage to his king (and patron) by showcasing the wealth of his territories, on the other he reveals a true interest in his subject-matter, praising specialities such as the *maccheroni* from Torre Annunziata, the chocolate cakes of Aversa and cheese and mozzarella from Cardito.[29] Vegetables come to the fore in *Del cibo pitagorico ovvero erbaceo per uso de' nobili, e de' letterati* (Pythagorean

Food [that is to say vegetarian] for the Nobles and the Literati, 1781), where Corrado presents them as healthy and worthy of the most sophisticated tables.

In the preface to *Il Credenziere*, Corrado expounds his theory on the historical evolution of cooking. He argues that the age of temperance and moderation, when people ate simply and according to their needs, was short-lived.

> The custom of eating always the same things, and prepared almost in the same way, caused disgust. Disgust spawned curiosity; curiosity led to having experiences; and experience generated sensuality. Man savoured, tasted, diversified, chose to his satisfaction.[30]

The result was cuisine, which Corrado considered a simple and natural art that the ancient Romans had perfected with sumptuousness, delicacy, variety and magnificence. For the Neapolitan chef, the Italians inherited the Roman passion for food and transmitted it to the French, eventually surpassing their masters.

Francesco Narici(?), *Giacomo Casanova*, 1767(?), oil on canvas.

The interest in food as a source of pleasure and entertainment is apparent from one of the most infamous libertines of the period, Giacomo Casanova, who used the table as an occasion for witty conversation and seduction.[31] The positive evaluation of culinary refinement contradicted the theories expounded by Louis de Jaucourt in his entry about cuisine in the foundational text of the Enlightenment, the *Encyclopédie*. For de Jaucourt culinary excesses, decadence and preoccupation with what one eats, introduced to France with the arrival of Caterina de Medici, were a sign of degeneration.[32] Many Italians shared de Jaucourt's scorn for the excessive sophistication of food. Catholic conservatives considered culinary hedonism and the appreciation of artificiality as corrupting influences both on personal moral life and on social mores. Many members of the nobility preferred abundance in their meals – an appropriate reflection of wealth and power at a moment when their prerogatives and entitlements were questioned by unprecedented circumstances.

The slow and limited political and economic reforms of the Italian states were accelerated by the momentous events that shook France at the end of the eighteenth century, into the beginning of the nineteenth: the French Revolution – the decapitation of the king, the Republic, the Terror, the bourgeois reaction and finally the ascent of Napoleon. The French emperor extended his control over most of Italy, with the exception of Sicily, which was a British protectorate. Republics were instituted in the north and the centre of the peninsula but fell under the control of the French military, despite attempts by local revolutionaries to achieve autonomy. After Napoleon's defeat at Waterloo, the enemies of France met in Vienna for a congress that restored the European political system as it was before the French Revolution. At the same time, all the dynasties of Italy that had been dethroned were able to regain possession of their lost territories. However, the status quo was not to last for long.

Throughout the political upheavals, Italy maintained an astounding diversity of rural cultures and economic structures. In the valleys of the Alps and in the nearby hills, land ownership was fragmented; small farmers and shepherds took advantage of traditional rights regarding summer pasturage and exploitation of common plots. In the hilly areas south of the Alps, groups of several families lived and worked together on large farms called *masseria*, where the owner was entitled to half the production. Over time, these farms were broken down into smaller plots occupied by single nuclear families that were easier to control than larger groups. New contracts obliged farmers to pay a fixed quantity of wheat, the production of which often required the cultivation of more than half the farm. Farmers were forced to use their best land for wheat and base their diet on potatoes and maize. As a consequence, their standard of living plummeted and pellagra, a disease that can lead to dementia and eventually death with symptoms including diarrhoea and dermatitis, became widespread.[33] Pellagra is caused by vitamin B deficiency; when maize has not gone through the process of nixtamalization (as discussed in the previous chapter) the vital niacin (vitamin B3) cannot be absorbed. Maize was often excluded from the culinary repertoire of the upper classes and closely identified with poverty.

In the plains around the Po River, agriculture was mostly oriented to produce for commercial markets. The investment in irrigation and public works made this area the most advanced in Italy. Laws facilitated the sale and acquisition of land, and modern techniques were used that integrated agriculture with intensive cattle herding. The situation was ripe for the intervention of entrepreneurs, called *affittuario* or *fittavolo*, businessmen who rented medium or large farms (*cascine*) from absentee owners and managed them to maximize returns on investments. Often paid by the day, fixed-wage workers (*braccianti*, from the word *braccia*, arms) provided most labour. In central Italy, traditional sharecropping (*mezzadria*) remained prevalent; the land was divided into units called *podere* or *fattoria*, which included a home for the farmer's family and other productive structures such as barns and stables. Sharecropping did not boost investments, since owners only had the right to half of the product. Furthermore, as farmers often lived in relative isolation and their production was geared towards self-sufficiency, the arrangement was not favourable to the expansion of cash crops for the market. As a consequence, the continuous rotation system that was becoming prevalent in the north did not expand to Tuscany and central Italy. Fallow periods remained prevalent in the *alberata* landscape, composed of narrow fields where many trees were planted and vines were festooned between trees. In southern Italy, nobles and ecclesiastic institutions still owned most of the land, as only a small portion had been expropriated during the French occupation. The rural poor had to work as salaried labour since they owned no land. At times they rented tiny plots but it was frequently not enough to guarantee self-sufficiency. They commonly lived in villages located on hills or on the slopes of mountains, and they had to commute daily – on foot – to their plot or to the land they were paid to

In the 19th century corn was grown all over Italy,
often consumed in the form of polenta.

till. The only exceptions to the desperate situation of southern agriculture were found along the coasts, where fruit and olive trees, together with vines, provided high-quality products that commanded good prices on the market.

Overall, in the century preceding the unification of Italy, agriculture saw a slow but unstoppable penetration of the capitalist mode of production due to the intervention of economic factors that shattered the traditional customs regulating the lives of rural workers. Land privatizations, new contracts and the reorganization of production worsened the living conditions of farmers, precisely when the decline in mortality rates was causing the population to grow.[34]

## THE PROCESS OF UNIFICATION AND ITS CONSEQUENCES

Starting in the mid-1800s, the complex and varied rural landscapes described above became part of a single country, the Kingdom of Italy. At the Congress of Vienna, the Savoy rulers were able to extend their territories to the former republic of Genoa. While the Savoy territories already included Piedmont and Sardinia, this final shift marked the end of the Napoleon era and an end to Genoan independence – just as had happened with Venice, given to Austria by Napoleon. In 1848, following

Italy, 1837.

a period of conspiracies and revolts aiming to eliminate foreigners and absolutist regimes from the peninsula, the Savoy kings initiated wars that led to the annexation of large areas in northern and central Italy. In 1860 an expedition led by Giuseppe Garibaldi landed in Sicily and moved north, causing the fall of the Bourbon Dynasty and ushering in the proclamation of the Kingdom of Italy in 1861. After the conquest of Veneto in 1866, the Italian troops penetrated Rome in 1870. The pope was left with the Vatican State, diplomatically isolated from Italy until the Lateran Treaty of 1929, which restored official realations between the Vatican and the Italian State.

If the peasants in central and, above all, southern Italy hoped that the unification and the arrival of Garibaldi's troops would bring change, they were quickly – and brutally – disillusioned. When Garibaldi landed in Sicily, needing the help of the locals to overthrow the Bourbons, he announced that lands would be redistributed to the needy. However, when in the town of Bronte social unrest turned into riots, the Italian army general Nino Bixio doled out harsh punishment and executed some of the rebels in order to quash the movement. While the properties of the nobility did not undergo any major reform following the occupation of Rome in 1870, the liquidation of ecclesiastical lands increased the patrimony of a growing bourgeoisie in the centre and south of the country. However, most new owners did not introduce

Giuseppe
Garibaldi, 1861,
photographic print
on a *carte de visite*.

modern farming techniques but modelled their management on the style of previous landowners, all the while eliminating the remnants of farmers' traditional access to open fields and asserting property rights in a modern and business-oriented manner.

The first governments of the unified country left agriculture to private initiatives. In Piedmont, a network of canals named after the former prime minister, Camillo Benso di Cavour, was completed between 1863 and 1866, and in 1878 the drainage of the Fucino lake in Abruzzo was completed. Only in 1882 did the state dedicate limited funds to the reclamation of marshy lands with the manifest goal not of increasing agricultural output, but of getting rid of malaria. Blatant inefficiencies eventually forced the government to entrust the operation to private consortia. Large territories were reclaimed in Emilia Romagna and in the countryside near Rome, where an important private agrarian enterprise was established in Maccarese. Laws were introduced to control the reforestation of mountain slopes to avoid landslides – a problem that still plagues Italy, as the destructive flood that swept through the Cinque Terre villages in October 2011 sadly demonstrated.

In the years following the unification, internal borders and custom fees were removed. The construction of railways eased the movement of goods and pushed landowners to specialize their productions for the market. In the south, citrus and almond plantations acquired large-scale dimensions, while sizeable areas in Piedmont and Lombardy focused on rice, which had all but disappeared in Veneto and Emilia. Olive oil and wine production increased, but most of it was consumed locally. Conversely, pasta and cheese were increasingly appreciated abroad.[35] Italian agriculture still suffered from inadequate transportation, intricate distribution networks, lack of storage facilities, insufficient availability of credit and a mind-boggling array of taxes and levies. The growing integration of Italian agriculture into global trade exposed the rural world to the uncertainties of market economies. A global over-production crisis in the 1880s depressed agricultural incomes and pushed rural workers to abandon the countryside and resettle abroad, mostly in the United States, Canada and South American countries such as Venezuela, Brazil and Argentina. It was the beginning of a long history of migration that would scatter Italians all over the globe. The crisis caused the decrease of average daily calorie consumption for Italians from 2,647 in the 1870s to 2,197 and 2,119 respectively in the two following decades.[36]

The unification of the country did not correspond to a sudden integration of its citizens. Most inhabitants of the countryside and large numbers of urban dwellers were illiterate and unable to speak standard Italian. Social and political systems were so radically diverse that the government had to fight for years to establish its authority, especially over Sicily and the south, where bands of brigands took to the mountains, often backed by the locals. The diet in the countryside was very limited, both in terms of variety and calories. Wheat production was mostly directed to middle-class urban consumers, while rural workers ate maize, barley, millet, buckwheat, chestnut, lentils, fava beans and chickpeas, also grinding them into flours that were used for porridges, dumplings, breads and focaccias. Beans and rice also provided some nourishment. Only peasants in Sicily and Apulia had access to wheat, the production of which was concentrated in those areas, but their living conditions were no better, as suggested in the poem *Il canto dei mietitori* (The Reapers' Song, 1888) by Mario Rapisardi from Catania:

We are the reapers' army
And we reap the crops for your Lordships.
Welcome is the scorching sun, the sun of June
Which burns our blood and darkens our snouts
And makes the hoes in our fists red hot
While we're reaping the crops for your Lordships . . .
Our little children have no bread
And, who knows, might die tomorrow,
Being jealous of your dogs' meals.
And we keep on reaping the crops for your Lordships.
Drunken with sun each of us staggers:
Water and vinegar, a piece of bread and an onion
Are enough to quench our thirst and appease our hunger.
They even fill us up.
Let's reap the crops for your Lordships . . .[37]

Workers were provided with larger meals to ensure their productivity during the long days of the grape harvest, the gathering and squeezing of olives and the killing of pigs.[38] Realist writer Giovanni Verga gives us a good description of a grape harvest in Sicily in his short story '*La Roba*' (The Stuff, 1883):

At the time of the grape harvest whole villages came swarming to his vineyards, and wherever you hear people singing on the land, there was singing as they picked Mazzarò's grapes. As for the wheat harvest, Mazzarò's reapers spread out across the fields like a whole army, and you needed fistfuls of money to provide for all those people, with their early-morning biscuit, their bread and Seville oranges for breakfast, their picnic lunch, and their lasagne in the evening. The lasagne had to be served up in bowls as big as wash basins.[39]

The central government tried to achieve a better understanding of the situation of the Italian working class by financing surveys and ethnographic research including the agrarian inquiry into conditions of the rural classes led by Stefano Jacini between 1881 and 1886.[40] Around 80 per cent of the working-class household budget was spent on food, with most concentrated on basic staples.[41] *Maccheroni* were sold on the streets of workers' neighbourhoods in Naples, often eaten outdoors on the

Tripe became an important element of the lower classes' diet at the end of the 19th century.

spot. Meat was consumed in small quantities and only on special occasions. In 1892, a massive slaughterhouse was inaugurated in Rome to satisfy the demand for meat, connected with the city's status as the capital and the influx of employees and bureaucrats in the new government offices and ministries. Yet most workers did not have access to the best cuts they butchered, but could only afford the offal, ironically defined as *quinto quarto*, the fifth quarter left after the animal's quartering. The availability of ox tails, suckling veal intestines and tripe were soon incorporated into low-class Roman cuisine with dishes like *coratella* (lung and heart of lamb, sautéed with slivers of artichoke), *coda alla vaccinara* (braised ox tail with herbs, lard and chopped tomato, in some versions with the addition of cocoa powder and pine nuts), and *trippa alla romana* (tripe [cow stomach] stewed with tomato sauce and mint, and served with grated pecorino romano).[42]

Italian intellectuals and politicians often framed the analysis of undernourishment in terms of differences between north and south, developing what historian Carol Helstosky aptly defines as 'a tale of two diets'.[43] However, class distinctions were more relevant than geographical environments, with blue-collar and rural workers suffering from endemic food scarcity. This situation frequently caused turmoil, as happened in 1868 when the government reinstated a milling tax based on the number of turns of the milling stones; in 1887 because of a duty on cereals; and in 1898 when, under the effect of the agricultural depression of the 1880s, prices rose quickly and riots exploded in many major cities, culminating in a massacre of protesters in Milan.[44] As social historian Paolo Sorcinelli acutely observed: 'In order to eat, Italians had to learn to demonstrate and to dissent.'[45] In the Po plain, where fixed-wage labour was prevalent, workers organized themselves to launch strikes and negotiate with their employers for better pay.

The end of the nineteenth century saw the rise of industrial food-manufacturing companies, despite the fact that most agricultural production was consumed locally, either fresh or as dried or cured goods.[46] Distribution infrastructure was also lagging. The first large, refrigerated warehouse was inaugurated in Milan in 1897, much later than in other European countries, followed by similar initiatives in northern Italy, particularly for the conservation of butchered animals, as frozen meat was still regarded with suspicion. Yet the need to feed Italian troops in the First World War changed this attitude, forcing the use of frozen and canned meat at the front.[47] Pasta stayed at the vanguard of more

A pasta factory in Naples, 1875, photo by Giorgio Sommer (1834–1914).

efficient distribution networks, as it had already experienced technological innovations in the previous centuries. Steam- and electricity-operated
machinery, such as the wheat sifter, the mechanical kneader and the
drier, produced pasta that could travel well nationally and even satisfy
the demand from migrants all over the world. Gragnano and Torre
Annunziata remained the main centres of production, and new factories
opened in Abruzzo (de Cecco and Cocco), Emilia (Barilla) and Tuscany
(Buitoni). Pasta, a product that had traditionally been perceived as
southern, was increasingly embraced as a national speciality, although
different shapes and lengths maintained elements of localism. Consumers
were able to choose among pasta made of semolina or flour, or a mix of
the two, at times dyed yellow with saffron, red with tomato and green
with spinach. Industrial *pasta all'uovo* (with the addition of fresh or
powdered eggs) and stuffed pasta made their appearance, while companies
tried to differentiate their products by adding gluten, iron, calcium,
beer yeast or anything that was supposed to increase nutritional values.[48]
From the Naples area, the custom of pairing pasta with tomato sauce
rapidly spread northwards.[49] Canning technology, based on the discoveries by Nicolas Appert, offered an alternative to the traditional production
of *conserva nera*, the dark paste made from boiling and sun-drying

tomato pulp, used for sauces during the winter. As grain prices plummeted following the 1880s crisis, farmers looked for profitable crops, and tomatoes took centre stage in the areas of Naples and Salerno in the south, and around Parma and Piacenza in the north, generating a lively canning industry. Cirio, founded in Turin, embraced tomato canning and opened plants near Naples, quickly establishing an international network of distribution. Italians are still familiar with brands that were launched during this period, like Perugina chocolate in Perugia; Caffarel chocolate-and-hazelnut *gianduiotti* and Martini & Rossi and Cinzano liquors in Turin; Lazzaroni cookies in Saronno, Lombardy, and Stock brandy in Trieste.[50] These products, renowned and appreciated abroad, helped establish a small but growing high-end consumer culture shared by the upper and middle classes all over Italy, who relied on brands as a form of protection against the growing plague of adulteration.[51] The wine industry was still lagging, with most of the production focused on *vini da taglio*, wines with a high alcoholic content that were exported to foreign countries to be mixed with local products, and *vini sfusi*, table wines resulting from the mix of different grapes and varieties grown more for quantity than for quality. When the grapevine disease phylloxera spread to France in the 1870s and to Italy in the late 1880s, growers were pushed to reorganize and streamline their vines. The reorganization improved production, but also pushed many low-yielding local varieties to the sidelines.[52] Some areas showed signs of commercial expansion. In western Sicily the local Florio family established a popular brand by embracing a product launched by the British during the Napoleonic occupation: fortified *marsala* wines.[53] Marsala became the drink of choice for the bourgeoisie, together with vermouth from Piedmont, where companies like Gancia and Cinzano stimulated farmers to improve their crops.

The central government contributed to the unification of food habits, as a side effect of the mandatory military service. Young men had to leave home for five years – three after 1875 – for training and stationing, shipped to faraway locations where people spoke unintelligible dialects and had different customs.[54] Italian military leaders clearly understood the importance of living conditions – and in particular food – for troop morale.[55] For many recruits, it was the first time they had access to three nutritious meals a day. Some of the victuals were not particularly popular, in particular canned meat, but others like coffee, pasta (with tomato sauce) and cheese became everyday items for recruits. At the end of military service, many former soldiers returned home with a taste for them, a symbol of the national identity that the country was still struggling to achieve.

Little information is available about the quality and quantity of food consumed among middle-class citizens as the government, cultural researchers and charitable institutions were much more concerned about the diet and nutrition of the lower classes. However, we can use newspapers, magazines and cookbooks to understand their culinary habits, their table manners and, above all, their inspiration as they shaped their cultural and social identity as citizens of a new country. In the years preceding unification, cookbooks tended to reflect local practices and ingredients, both for the aristocracy, like Ippolito Cavalcanti's *Cucina teorico-pratica* (Theoretical and Practical Cuisine, 1837), and for larger audiences, like *Il cuoco senza pretese* (The Cook without Pretensions, 1834). Others, like *Il nuovo economico cuoco piemontese e credenziere napoletano* (The New Economical Piedmontese Cook and the Neapolitan Butler, 1822), attempted to connect different regional traditions.

The first book that contributed to defining a national cuisine for the Italian bourgeoisie was *La scienza in cucina e l'arte del mangiar bene* (Science in the Kitchen and the Art of Good Eating), published by Pellegrino Artusi in 1891. Artusi was born in 1820 in Forlimpopoli, a town near Forlì. The son of a successful merchant, he moved his business to Florence in 1852 where he lived until his death in 1911, enjoying his wealth and dedicating himself to literature and cooking. As he could not find an investor for his recipe collection, Artusi published it himself, selling 1,000 copies of the first edition in four years. Soon the book was discovered by middle-class cooks and by the time Artusi died more than 200,000 copies had been sold – a huge number for the time, considering how few Italians were literate. The volume went through fourteen editions, growing from 475 to almost 800 recipes. Despite the fact that he was most familiar with the cuisines of Tuscany, Emilia and Romagna, Artusi included recipes from all over Italy, single-handedly creating a nation-wide Italian vocabulary for food and cooking. The recipes, although at times not very precise, are lively, entertaining and full of stories, making for a pleasant read. Artusi's repertoire included *costoletta alla Milanese* (Milanese-style veal cutlet) and eel in the style of his native Romagna, as well as southern dishes like couscous from Sicily (*cuscussù*, identified as a Jewish speciality) and what he considered as Neapolitan pizza, a dessert with almonds and ricotta cheese. The author, who avoided hot peppers and did not even mention Sardinia, provided a few foreign recipes such as roast beef and soufflés, revealing the influence of international cuisine on Italian bourgeois cooking. Artusi's books reflected not only the cultural and social values of the middle classes, but also their access to food and spending power. The author adopted an educational approach, mixing home economics tips, hygiene counsel and medical advice aimed at sobriety, temperance and good management of domestic finances. His tone is light and entertaining, offering side notes that give us a better sense of the culture of the time. Reading his recipes, including the two I have translated below, it is noticeable how Artusi gave vague indications about quantities, assuming that readers, mostly women, would know exactly how to measure the ingredients.

Bourgeois families embraced the model of the shared family meal, which reinforced the patriarchal structure of the nuclear family and distinguished them from lower-class individuals, both rural and urban, who tended to eat alone and more frugally (except on festive occasions), depending on their work schedule and location.[56] Historian Paolo Sorcinelli ironically points out that the way workers ate, quickly, voraciously and without great attention to manners, resembled more the ethos of contemporary fast food than the imaginary ideals of the traditional family sitting around the table and taking the time to eat together.[57] The proper meal, both in restaurants and private middle- and upper-class homes, slowly acquired a structure based on the sequence of antipasto (appetizers), *primo* (usually a soup or a pasta dish, less often rice), *secondo* (meat or fish) with *contorni* (side dishes, often vegetables) and dessert at the end. Antipasti were reserved for special occasions, but in the south it was normal to keep finger food on the table before the meal or between meals: olives, slices of salami, pieces of cheese. (Today, the meal structure has fundamentally remained the same, although now Italians tend to eat fewer courses, with the exception of special occasions and Sunday meals.) When guests were invited, the new meal structure allowed the host to decide its content and timing, controlling the quantities of food while at the same time demonstrating propriety. Bourgeois families, in some ways, tried to transform the Sunday meal into a special occasion, a minor version of important banquets. During the week, though, meals were much simpler, and recipes that allowed the recycling of leftovers were appreciated.

Hotels and restaurants flourished, becoming places of conspicuous consumption for the bourgeoisie. From the point of view of the table

### Florence-style Black Risotto with Cuttlefish

This invertebrate (*Sepia officinalis*) of the order of molluscs and the family cephalopods is called *calamaio* (inkwell) in Florence, perhaps because (as the beautiful Tuscan language often forms vocabulary based on similarities) it contains a little bladder, which nature gave it for defence, containing a black liquid that can serve as ink. The Tuscans, the Florentines in particular, are so passionate about vegetables that they would put them everywhere and consequently they put beetroots in this dish, which I think fits in it as *pancotto* (bread soup) fits in the Creed prayer. I would not want that this excessive use of plants be one, and not the least, of the causes of the flabby constitution of certain classes of persons, who, under the influence of some illness, cannot stand its brunt and are seen falling thick as leaves in late autumn.

Peel and separate the cuttlefish to clean them of the useless parts, such as bone, the apparatus of the mouth, eyes and digestive tract; put aside the ink bladder. After washing them well cut them into small squares, and the tails into pieces. Chop two large onions minutely, or rather one onion and two cloves of garlic, and put them to the fire in a saucepan with fine and plentiful olive oil. When the onions have browned, add the cuttlefish. Wait for them to boil and turn yellow, then add about 600 grams of chard, without the thicker ribs and chopped in large pieces. Stir and let it boil for about half an hour, then pour 600 grams of rice (which will be the weight of the cuttlefish before cooking) and the ink, and when the rice is well soaked in the sauce, cook it by slowly adding hot water. Rice, as a general rule, needs to be under-cooked, and when we say dry it should form a mound on the tray in which you serve. Always season it with grated Parmesan cheese, but if you have a sensitive stomach, refrain from using it: when it is cooked with these and similar ingredients, it is not easy to digest. Now I will show you another way to make this risotto, so that you can choose the one you like between the two. No chard, no ink, and when the cuttlefish, as we said, are beginning to turn yellow, add the rice and cook it by slowly adding hot water and tomato sauce or paste, giving it more grace and flavour with a bit of butter; when it is almost cooked add the Parmesan cheese. If you want it even better, at two thirds of cooking add the peas we mentioned in the risotto with the tench.[58]

### Stuffed Potato Croquettes
potatoes, 300 grams
parmesan cheese, two tablespoons well filled
eggs, two
a hint of nutmeg
flour, as required

Boil the potatoes, peel them and pass through a sieve, making them fall on top of a thin layer of flour. Make a hole in the mound of potatoes, add salt, give them the aroma of nutmeg and pour in the eggs and grated Parmesan. Then, using as little flour as you can, work the mix into a soft mass that you will divide into 18 parts. With floured finger, make a small hole in each of these and fill it with chopped meat. Pull the flaps over to cover the meat and, with floured hands, shape round balls that you will fry in lard or oil, sending them to the table as a side dish for a fried meat course. This dish is flashy, good and inexpensive, because you can also make the filling just out of a single chicken giblets, and when you happen to buy a whole chicken, you can grind its crest, the gizzard, the unborn eggs cooked with a little chopped onion and butter, and then add a diced slice of ham (both fat and lean). If you do not have a chicken, form the filling some other way.[59]

Carl Heinrich Bloch, *Osteria in Rome*, 1866, oil on canvas.

service, a new style known as 'Russian' became popular, where a succession of individual dishes – as opposed to the previous multi-dish services – were presented to all the guests at the same time. Those who could not afford elegant establishments would still patronize *osterie* or *trattorie*. Many city dwellers enjoyed Sunday excursions to the countryside immediately outside the cities, where *trattorie* offered simple meals and at times allowed customers to bring their own food if they bought wine. The quality of wine sold in these places varied, often proportionally to price. The less fortunate had access to water in which grape marc had fermented, or a mix of vinegary wine and water. Only after a tariff war with France in the early 1890s did large quantities of wine, previously exported, find their way into local distribution, at the same time becoming more affordable. Its consumption increased. Abroad, the most progressive members of the medical establishment identified alcoholism as a medical condition, but in Italy the cultural perception was much more ambivalent. While on the one hand wine was considered healthy, nutritious, effective against malaria and less damaging than stronger spirits, its excessive consumption was also branded as personally and socially destructive.[60]

Incomes and living conditions in the countryside were still worse than for urban blue-collar workers. Illiteracy was rampant, despite the law of 1879 that made elementary schooling mandatory. Overall, women and children suffered from undernourishment more commonly than men, who were considered the breadwinners and thus worthy of larger portions of the meagre family meals:

> Women (both single and married ones) ate standing, in the kitchen, in a corner, on the cutter, on the box for the fire wood, with the dish in their hands, or sitting on the floor and without silverware, reserved for the exclusive use of the males; they often ate what was left, alone, when – as a Piedmont female rural worker remembers – 'they [the males] were not at home'.[61]

While the agricultural crisis of the 1880s laid the basis for agricultural development in the Po plain, living standards for rural workers in the centre and the south worsened. Pellagra decreased in many northern areas, where rural families could count on higher income connected with seasonal employment in the growing industrial sector and could afford more varied food.[62] However, pellagra cases increased among sharecroppers in central Italy, especially on the mountains, where it had up until then been a rarity. The disease spread as farmers were forced to subsist on corn, growing cash crops on most of their land to pay taxes and buy commercial goods.[63] The myth of the Italian farmer as a strong, parsimonious and frugal worker became an excuse for the upper classes – including political leaders – to justify their failure to improve rural living conditions. At the same time, rural workers were depicted as lazy, indolent and lacking in initiative, ignoring the connection of these behaviours with insufficient nutrition. Yet at the turn of the twentieth century agriculture still employed the great majority of Italians, with industrialization and economic development still a long way off.

# FIVE

# From War to Miracle

## LA BELLE ÉPOQUE

In the first years of the twentieth century, production and prices picked up in Italy, reflecting fast developments at a global level. Life standards improved for larger segments of employees in the growing service sector, as office clerks and public bureaucrats enjoyed higher incomes. In 1912 all male citizens acquired voting rights. Also workers, both urban and rural, had access to better living conditions, thanks to higher wages and remittances from emigrants abroad. New industrial products were introduced on the market, such as concentrated meat stock, instant chocolate and baking powder, having great appeal as an expression of a burgeoning consumer culture.

Despite special laws to help the growth of industrial activities in Basilicata, Naples, Calabria and Sardinia, agriculture remained the main economic engine for the country. Major changes took place in this sector, especially in northern Italy, thanks to the introduction of mechanization, fertilizers and the systematization of the synergies between farming, cattle-raising and dairy production.[1] Meat played a secondary role in the Italian diet, especially when compared with other European countries, while cured and dried fish still provided a relevant amount of protein. Wine consumption increased across the board, though more so in urban centres than in the countryside. Maize consumption declined as sales of wheat and pasta increased despite higher prices, due in part to the fact that cereal imports more than doubled between the late 1800s and the beginning of the First World War.

Many Italians viewed the conflict, in which Italy participated from 1915 to 1918, as the 'fourth war of independence', as the country fought on the side of France and England against Germany and the Austro-Hungarian Empire to take control of territories in the northeast of the peninsula that Rome considered Italian, such as Trentino Alto-Adige and Venezia Giulia. The First World War caused a slump in food production. As most soldiers were rural workers, agricultural production suffered from lack of labour. Additionally, it was difficult to secure fertilizers and other supplies. During the war, the government managed all economic activities. Wartime industrial production ensured employment to men who were not at the front, and labour scarcity caused wages to rise. As a consequence, Italians had access to a healthier and varied diet, despite rationing and price controls (*calmiere*) that extended to wheat, meat, eggs, butter and sugar, among other products. In fact, bread became more affordable thanks to state subsidies, designed to avoid the social unrest that exploded each time the fluctuating prices went up.[2] Consumers adopted substitutes like margarine, saccharin and staples such as barley and rice.[3] Towards the end of the war, more food was directed towards the front, sparking protests among civilians. The book by Olindo Guerrini, *L'arte di utilizzare gli avanzi della mensa* (The Art of Using Leftovers, 1917), published just after the author's death, seemed to embrace the frugal ethos of the lower middle class, also integrating working-class recipes like bread-based soups.[4] However, a close reading reveals that Guerrini, a poet and a librarian, actually addressed relatively well-off readers. A section focuses on game. The introduction of the section about beef reads: 'The families that either by habit or for health reasons frequently or uninterruptedly use broth are sentenced to boiled meat for life.'[5] It is easy to imagine how many Italian families could only dream of being condemned to eating meat daily. The book offers as many rice recipes as pasta ones, revealing the northern origin of the author and pointing to dietary differences in the country.

The conflict brought together men from all over the country, exposing them to a diet that was perceived as 'national' and 'Italian', frequently very different from their local customs and culinary preferences, and most of the time far more abundant. Soldiers had access to meat, cheese, coffee, sugar and even liquors. The cultural shock was even stronger for soldiers from the countryside, where diets tended to be less varied and abundant than in the army. War rations reached 3,650 calories a day, with a supplement for the troops fighting on mountains.[6] For the first time, Italians participated in an international conflict as a unified country. The goal of liberating Italian territory (Trento and Trieste) from Austrian occupation contributed to the construction of a national identity that would play an important role in the following decades.

The aftermath of the war saw the expansion of consumer culture among the most affluent segments of the population, who were quick in embracing new products and trends. Beer is a good example of these shifts. Although several Italian beer brands vied for customers' attention, production had plummeted during the war because malt imports were affected by the conflict. When the war ended, however, beer consumption boomed. Important factories like Dreher in Trieste and Forst in Merano had become Italian, following the annexation of former Austro-Hungarian territories, and also brands like Ichnusa in Cagliari, Menabrea in Biella, Moretti in Udine, Peroni in Naples and Wührer in Brescia enjoyed great popularity.[7] Italian liquors and spirits boosted their sales, taking advantage of the growing impact of advertising both in newspapers and magazines – a marketing tool that had become more effective as literacy increased. Early ads, mostly in printed media, had been wordy and focused on describing the technical and sensory quality of the product, often including prices and places where the item could be purchased. In the 1900s advertising also took the form of mural posters that promoted products to those who could not read. Artist Leonetto Cappiello was among the first to create branded posters that made products memorable, including those for Cinzano Vermouth, Chocolate Klaus, which became famous for 'the woman in green' it represented, and Bitter Campari, with a pixie coming out of orange peel. Later on, images made popular by posters appeared also on postcards, playing cards and calendars, while the posters themselves grew in size to become billboards. Artists like Marcello Nizzoli and Severo Pozzati abandoned the Art Deco style in advertising to embrace a more abstract approach to communication. In 1919 Fortunato Depero founded the House of Futurist Art, a graphic lab for advertising that became famous for a series of advertising images for Campari.

## THE FASCIST CONSENSUS

After the end of the First World War, the government went back to its laissez-faire approach. Italians, however, preferred to pay higher prices rather than give up the goods they had grown used to during the war.[8] Although remittances from migrants ebbed and demographic pressure in the countryside caused land occupations and instability, rural incomes remained stable under the effect of the moderate increase of prices for staples and other agricultural crops. Factory workers' wages and security

Advertising poster
for Campari by
Leonetto Cappiello,
1921.

improved, also thanks to the activities of unions and the Socialist Party.
At the other end of the spectrum, the industrial groups that had grown
and profited from their business with the army invested and consolidated,
both horizontally and vertically, generating semi-monopolistic conglomerates. The middle and low bourgeoisie suffered the most from the
inflationary trend and the concurrent currency devaluation as their standards
of living depended on fixed salaries. When in 1919 the state tried to
abolish the subsidies that kept the bread price under control, the political
reaction was so violent that it caused a change of government. Consumer
cooperatives, which had started in Italy in the 1850s, expanded in this
period as a reaction to higher prices. Just like a joint-stock company, they
gathered up commercial capital to buy wholesale, obtaining better prices
than small shops. At the same time, they established well-organized
distribution networks that allowed the budding Italian agro-food capi-
talism to find easy outlets for their goods. In 1920 social tensions were
at breaking point. Factory occupations and rural unrest led to the

establishment of the associations of industrialists (*Confindustria*) and of landowners (*Confagricoltura*) and, the following year, to the foundation of the Communist Party of Italy.

This unstable background allowed Mussolini and the Fascist Party to gain power in 1922 by taking advantage of the middle-class discontent and social tensions. To do so, they practised widespread violence and intimidation, largely directed at newspapers, political organizations, unions and rural workers' organizations. The Fascist government outlawed strikes and replaced unions with 'corporations' that included both workers and owners, with the goal of eliminating any contrast in labour negotiations. The regime revalued the Italian currency, the lira, which caused a reduction of production and exports, a slump in wage levels and the increase of prices, a situation made worse in 1929 by the worldwide Great Depression. In an attempt to control prices, the government embraced commercial protectionism, increasing tariffs on wheat imports and launching the so-called *battaglia del grano* (the grain battle) in 1925, aimed at boosting national wheat production. The policy, however, was adopted precisely when wheat prices were decreasing worldwide, due to a global surplus.

When the regime realized that these measures were not enough to provide the necessary amount of grains, it launched a *bonifica integrale* (comprehensive reclamation) of marshlands, which was supposed to involve both the state and private landowners. The initiative was successful in the Agro Pontino area, south of Rome, where 3,000 plots were distributed to farmers, who often came from the northeast. To this day, the villages around Latina and Sabaudia, the two major cities built by Mussolini in the area, have names that echo the origins of the settlers, like Borgo Sabotino, Borgo Piave and Borgo Carso, towns and places in northeast Italy. At the same time, policies were introduced to facilitate the sale of plots to more efficient farms by owners who did not have the financial means to cultivate them. The goal of these interventions was not only to increase land for wheat production, but also to limit the relocation of farmers into industrial cities, especially in the north, at a time when the regime was trying to stop emigration to other countries in an effort to increase Italy's population. The concentration on wheat, however, limited the government's investment in animal husbandry and other crops with greater commercial value on the international markets, such as grapes and citrus. A national rice board (Ente nazionale risi) was created to promote rice consumption in central and southern

Italy, where it was consumed less frequently. As late as 1937, a third of internal wheat consumption still relied on imports.⁹ Bread became a focus for Fascist propaganda, which prompted citizens to be more conscientious about its use. Italians were invited to eat wholewheat bread as a heartier, longer-lasting, more nutritious alternative to white loaves. Schoolchildren were taught a small poem that Mussolini wrote for the Bread Day of 1928, a day dedicated to the appreciation of the precious food:

> Love bread, heart of the home, aroma of the table, joy of the hearth. Respect bread, sweat of the brow, pride of work, poem of sacrifice. Honour bread, glory of the fields, fragrance of the earth, feast of life. Don't waste bread, wealth of the mother-land, God's sweetest gift, the most sacred prize of men's toil.¹⁰

The language and tone exemplify the rhetoric of Fascist propaganda, which had a deep influence on the media. Mussolini had a great appreciation of the power not only of graphic design, posters and radio, but also of the moving image, as movies had become a very popular form of entertainment. He was one of the first world leaders to use his own body in pictures and newsreels to promote policies and political campaigns. During the *battaglia del grano*, Mussolini appeared at harvest season on wheat fields, where he was filmed shirtless as he helped the workers.¹¹ As early as 1924, the Fascist government founded the Istituto Luce to produce feature-length and short films shown in cinemas all over Italy.¹² Many documentaries focused on the life and production of rural workers, symbolizing the backbone of the country.¹³ The leaders of the propaganda machine built Cinecittà, a large area with modern sound stages that was to become the 'Hollywood on the Tiber' during the 1960s. The regime also launched the film school Centro Sperimentale di Cinematografia, which taught many of the movie-industry professionals who would become famous in the following decades.

Scientists and nutritionists rallied in support of Fascist policies. They theorized that the metabolism of the average Italian was slower, and therefore required a lower daily caloric intake, than for people of other descents.¹⁴ The frugal customs of the Mediterranean populations were not the result of poverty, but rather based on physiological differences. After all, ancient Romans, whom the Fascist propaganda framed as cultural models, praised the benefits of frugality. Eating genuine foods,

Demonstration against sanctions, Rome, 1935.

exercising their bodies in their daily activities and with innately simple culinary tastes, farmers were supposed to be healthier – and even more sexually potent – than urban workers.[15] At any rate, eating little was thought less dangerous than excessive eating.

In 1935, a possible solution for food scarcity was indicated in the occupation of Ethiopia, which was supposed to provide cultivable land for Italian farmers, while realizing Mussolini's colonial design.[16] The military campaign led to the conquest of Somalia and Eritrea and to the proclamation of Italian East Africa as part of the Empire. However, the Society of Nations retaliated by establishing economic sanctions against Italy that affected imports and exports of strategic goods. In reaction, Mussolini launched a campaign to establish *autarchia* (autarchy), complete self-reliance on Italian products, by further raising tariffs on imports and discouraging shoppers from buying foreign goods.[17] Food shortages and higher prices ensued, especially for meat and dairy, stoking discontent among Italians. The regime inaugurated soup kitchens and distributed victuals to the needy, more for propaganda purposes than for actually dealing with the crippling food scarcity. Resources were diverted to Africa to support the colonists, who were facing lower yields than expected because of lack of investment and infrastructure. Bananas, *karkadé* (hibiscus flower tea) and peanuts were shipped back to Italy, but they were not enough to make the new colonies profitable.

## Food Culture under the Regime

Inevitably, the connection between food consumption, frugality, patriotism and moral qualities became a focus of Fascist propaganda. Homemakers (*massaie*) were basically given the task of bringing the economic policies and the Fascist ideology into the daily life of Italian families:

> Never before as much as in this crucial time, all that constitutes active and effective moral strength acquires a transcendental power on the road toward sacrifice. Your mission as housewives has never been so important, connected in the most diverse ways with the urgent interests of our Nation. As you turn your activities and your spiritual potential into the core of family life, we want you to be an example to convince even the indifferent and the irresponsible to rigidly observe the rules of parsimony we have imposed on ourselves till victory is ours![18]

The propaganda efforts also reached rural women. The movement of *Massaie rurali* (rural housewives) organized women in the countryside, as there was a growing demand for female workers in agriculture while men were increasingly occupied in factories, at least for part of the year.[19] The aspiration to better organize household budgets and eating habits spurred a new interest in the rational and technological aspects of cooking, following the example of the home economics movement in the United States. In 1926, the National Agency for the Scientific Organization of Work was founded, aimed at modernizing households, including kitchens where electric stoves, electric boilers, aluminium pots and pans, clocks, scales and other appliances were introduced. Refrigerators were almost unheard of, but many households had iceboxes. The advancement in aluminium technology allowed the mass production of domestic objects that soon invaded Italian kitchens, like the Bialetti Moka Express that made espresso-like coffee on kitchen stoves. Espresso machines, first patented in 1901 by Luigi Bezzera for restaurant use and

Under the Fascist regime, modern kitchen appliances became a status symbol for Italian housewives.

operated by trained staff, and later improved on by Francesco Illy with the use of compressed air, were too large and expensive. The new stovetop coffee maker allowed households to enjoy a similar brew, replacing the traditional *napoletana* contraption, a pot brought to boil and then flipped over so that the water trickled down through the grounds.[20] Following the autarchy, however, coffee became scarce, prompting women's magazines to advise their readers to use less:

> Coffee is not necessary to our dynamic, active, alert race, which does not need excitant or stimulating substances . . . Coffee does not represent for us a necessity but rather a delicacy and a habit born from the preconception that it heals sickness and it provides indispensable help to those who work. But we are not afraid of work even when it is unnerving and unrelenting and always the same. We do not need any pause at the espresso counter to accomplish it in good health.[21]

Housewives also appreciated the mechanical pasta maker, operated with a crank, which pressed dough between metal cylinders into thin sheets. This is an implement that can still be found in households where pasta is handmade, at least for special meals or weekends. Under the embargo, it became necessary to create cooking contraptions, called *cassette di cottura* (cooking boxes) to save coal and gas: these were wooden boxes tightly stuffed with cotton, cloth and paper to create an insulated space where pots could be moved to simmer or finish preparations that were started on the stove.

Fascism made sure that women were taught 'modern' culinary habits and new, more efficient, ways to cook.[22] Many radio shows were geared towards them. While women were invited to reduce consumption and avoid unnecessary purchases, advertising promoted fashionable brands – albeit Italian ones – and food companies sponsored radio concerts of famous singers.[23] In 1922 ACME, the first advertising agency, launched its operations, introducing slogans as short and catchy sound bites. Advertisers embraced marketing methods with scientific and techno-logical undertones, considering consumption not just as a means to satisfy personal whims and desire, but as a vehicle for nation-building.[24] In 1934, Buitoni-Perugina sponsored a radio spoof of Alexandre Dumas'

Bialetti Moka Express, the stove-top coffee maker that is still used in most Italian house-holds.

*The Three Musketeers*, and printed 100 collectible cards representing the characters in the show. The listeners who managed to gather all the cards got a prize, but those who completed several collections received greater rewards, winning trophies as grand as the Fiat Topolino car – worth 150 collections. Italians went crazy for these cards, especially for the *Feroce Saladino* (fierce Saladin), which was the rarest of all. Eventually, in 1937, the government prohibited this kind of promotional campaign. The expanding consumer culture clashed with the backwardness of the food industry. With the exception of the brands launched at the turn of the previous century, most businesses were small or very small, limited by exclusively local distribution networks and modest access to technological innovation.[25]

Cookbooks and women's magazines played an important role in educating women of all classes, spreading bourgeois ideals of propriety and thriftiness while making local recipes and ingredients known all over the country. The publishing industry contributed to normalizing the food policies of Fascism and motivating Italians not only to embrace efficiency and modernity, but to cook in more frugal ways. Housewives had to negotiate between the call to reduce waste, eating according to the regime's patriotic directives, and the need to maintain the family's health and morale, impressing guests (*fare bella figura*) even on a tight budget. Fernanda Momigliano's *Vivere bene in tempi difficili* (Living Well in

During the embargo caused by the invasion of Ethiopia, even food magazines like *La Cucina Italiana* embraced the regime's propaganda.

174

Hard Times, 1933) advised readers by imagining an urban family of four living on a modest income. Cookbooks were published that embraced the refusal of meat as a fashion and a symbol of modern consumption, following the establishment of the Italian association of vegetarians in 1905.[26] In 1930 Duke Enrico Alliata di Salaparuta published *Cucina vegetariana: manuale di gastrosofia naturista* (Vegetarian Cuisine: A Manual of Natural Gastrosophy), in which the dietary choices were not dictated by the Fascist call to sobriety, but rather by philosophical choices and refined upper-class overtones. In 1929, the monthly magazine *La cucina italiana*, printed on thin, foldable paper like a daily, presented itself as 'a magazine of gastronomy for families and gourmets', negotiating a middle ground between the interests of upper-class consumers and the needs of middle-class housewives. In 1932 the magazine was sold to the newspaper *Giornale d'Italia* and became an amplifier for Fascist food-related policies. One of the most popular books of the period was Ada Boni's *Il talismano della felicità* (The Talisman for Happiness), first published in 1925, which already in its title promised domestic bliss to all those who cooked following its recipes. Boni's volume, which is still considered a classic and is often given as a present to newlywed women, went through many reprints and changes over time. After the demise of Fascism, the more patriotic and propagandistic overtones were eliminated to make the new editions of *Il talismano* acceptable. Ada Boni, a Roman lady who paid great attention to trends and novelties, had already launched the magazine *Preziosa* in 1915, promoting an interest in practicality and domestic advice for women that resonated in autarchy times. Other female food writers acquired great notoriety in this period. In 1929 Amalia Moretti Foggia della Rovere, famous under her nom de plume Petronilla, started writing for the weekly magazine *La domenica del corriere* about health and nutrition. One of the first Italian women to earn a university degree (in biology and medicine), she worked as a paediatrician in Milan, garnering a faithful readership when she started her column 'Tra i fornelli' (At the Stove). Her personal and refined tone struck a chord among housewives who wanted to maintain propriety even during the hard times of food rationing and autarchy, a situation the author barely acknowledged.

Ada Bonfiglio Krassich authored a series of books that promoted 'economic and healthy' cooking. Here are two recipes from the 1937 edition, when autarchy was already the war cry for patriotic housewives. Note the tiny quantities suggested for more expensive products, like

## Economic Gnocchi in a Baking Pan

Put a pot on the stove with 150 grams of white flour, stirring two whole eggs and two litres of milk in it, a little at a time to avoid lumps. Add 50 grams of diced Gruyère cheese and, while stirring, cook on a moderate flame till you see the mix become denser. Emulsify 30 grams of butter in it, add a little salt and remove from the flame. Pour the mix on a baking sheet, and after letting it cool spread it so that is has the same thickness. Cut it in big dices and place them in a baking pan that you will have greased with butter. Sprinkle it with little pieces of butter and grated parmigiano cheese, place the pan in the oven and bake till the gnocchi have become a nice golden colour.[27]

## Economic Meatloaf with Peas

Take a nice slice of beef, wide and thin, and after sprinkling it with some salt cover it with slices of mortadella (around 70 grams). Place thin slices of Gruyère cheese here and there (around 50 grams) then roll the meat into a cylinder that you will tie very tight with twine. Put a big piece of butter, a diced slice of pancetta, and an onion sliced in rings in a casserole and place it on the flame. When the ingredients start browning, add the meat roll that you will have passed in flour. Make it brown then add a cup of warm water in which you will have dissolved a teaspoon of tomato paste. Cover the casserole and let it simmer on a low flame for an hour. Then add 300 grams of fresh peas, adding some tablespoons of warm water if the sauce is too thick. Add salt, pepper and let it cook slowly. If they are tender, the peas will be ready in half hour. Reduce the sauce and serve with good polenta.[28]

Gruyère cheese and mortadella. Nevertheless, consumers were still assumed to have access to meat, butter and other goods that would become largely unavailable in the following years.

At times, the Fascist propaganda machine intervened directly on the food scene, publishing pamphlets like *Sapersi nutrire* (How to Nourish

Oneself), *Perché bisogna aumentare il consume del pesce* (Why It Is Necessary to Increase Fish Consumption, 1935) and *La cucina economica in tempo di sanzioni* (Thrifty Cooking in the Time of Sanctions, 1935). Before Mussolini issued racial laws in 1938, Jewish cookbooks also strived to represent the community as part of the Italian nation, proposing menus for traditional holidays that were structured according to the usual Italian meal sequence of antipasti-*primo-secondo* and *contorni*-dessert.[29]

The party emphasized the wealth of specialities and recipes that made Italy unique, as an expression of national pride and an invitation to promote the consumption of local products. Festivals were organized to highlight traditional customs and folklore, especially when connected with agriculture. In 1931 the Italian Touring Club published *Guida gastronomica d'Italia* (Gastronomic Guide to Italy).[30] The volume aimed to boost the knowledge and the diffusion at the national level of local foods that were otherwise limited to specific areas.[31] This approach revealed a new mentality that looked at traditional products as 'specialities' and 'typical products' that could attract tourists and that presupposed mobility, disposable income and an efficient transportation system. The railway system, one of the priorities for the Fascist regime in terms of national development, had spurred the success of modern establishments attached to the train stations that often offered 'Italian' food rather than local dishes.[32] The idea behind the *Guida gastronomica d'Italia*, as scholar

My moustachioed great-grandfather at a local market in Rome in 1933.
Canned and packaged goods had become common.

Alberto Capatti has noted, did not clash with the modernization of transportation, rural development, the industrialization of food productions or with the self-reliance project that Fascism would embrace shortly after the publication of the guide:

> From the point of view of the autarchy, the food industry works for the wealth of the country, protects consumers from foreign competitors, and does not destroy small rural and mountain manufactures. Artisans, food technicians and housewives all give their individual contribution to a collective economic project.[33]

The desire to showcase the culinary wealth of Italy was also reflected in journalist Paolo Monelli's *Il ghiottone errante* (The Wandering Glutton, 1935), the *Almanacco della cucina regionale* (Almanac of Regional Cuisines, 1937), a cookbook for housewives by Ada Bonfiglio Krassich, and *Trattorie d'Italia*, a restaurant guidebook published in 1939 by the Fascist National Federation of Public Establishments.[34]

All kinds of establishments provided wine and food. At the *osteria*, abundant and cheap wine – often of poor quality and sold on credit – could be bought and consumed with the food that customers brought from home. At times, *osterie* provided both wine and food, either from nearby frying shops, bakeries or other kinds of food manufacturers, or from a kitchen on the premises (*osteria con cucina*). *Osterie*, more common in cities than in the countryside, and more numerous in the north than in the south, frequently became the object of temperance campaigns led by the socialists, who wanted to free workers from alcoholism and bring them to culture and political engagement, following the motto *libro contro litro* (a book instead of a litre). At the same time, these watering holes offered a place to meet with friends, play cards, discuss the current situation and socialize away from home, a necessity in the new neighbourhoods in northern Italian cities where factory workers lived in close, if not cramped, quarters.[35] Especially in the south, *osterie* were perceived as male spaces. Even when women were involved in running the *osteria*, they often stayed in the back of the house and the kitchen, while men dealt with customers. This division of roles is reflected in Luchino Visconti's first movie, *Ossessione* (1943), an early example of the Neorealist film style. The movie opens as a handsome and muscular vagrant in a singlet is visiting a roadside *osteria* and enters the rear kitchen uninvited. He startles but also intrigues the gorgeous and coquettish wife of the

My great-grandparents enjoying an outdoors snack in the 1930s. Even during shortages,
city dwellers enjoyed picnics in the countryside and outings to *osterie* and *trattorie*.

owner, who is also the cook. In the kitchen, the vagrant eats directly from the pot, an attitude that the woman clearly interprets as a form of sensual flirting. The break of the social norm foreshadows the torrid passion that will develop between the two and that will eventually push them to kill the woman's stolid and overweight husband.

Drinking shops were also called *bettola*, when they were particularly small and carrying a bad reputation, or *taverna*, a word that over time acquired more positive connotations. Dining establishments that wanted to distinguish themselves from the vulgar *osteria* and *taverna* adopted the names *trattoria* and *ristorante*, serving both Italian and French food, with a greater attention to service and dish presentation. When the Fascist regime tried to protect the Italian language from foreign expressions, *trattoria* fell into disfavour and the word *ristorante* was officially eliminated in 1941 by the Royal Academy of Italy.[36] At any rate, as early as 1921, the German author Hans Barth was already complaining about the gentrification of eateries in his volume *Osteria*, the reprint of his groundbreaking guide from 1908 to this specific Italian culinary institution.[37]

While Italy was struggling to adapt to the food policies of Fascism, a very visible art movement, Futurism, embraced the regime's priorities regarding food consumption, but it did so by adopting a very iconoclastic approach that expressed a deep fascination with modernity, machinery and speed. In 1930, artists Filippo Tommaso Marinetti and

## From the 'Manifesto of Futurist Cuisine' (1930)

We first need the abolition of pasta, the absurd Italian gastronomic religion. Perhaps stock fish, roast beef and pudding benefit the British, meat cooked with cheese the Dutch, sauerkraut, lard and smoked sausage the Germans, but pasta does not help Italians. For example, it contrasts with the vivacious wit and passionate, generous, intuitive soul of the Neapolitans. These were heroic fighters, inspired artists, enthralling speakers, witty lawyers and tenacious farmers in spite of the massive daily pasta. In eating it, they develop the typical ironic and sentimental scepticism that often truncates their enthusiasm. A clever Neapolitan professor, Dr Signorelli, writes: 'Unlike bread and rice, pasta is a food that you guzzle, instead of chewing. This starchy food is mostly digested in the mouth by saliva and the work of transformation is carried out by the pancreas and the liver. This leads to an imbalanced disorder of these organs. The result is weakness, pessimism, nostalgic inactivity and neutralism.'

We require the abolition of the mediocre daily habits in the pleasures of the palate. We call upon chemistry for the duty to quickly provide the body with the necessary calories by equivalent nutrients, free and given by the State, in powder or pills, albumen compounds, synthetic fats and vitamins. So we will achieve a real fall in the cost of life and in wages, with a relative reduction of working hours. Today, two thousand kilowatts need only one worker. The machines will soon constitute an obedient proletariat of iron, steel and aluminium serving people who will be almost totally relieved from manual labour. This, being reduced to two or three hours, allows you to refine and ennoble the other hours through thought, the arts and the foretaste of perfect lunches. In all walks of life, lunches will be spaced but perfect in their daily equivalent in nutrients.

Fillia (Luigi Colombo) published a daring manifesto entitled 'Manifesto of Futurist Cuisine' in the *Gazzetta del popolo* in Turin, which was as controversial as their dinners, in which performance and bombastic declarations were as important as the actual food.[38]

The book *La cucina futurista* (The Futurist Cookbook, 1932) proposed dishes and menus that repudiate all Italian traditions. In its introduction, the cookbook stated:

> Against the criticism already expressed and that can be expected, the futurist culinary revolution, illustrated in this volume, proposed the high, noble and useful aim of radically modifying the food of our race, to make it stronger, more dynamic and more spiritual with brand new dishes where intelligence, experience, and creativity replace – in an economic way – quantity, banality, repetition and cost. Regulated for high speed like the engine of a hydroplane, this futurist cuisine of ours will appear to some trembling traditionalists as crazy and dangerous; on the contrary, its goal is to create harmony between men's taste and their lives, today and tomorrow.[39]

As a matter of fact, many of the Futurist culinary creations appear far-fetched and unappetizing, such as the *Paradosso primaverile* (springtime paradox), a cylinder of ice cream topped with bananas and plum-filled hard eggs, or *Parole in libertà* (free words), composed of sea cucumbers, watermelon, radicchio, a cube of parmigiano, a sphere of Gorgonzola, caviar, figs and amaretto cookies, 'all neatly placed on a bed of mozzarella, to be eaten with your eyes closed, grasping here and there, while the great painter and "free-worder" Depero will declaim his famous song "Jacopson"'.[40] The recipes proposed were mostly daring assemblages, with frequent sexual, lavatorial or belligerent innuendos, such as in the case of 'raw meat torn by the sound of trumpet'.[41]

> Cut a perfect cube of beef. Spike it with electrical currents, keep it soaking in a mixture of rum, cognac and white vermouth for 24 hours. Take it out of the mixture and serve it on a bed of red pepper, black pepper and snow. Chew each bite thoroughly for one minute, separating them by impetuous notes of the trumpet blown by the eater.
>
> When waking up, fighters will be served platters of ripe persimmons, pomegranates and blood oranges. While these disappear into the mouth, the room will be sprayed with suave aromas of rose, jasmine, honeysuckle and acacia, whose nostalgic and

decadent sweetness will be brutally refused by the fighters, who will immediately wear their gas masks.

Before leaving, they will swallow a *scoppioingola* [burst in your throat], hard liquid constituted by a little ball of parmigiano cheese soaked in *marsala* wine.[42]

Mussolini never took part in any of the extravagant dinners, but expressed his appreciation for the Futurists' work.[43]

### Mayhem and Reconstruction

Despite the political and economic ties with Hitler's Third Reich, at the beginning of the Second World War Mussolini proclaimed non-belligerence and waited until June 1940 to join his ally against Great Britain and France. The Italian intervention proved a disaster: the military conquest of Greece failed, and the Italian battalions sent to Russia to take part in Hitler's attack against Stalin were defeated. In July 1943, following the massive bombardments of Italian cities and the landing of the Allies in Sicily, Vittorio Emanuele III dismissed Mussolini, who was taken prisoner to Abruzzo. In September the new government, guided by Marshall Pietro Badoglio, signed an armistice with the Allies. The German troops immediately occupied all of northern and central Italy, including Rome, while the Allies and the Italian government took control of the area south of Latium and Abruzzo. Mussolini was freed and established a puppet state in northern Italy with Salò, on Lake Garda, as its capital. National Liberation Committees, which gathered militants (*partigiani*, 'partisans') from all political parties, were formed in the occupied areas and fought a guerrilla war against the Nazis and the remnants of the Fascist troops.

War inevitably brought hunger; food availability decreased dramatically as agricultural production slowed and rural workers departed to the front. Hoarding became a widespread phenomenon and rationing started as early as 1940, with coffee and sugar first, then oil, rice, pasta and bread. The government distributed food stamps that could be redeemed with basic products, but the system did not function properly. Faced with widespread meat scarcity, those who could raise chickens, rabbits and pigs did so for their own consumption and for sale. Farmers created parallel distribution networks to bring their goods into the cities, selling them to entrepreneurial individuals who resold them at much higher prices,

The black market (*borsa nera*) in Rome after the war.

and shop owners sometimes hid rationed provisions to sell them on the black market.[44] Hotels and restaurants at times managed to stay open and offer full menus to whoever could afford them. The black market system (*borsa nera*) worked thanks to the connivance of state functionaries, from mill inspectors to policemen and city guards, who enjoyed food kickbacks. Research on access to food during the war reveals that the black market became the main source of procurement, limiting options for Italians living on a fixed income.[45] A diet relying exclusively on rationed food from the government would have ensured only around 900 calories a day.[46] The urban dwellers that had family in the countryside moved out of the city, hoping to tap into the relative availability of food and the higher living standards of the rural world. In the Nazi-occupied areas the situation was even worse, as the German troops requisitioned great quantities of provisions for their own use and rounded up males to work for them.

In June 1944, Rome was liberated and the occupied area shrank north of the 'Gothic Line' between Rimini in Romagna and Forte dei Marmi in Tuscany. Finally, on 25 April 1945 (a date celebrated with a national holiday in Italy), the general insurrection against the Nazi occupation was proclaimed. The German troops surrendered and Mussolini was captured, executed, and his corpse hung by the feet in a square in Milan where the Nazis had shot fifteen *partigiani*. In 1946

An American GI embraces a girl after the end of the Nazi occupation in 1945.

Italians voted to become a republic, and in 1948 the new constitution was passed. With the arrival of the American GIs in the south, and later in the rest of the country, condensed milk, cookies, chocolate, coffee and other victuals suddenly reappeared, albeit sparsely. Much of the distribution network was still so inefficient that most consumers kept on buying what they needed on the black market. Great efforts were focused on bringing food from the countryside into the cities through legal channels, but it was to little avail. The Alto Commissariato dell'Alimentazione (High Commissariat for Food Provisioning) and the United Nations Relief and Rehabilitation Administration (UNRRA) struggled with the sheer amount of food needed. Federconsorzi, the Italian federation of rural consortia that since the 1890s had helped farmers get credit, seeds and raw materials, was involved in the distribution of staples and crops.[47] Numerous Italians were fed in soup kitchens and other institutions run by political parties and by the Catholic Church, like the *Refettori del Papa* (pope's dining halls).

The decade 1945–55 was defined as *ricostruzione* (reconstruction). Italy, with its powerful Communist and Socialist parties, found itself at the hinge of the Western and the Eastern blocs during the cold war. It was crucial for the U.S. that Italy stayed in the Western camp. The result was the inclusion of Italy in the European recovery programme, also known as the Marshall Plan, to funnel financial aid towards the reconstruction of the productive system in order to avoid unemployment and social turmoil. Great efforts focused on state-led initiatives to rebuild the industrial system, which was already concentrated in the industrial triangle between Milan, Turin and Genoa. Food became crucial in the political debates that surrounded the first democratic elections for the new parliament: the Christian Democrats, a party of Catholic inspiration, underlined its connection with the U.S., a source of aid and food provisions, unlike the Communist Party's Soviet allies.

The rural world, particularly in the south, was ready to explode, as became clear with the police killing of farmers occupying uncultivated lands in Melissa, Calabria, in 1949. The major issues included the concentration of land ownership, the technological backwardness and the low wages paid to agricultural workers, who lived in conditions of

At the end of the war, Italians finally had access to food.

185

chronic undernourishment. *La terra a chi lavora* (the land to those who work it) was the slogan. The following year, a reform was launched after long negotiations between the leftist parties, which were against any sort of large ownership, and the Christian Democrats, who wanted to support rural families while defending private property.[48] The reform, which involved about 30 per cent of all available land, did too little, too late. Expropriated owners received public bonds with a 5 per cent interest rate, while farmers were given the opportunity to buy plots from the state with 30-year mortgages. Almost 1.5 million acres were transferred to small farmers whose traditional methods frequently could not keep up with the modernization in the sector. The reform was more successful in coastal areas, where the government was building public infrastructures using a special fund, Cassa del Mezzogiorno, for the development of the south. Agricultural production only increased at a rate of 2.5 per cent a year, despite the government's efforts to amass wheat to keep its price high and support rural incomes.[49]

Most Italians were still sticking to what would later be known as the Mediterranean diet, mostly consuming grains, fresh vegetables and fruit from the neighbouring countryside, pasta, eggs and the occasional fish or piece of cheese. In the north the consumption of animal fats was higher. Nevertheless, in the early 1950s the average per capita consumption of meat was still limited. A survey on poverty, organized by the parliament after the launch of the land reform, indicated that over 50 per cent of families in southern Italy were to be considered indigent.[50] Many families still cooked in the hearth or in a coal burner; better-off households could afford a *cucina economica*, a coal or wood stove that also provided heat and hot water. Electric or gas burners were still luxury items.[51]

Young film-makers such as Roberto Rossellini, Vittorio De Sica and Luchino Visconti immortalized this situation of penury in sombre tones, often exaggerating the admittedly hard reality for political reasons. They rejected the propagandist approach of the previous period to reflect the world they saw around them; they chose to shoot on location rather than in studios, and preferred to hire non-professional actors when possible. By so doing, they established new film aesthetics that acquired worldwide renown under the name of Neorealism.[52] Their stories highlighted the vicissitudes of working-class characters. In *La terra trema* (The Earth Trembles, 1948), Luchino Visconti narrated the ruinous attempts of a poor fisherman's family on the eastern coast of Sicily to overcome their condition, while in *Riso amaro* (Bitter Rice, 1949)

Fishermen in Lampedusa, off the coast of Sicily. Some areas of Italy remained excluded from economic reconstruction after the war.

Rice gatherers, or *mondine*, the protagonists of the film *Riso amaro* (1949).

Giuseppe De Santis focused on the lives of rice gatherers and the union struggles of rural workers.

Paradoxically, the filmmaker could count on the eager audiences who had become accustomed to the Fascist-sponsored movies, both as entertainment and as a tool for political communication. In a famous scene from Vittorio De Sica's Neorealist masterpiece *Ladri di biciclette* (Bicycle Thieves, 1948), which takes place in Rome right after the end of the Second World War, a father decides to splurge and to take his young son to lunch in a restaurant they cannot afford. The child, looking at the lavish food consumed at a nearby table by snooty, upper-class people, enjoys a simple *mozzarella in carrozza*, a slice of mozzarella squeezed between two slices of bread and then fried. He also shares some wine with his father, knowing well that they are doing something his mother would disapprove of. The child, intimidated by the unfamiliar surroundings, almost stops eating out of guilt when his father mentions the dire straits the family finds itself in after the theft of the bicycle he used for work. The scene is particularly poignant, as we see a desperate father trying to hold onto his role as breadwinner, while being confronted with his poverty and his limited access to food. Many elements provide us with useful information about eating in public at the time: the service, the available dishes and the social discourse about food scarcity. Poverty is also the focus in De Sica's *Miracolo a Milano* (Miracle in Milan, 1951), where homeless people participate in a raffle to win a 'real chicken', which is eventually devoured by the lucky winner alone in front of the other hungry participants.

De Sica's more ironic and light-hearted approach to social issues became more common in Italian films, reflecting the improvement of the economic situation in the early 1950s. Luciano Emmer's *Domenica d'agosto* (August Sunday, 1950) turned its ironic gaze on Romans flocking to the beaches with huge amounts of food and displaying their newly found security but also their lack of education. Food and hunger, not urgent issues for the greater part of the population, soon turned into targets for comedy, as Mario Mattone's *Miseria e nobiltà* (Poverty and Nobility, 1954) clearly indicates. In the most famous scene, which takes places in Naples, a famished Totò, a well-known and beloved comedian, is so excited to be offered spaghetti with tomato sauce that he fills his pockets with it and eats it with his bare hands while dancing on a table. Movies also documented the influence of the u.s. as a dietary model and the spread of foreign foods during the reconstruction. The young

Totò in Mario Mattone's *Miseria e nobiltà* (Poverty and Nobility, 1954).

Roman protagonist of Steno's *Un americano a Roma* (An American in Rome, 1954) pictures himself as an American, comically mimicking words and behaviours to express his newfound identity. In a sequence that many Italians can still recite word for word, he expresses his desire to enjoy glamorous but unpalatable foreign foods such as yogurt and mustard. At the same time, he negotiates his attachment to traditional

189

Biscotti con crema
di marroni Zuegg
Ric. n. 244

After the war, new industrial products (like this chestnut paste in a tube)
fascinated Italians as symbols of modernity and progress.

fare such as spaghetti and wine, which he mocks as passé and uninter-
esting while craving them as a source of comfort. The famous line,
'Spaghetti, you provoked me, now I am going to devour you', is often
quoted in contemporary situations where Italians find themselves facing
globalized foods that are considered trendy and exciting but not as
satisfying as Italian traditional dishes.[53]

The mid-1950s saw the end of food shortages, with growing
industrial production of pasta, dairy, sugar, wine and liquors. Foreign
consumer goods such as Ritz crackers, whisky and Coca-Cola were
embraced as symbols of cosmopolitanism and abundance. Cookbooks
reflected this sensibility, offering exotic and daring recipes that were
supposed to surprise guests when entertaining. However, domestic food
habits did not change much. As historian Carol Helstosky underlines:

Consumers purchased more of the foods they consumed prior to the war but did not alter the content or structure of their daily meals. The Italian food industry reinforced existing habits by concentrating on producing and marketing the foods characteristic of the Mediterranean diet: pasta, olive oil, tomatoes, wine and bread.[54]

Women found themselves recast in the traditional middle-class roles of homemakers. Supposed to find satisfaction and self-expression in the expanding access to consumer goods, they were considered naturally responsible for the home and care-giving work.[55] However, the economic system was changing too fast for traditional gender roles to be maintained. In the 1960s and 1970s, women entered the job market in droves, triggering epochal changes in Italian society that led to the reform of family law, the introduction of divorce and women's unprecedented control over their bodies and sexual lives.

## La Dolce Vita

Life became easier for many Italians during the late 1950s when the country experienced the beginning of the so-called 'economic miracle', credited to international peace, currency stability and a growing internal demand for consumer goods. The average GDP growth rate was 6.3 per cent between 1958 and 1963, with a peak of 7.6 per cent in 1961. The unemployment rate plummeted as low as 2.6 per cent in 1963.[56] Most of the development happened in the industrial sector. In 1957 Italy joined the European Economic Community (EEC), which embraced a free-market model based on specialization and the expansion of consumer demand. The following year, the Common Agricultural Policy established a huge free exchange space for agricultural goods across several European nations but also incorporated a high degree of centralized decision making at the Community level, with a focus on efficiency that contradicted the goals of the land reform in Italy. European price support focused on cereals, milk, cheese and meat, mostly produced in the plains of northern Italy, while almost ignoring southern goods like olive oil and wine. In 1961 and 1966 the Italian government approved two *piano verde* (green plans) that emphasized technology, mechanization, fertilizers, pesticides and construction. These measures increased the rural demand for industrial products, then mostly flowing towards large agricultural enterprises.

Starting from the 1950s, Italy reconstructed its production system and
embarked on the industrialization of its agriculture.

The new European framework and the policies adopted by the Italian
government did not do much to improve the living standards among
small farmers, who frequently ended up selling their properties to larger
owners.

Despite a law of 1957 that established areas for industrial investment
in the south, the rapid growth in the industrial triangle around Milan,
Turin and Genoa stimulated a major wave of internal emigration of
southerners to the north. This rapid demographic shift compounded
the long-term movement of the population from the interior to the
coasts and from the countryside to cities that had started with the unification. From the 1880s on, during every decade, almost a million rural

residents relocated to urban centres. This figure increased to 3.2 million between 1951 and 1961, when the Fascist law against internal migration was struck down, and was 2.3 million in the following decade.[57] A total of around 9 million people changed residence between 1955 and 1971.[58] Despite the fact that agricultural jobs decreased from 44 per cent of the total workforce to 29 per cent between 1951 and 1961, rural productivity increased, providing goods for the growing consumer market. This trend also continued after the end of the 'miracle': by 1981, only 14.1 per cent of Italian jobs were in agriculture.[59]

Cinema took stock of this epochal migration, featuring food to express nostalgia, lack of understanding between newcomers and host communities, and the fear and struggles experienced when leaving one's native place to move to an unfamiliar destination. Among the films that reflect these issues we can mention Luchino Visconti's *Rocco e i suoi fratelli* (Rocco and His Brother, 1960), the dramatic narration of a family's life from Basilicata in Milan.[60] Other films offered a lighter and more comedic approach, like Camillo Mastrocinque's *Totò, Peppino e la malafemmina* (Totò, Peppino and the Shameless Woman, 1956), where the protagonists travel from Naples to Milan wearing heavy coats and fur hats for fear of the cold, bringing tons of southern food, and Mario Monicelli's *I soliti ignoti* (Big Deal of Madonna Street, 1958), about a motley crew of inexperienced thieves in Rome, many of whom were immigrants.

Mass internal migration gave rise to deep social changes and caused fissures in the family structure and the traditional values that sustained it. Many agricultural workers decided to abandon their farms for factory work, which provided stable and substantial revenues. But the sudden lack of agricultural labour triggered the neglect of low-yield crops that were too labour-intensive. Biodiversity suffered an unprecedented blow, while many food-related production techniques and artisanal know-how almost got lost.

Immigrants settling in the industrial north were often ambivalent about their own culinary habits, which depended on their personal situations, family stories, social integration in the host communities and financial constraints. Some wanted to forget their past and blend into the new environment; many considered the dishes they grew up with unfashionable, if not despicable and smacking of poverty. Others displayed an admirable attachment to their culinary heritage, going to great lengths to procure the necessary ingredients. During holidays, it was especially common for immigrants to prepare and share their more traditional dishes, as a way to remind themselves of their cultural identities. Nevertheless, these recipes belonged to the intimate sphere of family or close friends, and as the financial situations of immigrants improved, the recipes were often relegated to a more symbolic status, still prepared for tradition's sake but at other times barely consumed. Women, who in the past were usually in charge of cooking, frequently had to leave their homes and find jobs, dedicating less time to the preparation of meals. Furthermore, the rise of the feminist political consciousness pushed many women out of the kitchen, now considered a place of exploitation.

Nevertheless, the displacement of major portions of the population allowed regional and local foods to become known in other parts of the country. While this interregional exchange had always existed for the higher classes, farmers and artisans had tended to eat what was produced around them, familiar and affordable. Now southern communities in the north craved Mediterranean products, creating commercial demand for foods that otherwise would never have travelled: this is the case with buffalo-milk mozzarella, sun-dried tomatoes and olive oil. Many migrants found their first occupations around the outdoor markets in northern cities, frequently working illegally as street vendors and climbing up the ranks to manage and purchase their own legal stalls or stores.[61] Markets were places where newcomers could find jobs, congregate with other people from their village or area, speak their own dialect and loiter on Sundays, which raised suspicions and outright criticism among northerners.[62] Over time, southern entrepreneurs opened successful stores, restaurants, bakeries and pastry shops that not only catered to their own communities, but also played an important role as cultural mediators, introducing locals to unheard-of specialities and recipes.

Due to steadfast economic development, protein consumption rose at an unprecedented pace, even among migrants. Despite their prices being maintained at artificially high levels by European policies, milk, cheese and meat claimed a place in Italian diets that they had never had before. Meat consumption increased especially quickly, not only in terms of quantity, but also quality and types of cut. If in 1881 the average per capita consumption of meat was 11.25 kg (25 lb) a year, in 1974 it was 45 kg (100 lb).[63] Steaks and *fettine* (slices of veal or beef) became the affordable symbols of comfort and financial security, replacing more traditional cuts considered too tough or just not as juicy. New consumer products flooded the market, including snacks like Motta and Algida packaged ice cream, Pavesi crackers and Nutella chocolate spread. However, the growth of the food industry was restrained by the limits of agricultural production, with a few exceptions: Barilla, Buitoni, Ferrero and Cirio. The production of consumer appliances fared much better. Gas stoves became common and refrigerators found their place in households, often with small freezer compartments that slowly allowed the adoption of frozen food, especially fish and, later, vegetables.[64] Italians enjoyed displaying their financial stability by purchasing cars, travelling at weekends and taking longer vacations, frequently spending their month off away from home. In August the country basically shut down, with many immigrants going back to their places of origin. Tourism became a common leisure activity.

The inauguration of public TV broadcasting in December 1954 marked the beginning of a new era of consumer culture. As early as 1957, a ten-minute show called *Carosello* was launched, aired right after the evening news and before the main entertainment in the one network then functioning. *Carosello* was composed of short commercials (both

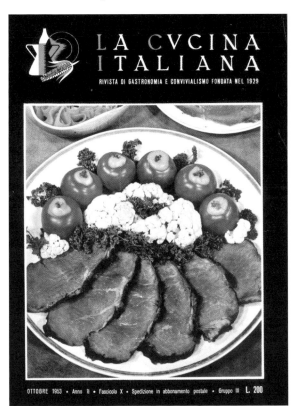

Cover from a 1953 issue of the food magazine *La cucina italiana*: after the war, the new abundance was symbolized by an increased use of meat.

with actors and cartoons) with only a few seconds dedicated to promote products. For this prime-time slot, advertisers created characters with stories and adventures that quickly became part of popular culture and established a solid position for the products they represented. It was usual for children to go to bed after *Carosello*, and it was a form of punishment to be sent to bed without watching the beloved show. The show ended in 1977, when long commercials became too expensive for advertisers to produce and air, and other forms of more direct promotion were adopted.[65]

Stimulated by advertising and enjoying their higher incomes, Italians familiarized themselves with the supermarket, an American invention that was introduced in Milan in 1957 with the participation of the International Basic Economy Corporation (IBEC), founded by Nelson Rockefeller.[66] Although the prestigious Rinascente department stores were inaugurated in 1917 and the less upscale UPIM and Standa had already opened during the Fascist period, the new food supermarkets required a transformation of the way Italians were used to shopping. Customers were expected to get goods from the shelves, an action performed by store staff in traditional grocers'; they were offered larger quantities of goods; furthermore, they had to acquaint themselves with food packaged in unfamiliar ways. Because of the small size of Italian industrial food production and the overall lag in the agribusiness sectors, supermarkets imported many goods from abroad or produced their own bread, coffee, sausages and cheese. Through their Confcommercio association, small shopkeepers resisted supermarkets, which they accused of depressing prices and ruining local businesses by pressuring local politicians. Consumer cooperatives also expanded their activities, reaching dimensions that allowed them to compete with private conglomerates. The League of Cooperatives, founded back in 1886, grew in the number of stores and purchasing power, becoming an important link between Left parties and consumers. Over the decades, the tension between the League and private entrepreneurs would be tainted by political tensions, with reciprocal accusations and legal battles.[67] In 1962 shopkeepers also founded their own cooperative, CONAD, which became a major player in the supermarket sector.

Following the economic miracle, *osterie* and *trattorie* almost disappeared, supplanted by new public places of consumptions like bars, where young people could congregate in an environment that was considered more modern and interesting. 'American bars' had made

My grandparents at a family meal, 1960s. The economic miracle became visible
on Italian tables, with more abundant food.

their appearance in Italy in the late 1890s, where coffee from espresso
machines was served at the counter by a barista.[68] Customers could
drink their espresso standing at the counter or sitting with friends. In the
1960s, bars once again became places to perform modernity, embracing
sleek design and materials such as linoleum, Formica and steel. Juke
boxes blasted pop music hits, while foosball tables provided cheap entertainment. Mass-produced carbonated drinks and alcoholic beverages
like beers, liquors, *amaro* and, more rarely, mixed drinks, replaced wine.
While traditional *osterie* disappeared, new establishments took the
name *hostaria*, with an 'h' that was supposed to suggest history and
tradition, proposing a domesticated and nostalgic version of the old
popular fare. From the 1960s, the ambivalent relationship between
tradition and innovation, between attachment to local identities and
the realities of globalization, became a constant element of the way
Italians experience food.

# SIX

# Now and the Future

While Italy changes, also diet rapidly alters styles, manners, conventions, processes and language. Hours and places, rhythms and pauses, cooking times and techniques adjust. The hands and the tastes of those who still work in the kitchen also change. The quick shift from a rural to a heavily industrialized country, together with the difficult transition from an archaic to a modern agriculture, has deeply modified the traditional balance between fields and orchards, markets and domestic kitchens.[1]

With his evocative style, this is how scholar Piero Camporesi described the rapid transformation that has shaken the Italian food system in recent decades. Nevertheless, the past still exerts a strong influence on the present, causing many consumers to feel ambivalent about their attachment to traditions and local identities and their commitment to modernity and progress in its more globalized aspects.

## AT THE TURN OF THE MILLENNIUM

The epochal changes of the 'economic miracle' left a deep and long-lasting mark on Italian society. In the period between 1964 and 1973, despite an average GDP growth rate of 4.8 per cent, production experienced a slight decrease compared to the previous years of fast development. Social tensions led to the strikes and the union unrest of the *autunno caldo* (hot autumn) of 1969. Conservative fringes opted for the so-called *strategia della tensione* (tension strategy), based on attacks, murders and other terrorist activities, culminating in the explosion of a bomb in a Milan square that killed seventeen people. The unemployment rate rose as workers who had temporarily moved to Switzerland, France, Belgium and Germany to work in mining and factories returned home. The state reacted by establishing a public welfare system that included retirement plans, healthcare coverage and other benefits for workers, many of whom enjoyed lifetime employment. The system survived until the early 2010s, when the economic crisis, the steep public debt and growing tensions about fiscal policy within the eurozone led the government to implement a series of unpopular measures that drastically shrank the reach of the welfare guarantees. From 1974 to 1982, production lagged and inflation spiralled due to the first oil crisis in 1973, causing union protests. The GDP shrank by 3.6 per cent in 1975.[2] As the Communist Party obtained over a third of the votes in the 1976 elections, social tensions exploded. Domestic terrorism by both Left and Right extremist groups became so terrifying that Italians still refer to this period as *gli anni di piombo* ('the lead years', referring to the metal used to make bullets).

The year 1983, which saw the advent of a centre-left government led by socialist statesman Bettino Craxi, marked the beginning of the 'Splendid Eighties', a period of political stability buoyed by moderate inflation, slight GDP growth and the increase of private consumption. The greater relevance of private life, success and financial security was referred to as *riflusso*, a 'reflux', from a period when everything was public and political. Individualism and hedonism were embraced by the yuppies that populated the elegant and exciting nightlife of Rome and Milan, where the minister of foreign affairs Gianni De Michelis was noticed for his infamous appetite and never-ending dinners. Food and its conspicuous consumption were important among socialites. In trendy restaurants, design and mood were more important than menus and dishes, in order to attract affluent customers who wanted to see and be seen.

An increasing interest in foreign food allowed French nouvelle cuisine to extend its influence to Italian tables. Chefs and housewives were eager to try new, seemingly brave, stuff, often with debatable results. It was fashionable to eat pasta with fresh cream and salmon, and to serve lemon sorbet between courses of formal meals. The following recipes were extremely popular while I was growing up in the 1980s. Although gourmets were already familiar with them in the 1970s, in the following years they trickled down to less exclusive tables. Compared to the more traditional fare that my mother cooked most of the time, I remember considering these dishes fancy and refined, and their ingredients

## Pennette with Salmon and Vodka

*For 4 people*

1 medium shallot
100 g (1½ sticks) butter
100 g (4 oz) smoked salmon
150 ml vodka
175 g (1 cup) cherry
tomatoes

1 tbsp tomato paste
130 ml (½ cup) fresh cream
chopped chives
450 g (1 lb) pennette pasta
1 tbsp chopped spring
onions

Finely chop the shallot and cook it in the butter until soft. Cut the smoked salmon into thin strips and add them to the shallots, then wet the whole with the vodka and let it evaporate. Cut the tomatoes into four pieces and sauté them for a few moments with the salmon, add a tablespoon of tomato paste and finally the cream. Turn off the heat after a few minutes and sprinkle everything with the chives. Meanwhile cook the pasta in salted water till al dente, drain it and add it to the pan with the salmon. Mix quickly and serve hot.

## Tortellini alla Boscaiola

*For 4 people*

450 g (1 lb) tortellini
100 g (4 oz) *prosciutto cotto*
(you can substitute with
cooked ham)
250 g (10 oz) button
mushrooms

200 g (7 oz) shelled peas
130 ml (½ cup) fresh
cream
salt, ground pepper
grated Parmesan cheese

Bring salted water to a boil in a large pot and cook the tortellini. In the meantime, cut the ham into cubes, slice the mushrooms and put them together with the peas in a pan with a thick bottom. Let them brown and add a little of the pasta cooking water if they stick to the pan. After about ten minutes, add the cream and season with salt and pepper. Cook for another 3 or 4 minutes and when the tortellini are cooked, drain and pour them in the pan with the cream sauce. Mix, sprinkle with grated Parmesan, and serve hot.

– including the pervasive fresh cream – quite exotic. Cholesterol was not yet a widespread preoccupation.

In the 1980s, foreign food corporations such as Danone, Nestlé, Unilever and Kraft started their penetration into the Italian market. Some historic brands lost their independence: Galbani cheese and Peroni beer were bought by Danone, Martini & Rossi by Bacardi. In 1985, McDonald's made its appearance in Italy with its first shop in Bolzano. The newcomer was perceived not only as an affront to Italian traditions and the country's way of life, but as an attack against labour organizations, local producers and the restaurant industry. To avoid a backlash, the American company acquired Burghy, a local fast-food chain with locations all over the peninsula, and bought meat from the Cremonini group in Modena, which also sells to Italian chains.

Behind the sparkle of the 1980s, public debt skyrocketed and social inequalities increased. The chasm in productivity between the north and the south became even larger than after the Second World War.[3] SME, the largest public food conglomerate, was privatized, turning it into the object of a long legal battle between the industrialist Carlo De Benedetti

McDonald's in Milan's elegant Galleria Vittorio Emanuele II.

and the media mogul and businessman Silvio Berlusconi. The impact of European policies was felt more intensely. To curb the distortive effects of price support for agricultural goods and the destruction of excess crops, both extremely expensive and disturbing for its citizens, in 1984 the European Economic Community revised its Common Agricultural Policy and introduced national quotas that limited milk production. In 1991 measures were adopted to decouple subsidies from agricultural output, with the goal of using them to support vulnerable farmers. Italian food consumption patterns changed so rapidly that nutritionists had growing concerns about health and increasing obesity rates, especially among children.[4]

Involving ministers and members of parliament, political and financial corruption was rampant, developing into an efficient system of bribery and illegal financing of political parties known as Tangentopoli (from *tangente*, 'kickback'). In 1992 a group of magistrates from Milan initiated a series of investigations, called Mani Pulite (clean hands), that eventually led to the demise of traditional political parties, an event that many welcomed – too hurriedly – as the beginning of a Second Republic. In 1994 the businessman Silvio Berlusconi decided to participate directly in politics and launched the Forza Italia (Go Italy!) party, winning the elections and forming a government that fell within eight months due to tensions among his political allies. Berlusconi was prime minister again between 2001 and 2006 and from 2008 and 2011.

It is still difficult to assess the effects of the global financial crisis of 2008, the strict fiscal policies adopted by Prime Minister Mario Monti, even in their milder version embraced by his successor Enrico Letta, and the following recession over Italian food production, distribution and consumption. The growing national debt, the rising unemployment rate (9.7 per cent in 2012, with a shocking 32.6 per cent for those between 15 and 24 years of age, according to the National Institute of Statistics, ISTAT), the crisis of the welfare state and the widespread disillusionment with regard to public institutions and politicians have darkened the outlook for the future.[5] The consequences are visible in food consumption. Italians waste less, making sure to consume more of what they buy. They shop more often and in lesser quantities to make the best use of all their groceries. They buy less beef and more cheap protein, such as eggs and legumes. Some have shifted to less expensive products, especially those on sale in high-discount supermarkets. Although inflation is quite stationary – around 2.2 per cent in 2012 – it might take time to recover from the crisis, as Italians brace themselves for the taxes introduced to finance the national debt. Growing inequalities in Italian society are reflected in the polarization of eating habits. According to the 2011 report by ISMEA (Institute of Services for the Agricultural Food Markets), the sales of high-end products increased 13.75 per cent between 2009 and 2010, just as all other food sectors began to stagnate.[6] While the few who can afford it enjoy spending at the table, many Italians might fully embrace the more restrained Mediterranean diet that their parents and grandparents were relieved to abandon during the decades of economic growth, as a mark of poverty and backwardness.

## WHERE TO SHOP, WHAT TO SHOP

One of the most visible changes in the Italian food system has been the development of different – and often competing – distribution networks. Supermarkets and self-service hypermarkets, high-discount stores and *centri commerciali* (shopping centres) have been displacing traditional outdoor markets and smaller family-run corner stores in both urban and rural landscapes. The Grande Distribuzione Organizzata (large organized distribution) profits from heavy purchase concentration through *centrali d'acquisto* (acquisition centres) shared by several distribution companies, which gives them an edge over producers during price negotiations.[7] Big players grow bigger, streamlining provisioning and management. They generate larger profits while creating oligopolistic inefficiencies that have an impact on consumers. Chains have been able to contain prices by launching products under their own label, often manufactured by the purveyors behind familiar, more expensive and heavily advertised name brands.[8] Furthermore, foreign businesses have acquired a dominant role in the hypermarket chains sector, such as the German Metro and the French Auchan and Carrefour. Their mammoth stores are usually located on the outskirts of large cities where land is cheaper and it is possible to build vast car parks, allowing customers to take their car and buy in large quantities.[9] Since the German chain Lidl's arrival in Italy in 1992, hard-discount retailers have opened all over the country, selling non-brand name products at low cost and in relatively small spaces, usually well within the city limits.

Most Italians do not shop daily any more but go to supermarkets at longer intervals to save time and fuel, especially as the biggest hypermarkets are located outside urban centres. Convenience, affordability and practicality have become the new goals for the food industry, which responds to and reinforces the sense that there is never enough time, and that Italians are living at an increasingly fast pace. The widespread availability of freezers has supported these trends. Moreover, industrial production has made local specialities available all over the country: soft cheese like *robiola* and *stracchino* from the north, *scamorze* and mozzarella from the south can be easily found in any region, together with a dazzling variety of salami, prosciutto and sausage.

The more traditional distribution channels have not disappeared, catering to different consumers' needs. Neighbourhood stores, where the shopkeepers know the clients and their preferences, are closer and easy to reach on foot. They work quite well for quick purchases limited to a few items. Corner shops managed by immigrants, who work late at night and at weekends, are able to offer low prices thanks to the limited profits that they are willing to accept. Some independent stores in the most affluent urban areas have turned into gourmet meccas, focusing on high-quality, high-status and value-added items appreciated by demanding and knowledgeable clients with higher disposable incomes. Although most have the same dimensions as traditional neighbourhood shops, in the past few years a chain of larger retail spaces, Eataly, has expanded from its first location in Turin to several stores across the country, including a multi-storied former train station in Rome, and branches in Tokyo and New York City. Eataly merges the structure and organization of a supermarket with the careful choice of high-quality products – often locally produced, artisanal or semi-artisanal – and the presence of restaurants that have become an attraction and a form of entertainment in themselves.

Eataly tries to reinterpret the sensory environment, the shopping experience and the atmosphere of markets, which still play an important role in the shopping habits of Italians. In urban centres, many markets have been moved by local authorities from outdoor spaces to new, supposedly more hygienic and efficient indoor buildings. The shift has rarely been accepted without a fight: during transition periods, owners of market stalls have feared that the often lengthy renovations would cause clients to shop elsewhere and resent the higher costs and fees connected with the more modern structures. However, shoppers seem to appreciate the better-organized and easy-to-navigate indoor markets, which can now accommodate other businesses in addition to food. Outdoor markets are still commonplace, operating daily, weekly or even monthly in smaller urban centres. A few outdoors markets have banked on their

Eataly, Rome.

traditional and somewhat quaint appearance to attract tourists, especially in large cities; other markets in upscale neighbourhoods specialize, instead, in high-end items. In cities with large immigrant populations, stalls have been rented out to newcomers, who frequently sell merchandise that Italians are not too familiar with. Immigrants often find employment in markets as a first step towards their integration into the host community.[10] Others prefer instead to cater to their own community, giving a more cosmopolitan and multicultural atmosphere to markets, which used to be strongholds of traditional Italian food.

The food found in markets is generally purchased from central wholesale distribution centres that receive merchandise from all over Italy and abroad. Shoppers that prefer to buy *chilometro zero* (zero kilometre) goods, products from nearby areas and sold directly by the farmers, tend to patronize *mercati contadini*, at times known by the English expression 'farmers' markets', formally established by law in 2007.[11] Small producers who cannot provide enough merchandise to wholesale centres or who embrace organic agriculture (*agricoltura biologica*) gather at farmers' markets to sell directly to customers who are ready to pay a premium to sustain the local economy, limit the environmental

Markets still provide products that are otherwise hard to find, such as snails.

impact of long-distance transportation and assert their cultural and social connection with local traditions and the nearby rural communities.

The relevance for shoppers of a direct relationship with the people who sell them food has prompted many supermarkets to introduce counters where consumers can deal with a person, taste products and socialize, just like they used to do in the old neighbourhood stores or at the outdoor market. Other sections allow consumers to touch and pick their food (although the use of plastic gloves is required), recreating a sensory experience reminiscent of the open-air stalls. Italians find themselves at the hinge of different distribution systems, accessing them at different times to buy different things, according to personal, financial and political motivations. Socially and ethically conscious customers also express their values and priorities by buying from *gruppo d'acquisto solidale* (the equivalent of community supported agriculture), social farms, which focus on the rehabilitation and social integration of individuals suffering from addictions, former convicts and other at-risk individuals, as well as farms growing food on land requisitioned from the Mafia.[12] Fair trade networks (*commercio equo e solidale*) have opened stores in large cities, selling chocolate, coffee, tea and other products from developing countries.

## FOOD POLITICS

This rekindled interest in wine and food, culinary traditions and local produce is reaching new heights just as the European Union is undergoing major political changes aimed at increasing integration between the 27 member states, not only administratively but also economically and financially. The process is not painless, and food is not excluded from the negotiations.

From the late 1990s, events such as the BSE (mad cow disease) crisis stimulated a widespread awareness among European citizens about what makes its way to their tables. In 2000, the European Commission, the executive branch of the Union, presented a white paper that highlighted priorities in dealing with emergencies, food safety and consumer information. Following these indications, the EU implemented a series of regulations to ensure food safety 'from farm to fork', as a slogan says. Regulation 178/2002 imposed that all foodstuffs, animal feed and feed ingredients are to be traced through the whole food chain. To ensure traceability, each business in the supply chain must be able to identify its suppliers and its buyers, according to the so-called 'one-step-backward, one-step-forward' approach. To appease consumers' concerns about safety, the largest supermarket chains are particularly involved in implementing traceability measures, imposing their standards on producers, manufacturers and packagers in order to pinpoint responsibilities in case of emergency. The most widely implemented among these standards, the GlobalGap (previously known as EurepGap), is familiar to farmers all over the world that sell produce to European supermarkets, while the British Retail Consortium (BRC) and International Food Standard (IFS) also cover non-agricultural goods. Of course, traceability turns into value-added, allowing large distributors to charge higher prices, while enhancing their control and power over the commercial network. Traceability is not as effective at the distribution level, so while it is relatively easy for a major chain to know where a product comes from, it is more complicated to pinpoint in which specific stores it might have been sold.[13]

In 2002, the EU established the European Food Safety Authority (EFSA) as an independent point of reference in evaluating risks. The institution, with offices located in Parma, is entitled to formulate pronouncements about controversial scientific matters and help manage any emergency crisis at Union level. EFSA does not have any enforcement authority but can pass its recommendations to the European Commission. Nevertheless, the institution is granted the autonomous right of providing information directly to the public, although in cases of emergency it has to coordinate its communication with the Commission and the member states. In managing food-related risks, the EU has opted to apply the 'precautionary principle': if there are reasonable grounds for suspecting a problem, the European Commission, the Union's executive body, can act to limit the risk. Based on that principle, the EU banned the use of growth hormones in cattle as early as the early 1980s. Food safety laws have been reorganized under the General Food Law (regulation 178/2002), issued in 2002 and implemented in 2005, along with hygiene rules (regulations 852/853/854/2004) implemented in 2006. Despite the EU interventions, Italian consumers are still quite suspicious about what they eat – a consequence of the long-lasting lack of trust in institutions and politicians, considered nepotistic, inefficient and often corrupt. Frequently, it is up to marketers and retailers to reassure consumers, although the general discourse focuses more on issues of quality than safety.[14]

Since there is no definitive proof that genetically modified organisms (GMOs) are not harmful to humans, European authorities have tried to control GMO penetration in the Union's territories by applying the precautionary principle. This action has been met with very high approval rates from European citizens, a majority of whom are extremely apprehensive about anything potentially genetically modified. In 1999, the Union established a de facto moratorium pending the adoption of legislation on the matter. In 2001, however, the EU regulated the experimental release of GMOs in to the environment and measures to avoid contamination with conventional and organic crops. In 2003, the Union also legislated on genetically modified food and feed, imposing labels that disclose the presence of genetically modified ingredients when the content is above 0.9 per cent, considered a reasonable level of 'accidental presence'. Nonetheless, it is not necessary to label meats from animals fed with genetically modified grains. After a U.S. complaint ruled that EU restrictions on genetically engineered crops violated international trade agreements, under the pressure of the World Trade Organization, the EU lifted the moratorium in 2004 and passed regulations to test and introduce GMOs.

These decisions led to the approval of genetically modified maize, cotton, oilseed rape, potatoes, soybean and sugar beet varieties and allowed GMO feed. However, Austria, France, Greece, Hungary, Germany and Luxembourg have banned GMOs from their territories, invoking the so-called 'safety clause' included in the 2001 directive. Moreover, a few administrative regions in Spain, Italy, Great Britain and Belgium, as well as in member states that banned GMOs, have created a network, based on a political agreement with no binding juridical status, to safeguard their agriculture policies against the dangers connected with the introduction of GMOs.[15] In Italy, twelve regions and the autonomous province of Bolzano have joined the organization. The Italian government still requires farmers to ask permission before planning GMO crops even if they have received approval from the EU. Traditional farmers, especially those with smaller properties, are aware that they have little advantage in implementing high-yield, GMO crops for industrial use. Many are betting on value-added, local and often unique varieties that allow them to operate outside the commodity market, at times obtaining geographical indication recognitions and commanding higher prices.[16] Also, due to lack of innovation and connections with research institutions, small- and medium-sized rural farms frequently and pragmatically mix different modes of production and sales, in terms of scale and variety, in order to maximize their chances of success.[17] However, the multiplication of denominations and labels risks generating confusion among consumers, who do not always understand or care about the complexities of food production and regulations.[18]

Organic farming (*agricoltura biologica*), considered as part of the effort towards sustainable agriculture, has become an important issue in the EU. In 2009 the Union introduced new regulations defining the objectives and principles of this kind of production. Manufactured foods may only be marked as 'organic' if at least 95 per cent of their ingredients are organic. Producers of packaged organic food must use the EU organic logo, which can also be used for imported goods, as long as they are produced and controlled under the same or equivalent conditions. The development of organic agriculture in Italy has not always been straightforward. Between 1990 and 2000, stimulated by consumer interest and European subsidies to those who adopted organic agriculture, organic farms in Italy grew from 1,300 to over 56,000. Then, between 2002 and 2004, farms that had failed to grow organic products in the three-year conversion period were dropped from the subsidy provisions, causing the sector to shrink dramatically.[19] However, Italy still has over a million hectares (around 2.7 million acres) dedicated to organic agriculture, and organic food consumption increased 8.7 per cent between

2001 and 2009.[20] According to the report of 2012 by Bio Bank, a database on organic food in Italy, the three Italian regions with the largest number of organic operators are Lombardy, Emilia Romagna and Tuscany. Consumption between 2009 and 2011 has augmented across the board: 44 per cent more organic-focused *gruppi d'acquisto solidale* (groups for community purchases, equivalent to community-sustained agriculture), an expansion of 27 per cent in the e-commerce of organic products, a greater involvement of restaurants (up 17 per cent) and the growth of direct sales on farms (up 16 per cent) and in *agriturismo* (up 10 per cent). An important component is the 33 per cent increase in consumption of organic produce in schools.[21] In 1999, a law was passed that obliges school administrations to use organic and PDO/PGI products, although it did not specify the modalities or quantities.[22] The widespread popularity of this measure reflects the concerns parents experience about their children's food. Many young mothers prefer to buy organic food, even if it is more expensive, not out of preoccupation with the environment but because they are worried about the health of their offspring. In 2009 the Italian government launched the plan 'Scuola and Cibo' (school and food) to introduce food education in public teaching, from elementary to high schools. The project has been sustained also by initiatives such as 'Frutta nelle Scuole' (fruit in schools), to increase the consumption of fruit in school canteens, and 'Guadagnare Salute' (gaining health), to help students prevent the onset of chronic diseases.

An interesting compromise between organic and conventional production is the Italian experiment with *agricoltura integrata* (integrated farming). This programme involves the exploitation of natural resources to substitute the technological means adopted in conventional agriculture, especially fertilizers and pesticides, and only uses them when they are deemed necessary to optimize the balance between environmental and health requirements and economic needs. Regional governments regulated integrated farming until 2011, when the nationwide Sistema di qualità nazionale di produzione integrata (National System for Integrated Farming Quality, SQNPI) was established.

## CONSUMER CULTURE, GENDER AND THE BODY

Manufacturing technologies, new shopping modalities, the commercial standardization of products and political debates at the national and international level have determined profound changes in Italian consumer culture. Long-term social transformations have played a huge role, accentuated by the slow but unstoppable dissolution of the patriarchal family. Women's entry into the job market and the influence of feminism has been indicated among the causes. Furthermore, it is increasingly difficult for young people to find jobs and start their own families. Last but not least, growing numbers of individuals choose to remain single, a trend the food industry capitalizes on by introducing single-portion products, ready-to-sauté pastas and frozen soups.

Men from older generations still expect their wives to shop and cook even when they have their own jobs. Younger couples, however, tend to make different arrangements regarding food-related chores. In the patriarchal society of the past, women were in charge of transmitting their culinary knowledge and experiences to the following generations of female family members. There was little desire for innovative recipes, as Italians had to deal with limited resources and the lack of a modern distribution system. Recipes and techniques were transmitted orally and by practical example. Young girls were asked to help their mothers with the kitchen chores, starting from the easiest and least dangerous ones, advancing over time to more complex tasks. While learning culinary know-how from their elders, women also inherited the distinction of roles that sustained the patriarchal society, as they were supposed to be able to take care of the kitchen by the time they were ready for marriage. A woman with scarce culinary abilities was pitied and frowned upon.

When in the 1960s women entered the job market, they were still expected to take care of the kitchen and to gain respect and admiration through their culinary abilities. Many women came to consider the preparation of daily meals a chore that they hoped their daughters would not have to deal with. Likewise, young women did not want to perpetuate the patriarchal society that still forced their mothers into the kitchen, and instead concentrated their energies on their studies and careers.[23] My mother, who had a full-time job as a high-school teacher, never stopped cooking every meal, but she made sure my sisters and I all learned how to cook. When we had many guests (a pretty frequent occurrence) we would all be asked to participate in the preparation, and as we grew older we were given more complicated tasks. However, none of the males of her generation, including my father, were expected to give a hand in the kitchen, their involvement often limited to some shopping under very careful instructions.

My experience was not too common. In the 1970s and 1980s many young people, especially those from urban families, did not learn how to cook. The chain of transmission seemed irremediably broken. At the same time, cooking methods and preferences were changing as convenient and affordable industrial products became available. Transportation improved, allowing access to better and cheaper foods that were once unfamiliar. For instance, people who lived in areas in northern Italy without direct access to the sea only consumed freshwater fish. Now the fish market in Milan is the best provisioned in the country. Most perishable food transportation in Italy is still organized by trucks, with very limited use of the railway system. Many consumers have lost the sense of food seasonality because of year-round availability connected with refrigeration, freezing technology, glasshouse agriculture, the delocalization of food production and global trade. In the twenty-first century, Italians frequently acquire culinary skills and learn how to cook both new and familiar dishes through magazines, TV shows and cooking schools. It is not unusual to overhear

*Robiola di Roccaverano* DOP, a local product now available all over Italy.

## Cooking as a profession

While women have always played a crucial role in domestic kitchens, things are quite different when it comes to professional environments where cooking constitutes a respectable career. In Italy, successful restaurants are either managed as a family business, handed down from generation to generation, or – in more recent times – the work of chefs who start from scratch, even after other careers and without any formal culinary training. In the first case, women are often in the spotlight, like Nadia Santini at Dal Pescatore in Canneto sull'Oglio (Lombardy) and Valeria Piccini at Caino in Montemerano (southern Tuscany). However, we find fewer women at the helm of brand-new establishments, perpetuating a state of affairs in which the creative head in the kitchen is a man, while the humbler roles are reserved for women or young male apprentices. From the nineteenth century, the luxury restaurants and hotel chefs were always professionally trained men. On the other hand, in family-run *trattorie* and *osterie*, the cooks were prevalently women, with their husbands working front of house.

In the past, specialized instruction was almost exclusively provided by hospitality high schools (*scuola alberghiera*), whose style and techniques are increasingly considered old-fashioned and lacklustre. Graduates from these institutions are frequently too inexperienced, but too qualified to work in collective facilities like hospitals, schools and company canteens, which prefer to hire less trained but cheaper staff. They often end up working for hotels, cruise ships and other tourist facilities with little claim to fame. The whole industry is undergoing major changes with the rise of private professional schools in which students can enrol after leaving high school. Instructors are often well-known chefs who not only provide cutting-edge and exciting training, but also the possibility of landing prestigious internships and networking within the industry. Besides providing a better entrance to the professional world, these schools respond to the expectations of young men and women who have grown up on a mediatized diet of culinary reality shows, food magazines and celebrity chefs.

customers asking for basic cooking tips from sellers at the outdoor market or even at the supermarket.

Cultural changes have also affected the connection between food and body image, largely for females but also, and increasingly, males as well. The desire for slimmer and fitter bodies has determined the multiplication of diets and the preference for 'light' food, which is not necessarily fat- or sugar-free but simply culturally perceived as more digestible and less fattening. Mozzarella, for instance, often falls in that category, as do prosciutto *cotto* (cooked ham) and soft cheeses like *robiola*. The preoccupation with health and the medicalization of culinary discourse through the widespread attention paid to cholesterol, diabetes and obesity have profoundly shaken the deep-rooted idea that Italian food is inherently good for you. The desire for safe and unadulterated food also expresses itself through the diffusion of *mercati contadini* and the growing interest in organic food, in Italian called *biologico*, a word that points more to personal and environmental health than to systemic issues.

### New Venues

The appreciation of wholesome and safe food, and the newly revived interest in traditional fare as an expression of cultural identity, has stimulated many Italians to rediscover the countryside for quality of life, rest, slow rhythms and healthy eating. This trend is reinforced by administrative measures that follow the adoption of the new Common Agricultural Policy at the EU level, a set of measures that underline the cultural value and the economic advantages of safeguarding the environment, the rural landscape, high-quality produce and the diversification of rural activities. New forms of tourism that focus on food and wine as expressions of local culture and traditions have developed in the past twenty years. An *agriturismo* is a rural enterprise that offers food and lodging to visitors, using products from the farm and at times organizing recreational or cultural activities. National and regional authorities have promoted this new type of tourism hoping it will entice farmers to stay on their land and to take better care of the landscape.

According to the law that regulates this kind of business, farming and animal breeding must remain the main activity, with tourism as an additional source of income. Hence only farmers who actually work the land are supposed to start an *agriturismo*. It is not enough to own a farm or a property in the countryside: the land must be cultivated. Additionally,

Olive trees in Calabria. The new Common Agricultural Policy is changing
the EU system of agricultural subsidies.

only pre-existing structures can be renovated to provide lodging to tourists;
with a few exceptions determined by local regulations, new constructions
are not allowed. Small patches of unproductive land can be dedicated to
campsites for a limited number of tents. These new enterprises have
enjoyed instant success. They offer lodging and meals at very convenient
prices, often also selling products to visitors. *Agriturismi* have actually
played a very important role in attracting urban dwellers to the countryside, including remote areas that otherwise would have remained untouched
by tourism. It soon became clear that an *agriturismo* was a good investment.
Financial groups that had nothing in common with the local life and
traditions purchased abandoned properties, often resuscitating farming
activities that had been discontinued decades before. Using loopholes
in the local regulations, many *agriturismi* focused on the real source of
money: tourism. Upmarket facilities started sprouting all over the place,
offering jacuzzis and swimming pools along with refined dining experiences with a veneer of rural charm. Some establishments that do not
produce enough themselves even buy the ingredients used in their
kitchen from neighbouring farms. However, the role of *agriturismi* in

bringing new life to the countryside and greater fascination with local food is a win for all.

In 1987, the same kind of interest generated Città del Vino (cities of wine), an association originally established by 39 mayors but now including more than 500 townships, natural parks and communities, many of which have histories, traditions and cultures connected to vineyards and vine growing. The Movimento Turismo del Vino (movement for wine tourism) was founded in 1993, with more than 900 wine producers receiving guests on their properties. Local authorities, wine and food producers, hotels and *agriturismi* soon began cooperating to create enticing offers and packages to attract high-end visitors interested in the unique mixture of culture, traditions and good food of a specific area.[24] In 1999 a national law was issued to regulate these activities, now called wine routes (Strade del Vino), defined as 'signalled routes marking natural, cultural and environmental points of interest, vineyards and wine-producing farms open to the public'.

These initiatives bank on the renewed interest in wine among connoisseurs and amateurs, a trend that was at the forefront of the rediscovery of local productions. Most grocery shops and even supermarkets now offer choices of premium wine. Some specialized shops,

Wine cellar at the Abbey of Monte Oliveto Maggiore, Siena.
Wine tourism is a growing sector.

called *enoteca*, cater to a growing segment of curious consumers interested in tasting and knowing more about a realm that, until a few years ago, was reserved for a handful of aficionados and experts. *Enoteche* are the direct development of wine shops that used to sell bulk wine, served by pouring it into bottles provided by the clients. The first occurrence of the word *enoteca* was registered in 1934, in the magazine *Enotria*. *Enoteca* now mostly indicates a shop selling bottled wine, together with gourmet products such as jams, preserves, honey and other packaged delicacies. The expression 'wine bar' (in English) is used for an establishment serving food to accompany the wine. Many *enoteche* have an annexed wine bar which operates under a different business licence and is allowed to serve food for consumption on the premises. Partly to meet the burgeoning demand from clients and partly to make them even more passionate about their products, some *enoteche* and wine bars organize tastings and tasting classes. When these events take place in wine bars, small bites are also provided to give clients more ideas for their food and wine pairings at home.

The success of businesses that focus on high-end products, rural and artisanal manufactures, local traditions and wholesome food should not take attention away from other forms of consumption. Following the lead of McDonald's, other international enterprises have peppered Italian cities with their franchises, including Burger King and Subway. Italian franchises like Spizzico Pizza, Mr Focaccia and Sedici Piadina have embraced the fast-food model and applied it to Italian specialities, managing to offer food at relatively low prices.

Various kinds of public establishments have become popular, especially among the younger generations. Pizzerias offer an affordable traditional dish in relaxed environments. While classics like *napoletana* or *margherita* are still very much appreciated, the desire for originality and exploration has pushed pizza makers to experiment with new toppings, from shrimp to rocket. In recent years, a new trend has swept the pizza world: young chefs are playing with different flours, yeast varieties and toppings inspired by seasonality and of high quality. They make pizza lighter and more digestible by increasing the rising time of dough from 48 to 72 hours. Pizza can also be delivered or bought in takeaway shops that sell by the weight or the piece. Convenience has become a major selling point. Some grocery stores and supermarkets produce ready-made food to take away (home deliveries are still extremely rare). *Tavola calda* offer hot dishes to take away or consume on the premises. *Rosticceria* specialize

*Panino* with prosciutto.

in fried or roasted foods that would be too time-consuming or complicated to prepare at home. In large cities with visible immigrant communities ethnic restaurants are increasingly common, in particular Chinese and kebab eateries.

Establishments have developed around the Italians' growing passion for beer, reflected in the great number of artisanal breweries founded by young entrepreneurs who experiment with techniques, ingredients and interesting forms of marketing. Beer is the main alcoholic drink sold in pubs (the English expression is used), or *birreria*. The decor is usually different from other restaurants, with wooden benches and tables without tablecloths, and service limited to the essential. Dishes with foreign origins are served, such as sauerkraut with wiener sausages, hot dogs, hamburgers with French fries and chilli con carne. Pubs can also serve salads, pasta and above all Italian-style sandwiches (panini) to satisfy all tastes. Some establishments, called *panineria*, focus exclusively on sandwiches filled with creative ingredients, frequently served warm.

Other stores focus on *piadina*, an unleavened flatbread with lard or olive oil added to the dough, originally from Romagna, or *tigella* (also called *crescentina*), another flatbread from Emilia, accompanied by cheese and cold meats. Fried bites that used to be consumed as street food have engendered their own stores: from Roman-style battered cod to *arancine* (small fried rice balls) from Sicily and meat-stuffed olives from Ascoli.

## Culture, Media and Civic Movements

The commodification of these traditional products, now rediscovered and appreciated by large segments of consumers, responds more to curiosity and the desire for something different than to a specific interest in Italy's culinary past. In fact, after the rapid economic development in the 1960s, not much was left of the centuries-old agricultural and pastoral traditions, and in the 1970s and 1980s consumers gave more relevance to the price, convenience and at times even trendiness of their food. Unexpectedly, though, the situation radically changed starting in the late 1980s when food, instead of just being a means to display conspicuous consumption, became the object of interest from cultural and political points of view.[25] A small but growing sector of intellectuals, activists and professionals shared the sense that the process of modernization had moved too fast and that mass production and globalization were threatening local eating traditions and identities, together with good quality and safety. The Slow Food movement was able to channel these concerns, turning them into a coherent programme.

Slow Food started in 1986 in Bra, a small town in the Langhe wine area of Piedmont, under the name ArciGola. ARCI was the acronym for the Recreation Association of Italian Communists. In Italian, the word *gola* means both food and gluttony, referring to the pleasure of food. ArciGola was founded by Carlo Petrini, a union militant from the same area. The association first reached a larger audience through *Gambero Rosso*, the monthly supplement to the Leftist daily newspaper *Manifesto*, which was also launched in 1986. ArciGola and *Gambero Rosso* scandalized the mainstream Leftist organizations by affirming the social and cultural value of pleasure, as experienced in the convivial consumption of good-quality food.[26]

Prompted by the opening of a McDonald's restaurant near the Spanish Steps, in the heart of Rome, ArciGola became Slow Food on 9 November 1989 at the Opéra Comique in Paris, when representatives from many countries signed its manifesto. The document stated that only a staunch defence of quiet material pleasure, and the long-lasting and slow enjoyment of food, could constitute an antidote to fast life, which forces human beings to consume lacklustre, unhealthy and socially destructive food. Proponents of Slow Food argued that the first line of defence is at the table: consumers should develop their taste in order to appreciate and defend local food, artisanal know-how and the environment.[27] Far from being a relapse into pure hedonism to avoid engagement in the public arena, the defence of pleasure was to become a weapon to bring citizens back to social and political action.[28] The movement immediately adopted a little snail as its insignia.

In 1994, Slow Food acknowledged its appeal outside the Italian borders and voted to promote its associative model abroad by establishing Slow Food International. In the same year, the movement organized the *Laboratori del Gusto*, workshops to educate a growing audience of food enthusiasts on specific products or wines. In 1996, the organization launched the first *Salone del Gusto* in Turin, a vast food-and-wine event intended to increase public awareness about small manufacturers and traditional productions. *Salone del Gusto*'s cultural marketing, more

Slow Food founder
Carlo Petrini.

effective than the average purely commercial food show, was so successful that Slow Food decided that the event would take place every two years. Both *Gambero Rosso* and Slow Food helped to establish a cultural outlook that considers food not only through categories of fashions, market dynamics or economics, but also within a conceptual frame where collective enjoyment, sharing and community become the main points of reference.[29] In this kind of approach, food is what allows individuals to get together, to rediscover their bonds to vital traditions and to take their time in a world that moves at an increasingly fast pace.[30]

Responding to the interest for disappearing foodstuffs, the movement published the *Manifesto of the Ark of Taste* in 1997, a document that set up a methodology to identify products and crops in danger of extinction, and proposed policies to defend them. In 1999, a scientific commission determined the principles behind the selection of products for the Ark, including high quality levels, the connection to a specific territory and to the cultural practices of its inhabitants, manufacture in limited quantities carried out by small producers, and potential or actual risk of disappearance. For instance, in the u.s. list of products admitted to the Ark we find the Roman Taffy Candy from Louisiana, the Olympia native oysters from Washington State and the Crane Melon from California. The year 2000 marked the introduction of the Award for the Defense of Biodiversity and of the *presidia*, small projects designed to assist and support small artisan producers.

A paramount year for Slow Food was 2004, when the United Nations Food and Agriculture Organization officially recognized it as a nonprofit organization. Slow Food also set up the Slow Food Foundation for Biodiversity, to sustain the Ark, the *presidia* and the Awards. Later in the year, the University of Gastronomic Studies opened in Pollenzo, near the association headquarters in Bra. During the fifth *Salone del Gusto*, the first *Terra Madre*, defined as a 'world meeting of food communities', allowed thousands of farmers to meet with experts, chefs and cultural institutions to discuss how to promote agricultural models that ensure biodiversity, while defending the environment and respecting the health and culture of local communities.

Although Slow Food is widely acknowledged for returning food to social and political debates, for the immediacy of its concerns and its media-savvy public relations activities, many critics of the organization have accused it of elitism. Slow Food members are usually middle to upper-middle class, its initiatives and activities require a certain amount of disposable income and the products it protects and promotes through the *Presidia* are often expensive.[31] Other critics have attributed to Slow Food what has been defined as 'culinary luddism', claiming that the movement's goal is to stop the industrialization of food processes world-wide in order to protect traditional and ethnic food traditions and products, building on the ideological myth of a time that knew neither disruptions nor crises.[32]

Although Slow Food never took an explicit position on the topic, the defence of traditions and artisanal activities could also be used by other organizations as a weapon to marginalize the food and traditions of the thousands of immigrants who are settling down in Italy. Unfortunately, that's precisely what happened, to the dismay of anybody who holds a progressive stand on social issues (including Slow Food). In the next chapter, we will try to assess the impact of globalization, both in terms of the growing presence of immigrant communities and the diffusion of Italian food all over the world.

# SEVEN

# The Globalization of Italian Food

Our exploration of Italian food started with the renewed interest in tradition and local identities. We observed that those values and the experiences that sustain them are far less static and ancient than one would suspect. Even the very concept of *territorio*, which frames many Italians' understanding of the connection between food and its place of production, has been influenced by *terroir*, a French idea. As citizens of a member state of the European Union, Italians' ideas and practices regarding health, safety and sustainability are increasingly entangled in international debates. We took a look into the past, observing how ingredients, materials and skills related to food have been transferred since Italy's prehistoric beginnings. All along, diversity in geographical environments, natural resources and technology has motivated migrations, cultural exchanges and trade among populations. The Greek colonization, the expansion of the Roman Empire and the transit and settlement of Germanic tribes, as well as the inclusion in the Islamic cultural sphere, are only a few examples of how food customs and production in Italy have been moulded by its participation in larger cultural, economic and political networks. These dynamics worked both ways. Chefs and food artisans from Italy have moved to different parts of the world since the Renaissance. In other words, Italian food has long been the result of complex processes that today we tend to define as globalization. Yet we need to be careful about jumping to conclusions. There are substantial differences between the past and the present, especially in terms of speed and intensity of change, heralded by increasingly rapid technological advances in food production, transportation and communication. As historian Jeffrey Pilcher points out, 'The emergence of a "global palate" in the twentieth century represented not a radical

Vineyard in the Chianti Classico area, among the best-known *terroirs* in Tuscany.

Mulberry Street, Little Italy, New York, early 1900s.

departure from the past but rather the intensification of existing cross-cultural connections.'[1]

In the case of Italian food, a sudden acceleration of international movements and exchanges took place during the last decades of the nineteenth century when Italians migrated en masse to other countries, especially North and South America. Trying to create a home away from home, migrants developed food traditions that maintained a strong connection with their roots but were also influenced by their new environments. At the same time, Italian ingredients and dishes have been adopted and adapted by culinary cultures all over the world. In fact, globalization works in many directions. Growing numbers of migrants that settle down in Italy participate in the food business and open restaurants, exposing Italians to unusual practices, dishes and ingredients. As in the past, culinary identities are determined by visible and invisible interactions between apparently unrelated worlds.

## Diaspora

Between the 1880s and the Second World War, 9 million Italians, the equivalent of a quarter of the entire population, left the country. The majority made their journey between the 1890s and the 1920s.[2] In 1908, 1.2 million Italians had already emigrated to the u.s., 67 per cent of whom came from rural homes. Nevertheless, only 6.6 per cent were still occupied in agricultural activities, indicating their desire to move towards more modern sectors. Instead, 60 per cent of the approximately 1 million Italians

Sicilian emigrants leaving for Venezuela.

225

who settled in South American countries worked in rural jobs.[3] In the early 1900s, American scholar Alberto Pecorini had no doubt that Italian immigrants had a future in agriculture.

> That the Italian is immensely better adapted to intensive than to extensive agriculture cannot be disputed for a moment . . . He loves the land, he excels in those operations which can only be made by hand and require a great deal of patience, and he understands irrigation. He also prefers to live close to other persons rather than isolated and he ardently desires to own his little piece of land as soon as possible.[4]

In Louisiana, many Italians – mostly from Sicily – worked on sugar-cane and cotton plantations. Others were employed as bricklayers and wrought-iron workers in the city.[5] Some launched agricultural enterprises, such as the strawberry business in Tangipahoa Parish, near New Orleans, while others opened stores, restaurants and ice-cream manufactures, developing their own culinary style. The *muffuletta*, the traditional New Orleans sesame-seeded round sandwich filled with various cold cuts, sliced cheeses and olive salad, originated in this period.[6] In California, Italians from Genova and Piedmont, who had first arrived during the gold rush, found occupations in grape and fruit cultivation, as well as wine production.[7] The Italian immigrants who settled on the California coast, working in the fishing and canning industries, introduced dishes like *cioppino*, a local version of the fish soups and stews from Italy.

*Muffuletta* sandwich, New Orleans.

The Italian exhibit in the Agricultural Hall at the 1876 Centennial Exhibition in Philadelphia, albumen print.

Men usually migrated first, with the intention of returning home after saving some money, or eventually bringing their family over once they had secured a job and a home in their new country. With the goal of sending remittances back home, many Italian immigrants spent very little money on food and shared rooms with other Italians in boarding houses, frequently managed by employers from the same area in Italy. Migrants fresh off the boat were likely to be exploited by these entrepreneurs, referred to as *padrone* (master). As Italian communities grew in number and complexity, with more women and children joining the men, the demand for Italian specialities expanded, especially for olive oil, hard cheese, dried pasta and canned tomatoes.[8] The overseas markets stimulated food production in Italy, which had been lagging due to the limited size of the domestic market. In the early 1920s, partly to satisfy the preferences of the American migrants, Italian tomato manufacture shifted from paste to *pelati*, whole and skinned tomatoes canned in their juices. Hybrid tomatoes, best adapted to this use, were selected, such as the famous San Marzano tomato, now a priced PDO.[9]

Immigrants often maintained very close ties with their places of origin, and many went back and forth between America and Europe. Right after the First World War booklets like *Practical Italian Recipes for American Kitchens Sold to Aid All the Families of Italian Soldiers* were

*Meat Soufflé (Flam di Carne Avanzata)*

25 g (1 oz) butter

1 tbsp flour

570 ml (1 pint) milk

1 cup cold boiled or roast meat, chopped fine

2 eggs

grated cheese, to taste

salt, pepper

Make the butter, flour and milk into a white sauce by melt‐
ing the butter, cooking the flour in it until the mixture
bubbles and begins to brown, then adding the milk and
cooking until it is smooth. Let this cool. Brown the meat in
a saucepan with a little fat or dripping, salt and pepper.
Remove it from the heat and add the white sauce and the
eggs, well beaten. Season with grated cheese, salt and pepper.
Butter a mould and sprinkle it with breadcrumbs, fill it with
the mixture and steam or bake as custard for an hour. Serve
with any good meat or tomato sauce.

published to raise money for veterans in Italy, revealing the immigrants'
emotional connection with the tribulations their motherland was experi‐
encing and the preoccupations with food availability during and after the
war.[10] The recipe featured here is an invitation to use leftover meat.

Immigrants of disparate origins, speaking a mosaic of dialects and
with diverse food customs, shared the same living quarters and established
uncharted social connections. American natives tended to categorize
Italians as one single ethnic group with clearly identifiable traits. The new‐
comers showed a strong attachment to their traditional dishes and dietary
habits, which they maintained by buying imported goods and, when
necessary, producing food. It was not unusual for immigrants to raise
chickens or pigs in their basements.[11] They also foraged, gathering mush‐
rooms and greens in parks and empty lots.[12] When they succeeded in
buying property, they planted familiar plants in their gardens: fig, peach
and cherry trees graced their outdoor spaces, together with edible herbs and
vegetables.[13] In the U.S., social workers criticized Italian immigrants for not
consuming enough meat or dairy, which at the time were considered the

View of Madison Street in New Orleans, 1906. The area was heavily populated with Sicilian immigrants at the time.

Italian market, Mulberry Street, New York, *c.* 1900.

best nourishment for individuals engaged in heavy manual work.[14] Their customs became the butt of jokes, generating stereotypes and ethnic slurs.[15]

As their disposable income grew, immigrants consumed more of the food they were used to, including costly goods from Italy, rather than replacing their customs with those of the host community. Dishes that were reserved for special or festive occasions, particularly if they included meat, became everyday occurrences and acquired visibility on the menus of Italian eateries. Despite the attachment to their culinary identity, Italian immigrants took advantage of the food that was available at their destination. Meat loomed large, as it was rarely consumed back home, quickly making it a symbol of success and opulence. Italians in southern Brazil and Argentina sent pictures of themselves eating *churrasco* and *asado* to their relatives, and in the letters some even complained about the excessive consumption of beef.[16] Steak eating was so common in tales and reports from migrants in the U.S. that landowners in southern Italy feared that these notions would convince more workers to leave.[17] Substitutions were necessary and acceptable, and the mix of Old and New World elements generated original, vibrant cuisines.[18] Some practices, such as the preference for aromatic herbs – including garlic – and coffee, were maintained when possible.[19]

Food became one of the most important traits in defining the cultural identity of Italian immigrants.[20] Sunday dinner turned into an emblem of ethnic identity: family and friends gathered around abundant and leisurely meals, embracing and adapting a practice that only well-off people could afford in the old country. In the U.S., when families built their own homes, they often included two kitchens, one downstairs for everyday cooking and another upstairs that was only used on special occasions and when guests were visiting. The two kitchens clearly demarcated the difference between the private domestic sphere, where immigrants could practise more traditional customs, and a more public dimension where cultural negotiations with the host community could take place.[21]

New culinary cultures were not only emerging in domestic settings, as some immigrants chose the food business as their entry into the host society. At first they managed to insert themselves into food distribution networks by peddling fruits and vegetables, especially in their own neighbourhoods. When they had access to more capital, they opened grocery and speciality stores, together with small restaurants that catered, at first,

Italian bread pedlar on Mulberry Street, New York, *c.* 1900.

to people from their own communities. These places turned into gathering points for the following waves of Italian immigrants, while attracting locals with their exotic dishes, laid-back atmosphere and low prices.

Migration from Italy picked up again after the Second World War, having experienced a temporary lull determined by restrictive Fascist policies. Migrants frequently moved to other European countries such as Germany, Switzerland, France and Belgium, where cheap labour was needed to jump-start production after the destruction of the war. These countries signed agreements with the Italian government to obtain workers in exchange for coal and other raw materials that Italy needed for its reconstruction.[22] Although the flow of immigrants temporarily ebbed when a mining accident in Martinelle, Belgium, in 1956, caused the death of 136 Italians, migration was still noticeable until the mid-1970s, when northern European industries shrank under the shock of the oil crisis of 1973. In the 1950s and '60s, Italian ice-cream parlours, or *gelaterie*, became a fixture in German cityscapes, facilitating the introduction of Italian restaurants and pizzerias.[23] In the UK Italian coffee bars were popular until the 1960s, and were back in vogue in the mid-1990s.[24]

*Wafu Pasta with Yuzukosho Sauce*

For 4 people

225g (½ lb) spaghetti (Japanese portions are not as large as in other countries)

225g (½ lb) eggplant (aubergine)

110g (¼ lb) shimeji mushrooms (East Asian species, rich in umami compounds)

1 clove garlic (finely chopped)

2 tbsp olive oil

1 tsp *yuzukosho* (fermented paste made from chilli peppers, yuzu peel and salt)

4 tbsp sake

4 tbsp soy sauce

30 g (¼ stick) butter

5 or 6 leaves *shiso* (*Perilla frutescens*)

Cut the eggplant into ½ inch slices and soak them in a bowl of saltwater for 5 minutes to remove any bitterness. Squeeze each slice delicately to remove all salt water.

Pour 2 tbsp of olive oil into a pan, add the garlic, and place it on a low flame. Sauté until the garlic is lightly browned. Add the eggplant slices to the pan and sauté on a low flame until they become brown and soft. Add the shimeji mushrooms cook for another minute, then pour 4 tbsp of sake into the pan with the eggplant and the mushrooms. Keep simmering on a low flame until the alcohol evaporates.

In the meantime, heat salted water to a boil in a large pot to cook the pasta.

Wash the *shiso* leaves and pat them dry with a paper towel. Roll them and cut into thin strips that you will use to garnish.

When the spaghetti is almost al dente, add 2 tablespoons of boiling water from the pot in which you are cooking the pasta, 2 tbsp of soy sauce and 1 tsp of *yuzukosho* and turn off the heat. Drain the pasta and add it to the pan with the sauce. Add the butter and mix thoroughly. Serve with the sliced *shiso* as garnish.[25]

## Italian Products around the World

As discussed in the first chapter, Italian food is now globally popular, with products exported all over the world and young Italian chefs making their mark in foreign countries. Apprentices from countries as far as Japan and Korea go to Italy to learn how to cook from local practitioners and then open Italian restaurants in their own country. For instance, in Japan Italian food is replacing French cuisine at the top of consumer preferences, and pizza is made by both Italian and Japanese *pizzaioli*.[26] The love story between Japanese chefs and Italian food has become the topic of a manga comic book, *Bambino!*, which between 2005 and 2008 narrated the adventures of a young man who discovers Italian cooking during his internship in a fictional Italian restaurant in Tokyo. Japan has generated its own take on Italian cuisine with *wafu* pasta, cooked both domestically and in restaurants. As the recipe featured here shows, pasta is seasoned with Japanese flavourings and ingredients such as miso, sesame oil, dried kelp and various kinds of pickle.[27]

Italian food businesses are trying to capitalize on the growing appreciation for Italian cuisine. Some large Italian food companies have been able to successfully establish their presence in foreign markets, such as Barilla, Ferrero and Buitoni. Small and medium-sized Italian food- and

Wafu pasta, from *Gourmet Traveler* 88, 2010.

winemakers are putting great efforts into expanding their exports, though many are experiencing mixed results. Frequently, their marketing communication highlights not only the quality and authenticity of their products, but also their significance as symbols of a whole lifestyle.[28]

The greatest competition for Italian food abroad comes from entrepreneurs who have developed local versions of Italian specialities, including pasta, canned tomatoes and cheese that are less expensive than those coming from across the ocean. This phenomenon started in the first half of the twentieth century with companies launched by Italian immigrants. The u.s. offers interesting cases, but similar stories can be found wherever large Italian communities settled, from Canada to Australia. In the late 1920s, Ettore Boiardi di Piacenza, the owner of an Italian restaurant in Cleveland, sold pasta, tomato sauce and grated cheese in a package, and then produced spaghetti in a can under the name Chef Boyardee.[29] Other companies founded in that period are still active, such as La Contadina tomatoes and Ronzoni pasta. Prices for these overseas

An industrial pasta-dough mixer made in Brooklyn, New York, 1914.

productions were cheaper, not only because they did not include import tariffs, but also because they frequently applied modern technologies and took advantage of economies of scale connected with larger consumer markets. The lead of the Italian food manufacturers outside Italy increased when, in 1935, the Society of Nations imposed an embargo on Italian exports and, later, during the Second World War, when the Italian productive system basically shut down. Pizza is one of the best examples. The first recorded mention of pizzeria in the United States was Lombardi's, opened in 1905 in New York City. Pizzeria Uno in Chicago created deep-dish pizza in 1943, a franchise still successful today.[30] Frozen pizza was mass-produced in the u.s. in the 1950s, extending its reach to the rest of the world in the 1960s.

Gaining recognition as an 'Italian' product is a sensitive topic. Foreign products utilize the label 'Italian' along with Italian products that are made with foreign raw materials. The Italian government is supporting initiatives that promote 'made in Italy' food, but advocating for proper labelling is an uphill battle. Firstly, approaches to copyright and trademarks differ around the world. Additionally, small Italian companies often lack effective marketing strategies and knowledge of global distribution networks, giving an advantage to local competitors who easily challenge the high-priced Italian imports. In China, for instance, Italian entrepreneurs have tried to penetrate a complex market with limited success, despite the widespread appreciation for Italian food products.[31]

Italian-themed restaurants have expanded worldwide, exploiting specific traits of Italian culture to create recognizable brands and promote corporate casual dining. In order to counteract the perception of a mass-produced experience, Italian-inspired global chains try to create a positive impression built upon traits stereotypically considered Italian, such as family values, traditions, shared meals, warmth and vitality.[32] Dining at an Italian-themed corporate restaurant is presented as an antidote to the anonymity and trivialization of food that corporate culture has contrived to create in the first place. Nostalgia is expressed through references to freshness, authenticity and artisanal skills, at times evoking the good old days of the past.

Italian chefs working worldwide are attempting to counteract these corporate initiatives. In 2010, the GVCI, the Virtual Group of Italian Chefs, proclaimed 17 January International Day of Italian Cuisines (in the plural, hinting at the intrinsic plurality of Italian food) with the purpose of maintaining the identity of Italian cuisine and highlighting the work

Gallo Nero, the Chianti Classico logo.

of Italian culinary professionals. The group promoted an 'irresistible worldwide wave of *tagliatelle al ragù bolognese* to support authentic, quality Italian cuisine against the forgery and counterfeiting of Italian food and products around the world'.[33] That same year, the association organized the first Italian Cuisine World Summit, with chefs coming from all over the world.

As Italian specialities grow in popularity all over the world and their commercial value increases, producers in Italy are fighting to safeguard their goods from imitations and counterfeiting. Not all countries have adopted a model for the protection of geographical indications based on special legislation like the one adopted by the European Union. Big players like the United States, Canada, South Africa and Australia are committed to a system of privately owned commercial marks, considered an expression of entrepreneurial freedom and a guarantee for investment and creativity.

In the U.S., Collective Marks and Certification Marks may be owned by foreign authorities, and they are the legal instruments most commonly used by Italian producers to protect their goods in a system that does not automatically recognize the geographical indications from the European Union. For example, Chianti Classico producers registered the design incorporating the Black Rooster with the words 'Chianti Classico Consorzio Vino Chianti Classico' as a collective mark. However, they were not allowed to use the expression 'Gallo Nero' (black rooster, the traditional Italian visual symbol) because of the lawsuit filed by Gallo Winery. The associations of Prosciutto di Parma and Parmigiano Reggiano producers registered their products as a collective mark.

## Food Patrols

The valorization of local traditions has the potential to limit the impact of globalization and to defend diversity, but it can also be exploited by xenophobic agendas. While food has the ability to bring people and cultures together, it can foster segregation. At times, racism penetrates local politics through food. The Italian north–south tension acquired new urgency after the launch in 1989 of the Lega Nord (northern league), a political party with a platform of fiscal federalism and regional autonomy. Born as an alliance between local organizations in northern Italy who sought secession from central and southern Italy, the Lega Nord maintains a large constituency.[34] They accused the central government of lacking efficacy, favouring bribery and exploiting the entrepreneurial spirit, the work ethic and the financial strength of the north. The capital, spitefully referred to as *Roma Ladrona* (big thief Rome), became the symbol of a national project that was despised as corrupt and myopic. The party also based its claims on the supposed cultural difference between the Padania, the areas located around and north of the Po River previously inhabited by Celts, and the rest of Italy, historically under the influence of Rome. As Celtic expert Nora Chadwick noted:

> Nor is the twentieth century free from the creation of Celtic myth . . . 'Celt' is fast becoming a metaphor for European unity, abused by politicians and multinational companies alike. None of this preamble is a cry of despair. History lies in the eye of the beholder, and the differing interpretations through the ages of the term 'Celt' add a whole additional level of fascination to the reality. How close to that reality we can ever get is debatable.[35]

## Food fights in the global market

Under the trademark model, adopted in the U.S. and other major industrial countries, there are three main marks commonly used to protect agricultural goods. The first category, the trademark, requires that private ownership be granted to a rightful 'inventor' of a product, and can be bought and sold as a business asset. Trademarks are often used to protect brand names, such as 'Coca-Cola', but are typically not applied to basic foodstuffs because these goods often cannot be tied to a rightful owner.

A Collective Mark can be used to certify that the goods originate in the particular geographical region identified by the term. In the U.S., the Collective Mark is registered through the United States Patent and Trade Office (USPTO) by an association, board or a collective group that administers the oversight and quality control of the mark. Unlike the Trademark, no one enterprise can apply for full ownership of a Collective Mark.

Finally, Certification Marks are owned by a certifying entity rather than by the producers themselves. The certifier sets standards that users must meet but nobody can be excluded from the use of the certification mark as long as the characteristics of the product are maintained. Examples of Certification Marks include Florida Citrus, owned by the State of Florida's Department of Citrus and Vidalia Onions, owned by the State of Georgia's Department of Agriculture.

All geographical indications are protected under Article 22 of the Agreement on Trade-Related Aspects of Intellectual

For anthropologist Michael Dietler, the rediscovery of the Celtic heritage has been playing an ideological role in various areas of Europe. Emotionally charged references to a Celtic identity have been used to promote 'pan-European unity in the context of the evolving European Community, nationalism within member states of that community, and regional resistance to nationalist hegemony'.[36]

The Lega Nord also decries the dangers of large numbers of immigrants, especially undocumented ones. Due to the relevance of food in

Property Rights of the World Trade Organization (TRIPS). However, Article 23 of the same treaty provides a higher level of protection to wine and spirits. For instance, geographical indications cannot be followed by expressions such as 'kind', 'type', 'style', 'imitation' or the like. So, the expression 'Chianti Classico style' cannot be used on wine labels, while 'Fontina-type cheese' would be allowed. Within Europe, however, this has already been outlawed: cheese producers in England and Germany are not allowed to use 'parmigiano', 'parmigiano-type' or even 'parmesan', which is considered an established and long-standing translation specifically referring to the product from Emilia Romagna.

*Fontina*, one of the most counterfeited cheeses from Italy.

the Italian cultural context, it is not surprising that these issues are often framed in very tangible, food-related terms. In 2004, Lega Nord party members organized a demonstration in the city of Como where 36 kg (80 lb) of polenta (a porridge of ground maize flour), mixed with local cheese and butter, was served to passers-by to remind them of their roots and to underline the emotional and cultural value of a traditional dish that in the past was considered the quintessential staple of the poor.[37] The slightest suspicion that local restaurants might use non-local ingredients for this dish was newsworthy.[38] To some extent, polenta became the symbol of the resistance of traditional food practices against the infiltration of exogenous factors.

Besides their symbolic impact, food-centred issues have entered far-reaching policy debates. In the spring of 2009, the municipal council of the Tuscan city of Lucca passed regulations to ban all shops selling kebabs, fast food and other non-Italian and non-traditional fare from the historical quarter in the city centre. 'With a view to safeguarding culinary traditions and the authenticity of structure, architecture, culture and history, establishments whose activities can be tracked to different ethnicities won't be allowed to operate', observed Flavia Krause-Jackson of Bloomberg in a blunt description of the scenario.[39] Local politicians wanted to ensure that visitors would find, smell and taste what they expected in a centuries-old city. Food heritage is supposed to offer tourists a controlled and non-threatening experience of 'Italianness', and not another version of the globalized and postmodern foodscapes available all over the world.

Similarly, in 2009, the regional government of Lombardy decided that no food could be served outside formal restaurants after one o'clock in the morning. No more kebabs, but also no pizza or ice cream, in order to avoid any loitering outside the stores and to maintain public peace. Opposition parties, of course, saw the regulation as a new step in the master plan plotted by the Lega Nord to damage food businesses often owned by non-Italians.[40]

Lega Nord's Luca Zaia, the minister of agriculture under the Berlusconi government and subsequently governor of the Veneto region, was very active in food-related political scuffles. A heated debate was ignited after he proposed working with McDonald's to produce a McItaly sandwich for the Italian market, made with Italian bread and meat, Asiago cheese and an artichoke spread. The rationale behind the culinary creation was, on one hand, to promote Italian flavours among young people who favoured fast-food joints, and on the other, to make sure that McDonald's bought Italian products. The international press covered the business deal and Matthew Fort, author of the *Word of Mouth* blog for the *Guardian* newspaper, wrote a scathing post about it, accusing Mr Zaia of opportunism and lack of respect for those very traditions he claimed to uphold.[41] The following day Minister Zaia shot back with a letter in which he vowed that he and his followers would 'become modern Jesuits' and try to 'convert the infidel' of the Left, who had never dirtied their hands working in the fields. 'They are the same people who, after preaching against those who – like me – work to ensure quality as a right for everybody instead of a luxury for élite consumers, run towards the "Organic Food" aisles of supermarkets with their heavy wallets and light consciences.'[42]

That was too much for the founder of Slow Food, Carlo Petrini, who until then had entertained a cordial relationship with minister Zaia, based on the shared defence of Italian food against globalization, standardization and GMOs. A few days later, Petrini published an op-ed in *La Repubblica* where he pointed out some of the weakest elements in the minister's approach, noting that not even the presence of Italian PDO products in supermarkets ensures fair payment to their manufacturers. Furthermore, Petrini observed that the attempt to 'globalize' Italian taste in terms of cultural identity actually risked making it disappear in the long run, absorbed by the power of international trademarks. Turning an argument very dear to the members of Lega Nord against its very proponents, the Slow Food founder argued:

> Taste, like 'identity', maintains its value only when differences exist, because its value is a function of differences. In fact we can safely argue that an Italian identity in terms of taste does not exist – those who invented McItaly can put their heart at rest – because there are hundreds, thousands of different Italian identities.[43]

Attempts by McDonald's to exploit Italian traditions continued after the McItaly quarrel. In October 2011 the company teamed up with famed chef Gualtiero Marchesi, widely considered one of the fathers of contemporary high-end Italian cuisine, to launch two new sandwiches, Adagio and Vivace, named after expressions used in classical music. Adagio contained an aubergine mousse, sliced tomatoes, sweet-and-sour aubergine, a beef burger and ricotta *salata*, while Vivace had bacon, sautéed spinach, marinated onions, a beef burger and a mayonnaise sauce with mustard seeds. In the press release that announced the new products, Marchesi stated:

> Just like life, cuisine progresses in fits and starts. When you turn to consider the before and after, you realize that the transition was very rapid. You are already beyond. It was like that when I first introduced Nouvelle Cuisine to Italy, and when I started closely watching young people, without prejudice. Where

do they eat? What do they eat? These are simple questions that preceded my decision to work with McDonald's.[44]

Both Lega North and Slow Food point to the development and protection of local identities and traditions, including food production, as relevant political issues. While Slow Food embraces these themes as part of an agenda aimed at multiculturalism and the protection of diversity worldwide, Lega North uses them within a discourse that places the defence of local privileges, the exclusion of outsiders and political autonomy at its core. After joining the political establishment, Mr Zaia gave a more moderate voice to Lega Nord's approach in his book *Adottare la terra per non morire di fame* (Adopting the Earth to Avoid Starvation, 2010). He underlined how the 'ancient and emblazoned' Italian agriculture needs protection against the competition from 'Bulgarian and Romanian peasants' as well as against 'blind and ideological globalization'.[45] However, he insisted that his position was not the result of racism but derived from the fact that 'hundreds of years of toil, sweat, study, investments, and the patient revision of regulations' distinguish southern European agriculture from others.[46] From his standpoint, the federalism that Lega Nord promotes is 'a cultural predisposition towards friendship within difference'.[47] While he demanded an 'identity-based agriculture that cannot be ripped away from its own history' and that focuses on seasons and local soil, he approved of the 'pineapple strike' launched in 2008 by inviting all citizens not to buy pineapples or Chilean cherries for Christmas. The former minister's balancing act reveals the political power of food issues in Italian civic debates, as well as the polarization that they can engender.

## The Intriguing Case of Pizza Napoletana

Within the staggering array of traditional Italian food products, pizza has recently become the object of much attention, probably as a result of its iconic status. In many parts of the world pizza's Italian origins have been so mystified that it is now considered a truly global food with myriad local interpretations.[48] Toppings, dough, thickness and cooking methods vary all over the world, partly due to the popularity of fast-food pizza chains.

Challenged by these developments, pizza makers from Naples have lobbied to acquire global visibility and to reaffirm the Italian pre-eminence in the pizza business. In February 2010, their two associations, the Associazione Verace Pizza Napoletana (Association for the True Pizza Napoletana) and Associazione Pizzaiuoli Napoletani (Association of Neapolitan Pizza Makers) obtained the status of Traditional Specialty Guaranteed (TSG) for *pizza napoletana* from the European Union. According to the regulation, only three kinds of pizza are to be considered truly Neapolitan: *marinara* (tomato, oregano, garlic and olive oil), *margherita* (tomato, mozzarella, basil and olive oil) and *margherita extra* (with the addition of fresh cherry tomatoes). The ingredients, techniques and even sensory elements of the dish are highly codified.

'Pizza Napoletana' TSG is distinguished by a raised rim, a golden colour characteristic of products baked in the oven, and a tenderness to touch and to taste; by a garnished centre dominated by the red of the tomatoes, perfectly mixed with oil and, depending on the ingredients used, the green of the oregano and the white of the garlic; by the white of the mozzarella slabs which are laid either closer together or further apart, and the green of the basil leaves, which are lighter or darker depending on the baking . . . At the end of the baking process the pizza emits a characteristic aroma which is deliciously fragrant; the tomatoes, which have lost only their excess water, remain compact and solid; the 'Mozzarella di Bufala Campana DOP' or 'Mozzarella STG' are melted on the surface of the pizza; the basil, garlic and oregano develop an intense aroma and do not look burnt.[49]

Theoretically, pizza makers around the globe could legally use the denomination *pizza napoletana* only when adhering to the guidelines of the TSG. However, it is highly unlikely that the two associations, the Italian government or the EU, would invest much money or research into making sure that no infringements are perpetrated in any part of the world. The effort is partly motivated by a desire to promote the Italian products one should supposedly use to make a pizza, like the PDO *mozzarella di bufala campana* or TSG *mozzarella*. But, since the origin of most ingredients is not specified and the regulation mostly focuses on the process and the final product, the goal is also to appeal to national loyalties against globalized taste to reinforce the cultural role and traditional skills of pizza makers trained according to the Neapolitan way.

With the implementation of the TSG status, pizza can be represented and promoted as a quintessential Italian product. However, this recognition risks erasing – or at least partially hiding – many globalized aspects of pizza production. In many shops in Italy, pizza makers are

*Pizza Margherita.*

immigrants, reflecting the vast presence of foreign employees in the restaurant business. In 2008, the *New York Times* pointed out that some of the most successful and upmarket restaurants in Italy have hired chefs from countries such as India, Tunisia and Jordan, and that most restaurateurs do not find anything wrong with this as long as their employees embrace Italian food and its techniques.[50] Photographers Marco Delogu and Michele de Andreis dedicated an exhibition to foreign chefs working in Italy, showing how immigrants in Italian professional kitchens are not only washing dishes or clearing tables, but also cooking. With a clear polemic intent, the photo portraits celebrate male and female professionals from Albania, Morocco and Bangladesh as the new face of Italian food.[51] Delogu is not new to expressing civil engagement in his work. He also shot a series of portraits of immigrant shepherds living in Maremma and Agro Pontino, the plain south of Rome where much buffalo mozzarella is produced. The collection became an exhibition in 2007 and then a book in 2009.[52] Italian foodies are taking notice and at times even celebrating foreign chefs who express themselves in the culinary traditions of their homeland. The authoritative Italian food magazine *Gambero Rosso* dedicated an article to the Roman neighbourhood of Pigneto, an area that until recently was among the most depressed in the eastern suburbs of the capital city. Through a fast process of gentrification, it has turned into a hotspot for ethnic restaurants and nightlife.[53]

Not all pizza ingredients are necessarily Italian. Studies project that, due to climate change, Italy will not be able to maintain its present level of wheat production, which is already insufficient to meet demands.[54] Because of its bread and pasta consumption, Italy accounts for more than 80 per cent of all the wheat imported into the European Union.[55] Barilla, the biggest pasta producer in the world, acquires its wheat from the u.s., Canada and Eastern Europe.[56]

Following the supply chain of pizza, in addition to the shepherds who tend the cows and the water buffalo from whose milk mozzarella is made, African immigrants – often undocumented – pick tomatoes, including the famed San Marzano variety for the pizza sauce. For years, Italian growers have been hiring both documented and undocumented immigrant workers during harvest time. According to the Italian farmers association Coldiretti, in 2010, 90,000 documented immigrant workers from outside the eu worked in Italian fields, 15,000 of them with long-term contracts.[57] For years Italians ignored the massive presence of immigrants in their food system, but the issue was taken up with urgency after the events that took place in January 2010 in the town of Rosarno

Immigrants working in Italian agriculture are often exploited and forced to live in harsh conditions.

in Calabria. There, undocumented farm workers participated in violent riots sparked by a xenophobic raid, a manifestation of built-up frustration at the inhuman living conditions, the low pay and the 'protection' bribes extorted by local organized crime, the *ndrangheta*.[58] The revolt became the subject of a documentary film, *Il sangue verde* (The Green Blood), which was presented at the Venice Film Festival in September 2010.

### Ethnic Restaurants in Italy

Immigrants are much more visible in the distribution and restaurant businesses than in food-production chains. The presence of ethnic restaurants is a relatively new phenomenon, first limited to major urban centres but increasingly spreading to smaller towns. Until the 1970s, few foreign immigrants chose Italy to start a new life, with the exception of nearby North African and Middle Eastern citizens. Mostly Muslim, these immigrants did not have access to halal meat in Italy, but were able to purchase what they needed from Jewish stores that followed kashrut rules. Halal butchers are now opening where Islamic communities are more numerous and stable, especially in large cities.[59]

In the 1980s, a large wave of Chinese immigrants marked the beginning of arrivals from all over the world: south Asia, the Philippines, South America and many African countries (especially those connected with the colonial past of Italy, such as Ethiopia, Eritrea and Somalia). With the fall of the Berlin Wall, great numbers of Eastern Europeans trickled into Italy as well. In the 1990s, massive numbers of Albanians, crammed into tiny boats, made their way across the Adriatic Sea; the frequent shipwrecks along the coasts made Italians realize that the demographics of their country were changing. Despite the fact that the percentage of foreigners living in Italy is still pretty low compared to other European countries, Italians show growing xenophobia and widespread fear of loss of identity. Nevertheless, immigrant communities are a reality. Young students are exposed to the eating habits of classmates from other countries, babysitters from remote corners of the world are feeding Italian infants, and *badanti*, individuals taking care of the growing elderly population, frequently cook for the senior citizens they live with. It is difficult to gauge the impact of daily exchanges and cohabitation, but these interactions between cultures are likely to leave their mark on the future developments of Italian culinary customs.

With the exceptions of big cities like Milan, Turin or Rome, immigrant communities are frequently not large enough to sustain ethnic eateries. However, stalls and stores selling exotic products are more visible than they were in the past. Chinese grocery stores are the most common. The reasons are manifold: Chinese communities are pretty large (in the Tuscan city of Prato, for instance, they run the local leather and textile industry) and they tend to maintain a strong attachment to their traditions, including eating practices (at least in the case of first-generation immigrants). Chinese restaurants have become a fixture, both in the historical neighbourhoods and in the outskirts of large cities, increasing the demand for Chinese products and ingredients. Chinese restaurants, which assure low prices, a laid-back environment and the thrill of trying a new cuisine, constitute a viable and affordable alternative to the pub or the pizzeria for many Italians, especially the younger generations. However, these establishments are perceived as less prestigious than those showcasing other ethnic cuisines, such as Japanese or Middle Eastern.[60]

Chinese restaurants are definitely the most visible and numerous ethnic restaurants in Italy, granting employment to Chinese newcomers. Being Chinese-owned and -managed, they do not require their workers to speak Italian. Furthermore, they often provide food and lodging, essential to employees when salaries are meagre. Cooks, coming from the most diverse backgrounds, are not professionally trained and the average standard of food in Chinese restaurants is relatively low. This does not seem to stop Chinese immigrants from trying their luck in the kitchen, aware that very few Italians know what Chinese food in China tastes like. The complexities and refinements of Chinese cuisines, including any regional varieties, have been largely erased to create a hybrid set of dishes that are the same in most restaurants all over Italy: easy to make and exotic enough to please the clientele. Chinese cooks worked out which dishes fit the Italian palate and what changes were necessary to make them cost-effective. Italians expect Chinese food to be served quickly and without fuss, allowing cooks to use precooked or frozen items such as dumplings, spring rolls and seafood. These packaged foods are also available in Chinese grocery shops and supermarkets, together with a vast array of rice, noodles, sauces and dried vegetables, but for the average Italian these outlets are difficult to navigate.

Chinese restaurants in Italy have changed the traditional structure of the meal to adapt to Italian taste and eating habits. Appetizers in a Chinese menu in Italy consist of all kinds of dim sum, spring rolls,

Vietnamese cold rolls and dumplings (boiled, steamed and pot stickers). The *primi* section includes soups, noodles and rice dishes, modelling themselves on the concept of *primo*. The *secondi* category is organized by protein: chicken, beef, pork, fish and other seafood (usually shrimp). Italians do not cringe when served whole fish (with bones, head and tail), so Chinese cooks can stick to their traditions. Sides (*contorni*) include egg- or tofu-based dishes and, of course, vegetables, usually steamed or sautéed. For the *secondi* and *contorni*, portions are often measured for the single client, and not for the whole table, as is the case in China. Desserts, almost non-existent in a Chinese meal, consist of novelties like fried battered fruits and fried battered ice cream, along with exotic fruit such as lychee (mostly canned, even if fresh lychees are available). After the meal, clients are often offered sweet liquors, which take the place of the traditional Italian *amaro* (bitter, digestive liqueur) and grappa. No fortune cookies for Italians, at least so far. Chopsticks and bowls are sometimes found at the table, but more frequently waiters provide them upon request.

After a few years of adaptation and cultural transformation, Chinese restaurants in Italy, with their laid-back service, loud decor and cheap prices, seem to have reached widespread acceptance, with an established set of dishes that growing numbers of Italians are becoming familiar with. In 2003, however, many of these establishments were almost forced to close down when, as a result of the SARS scare, Italians temporarily shunned them. The owners resorted to all kinds of ruses to attract clients: some installed satellite TV so that customers could watch football matches on pay-per-view; others served pizza and other Italian dishes, offering cheap fixed-price menus. When the sanitary alert fizzled out, most restaurants went back to business as usual, but many kept the changes they had introduced during the crisis.

The status quo is being challenged by a new generation of trendy restaurants, usually owned and managed by Italians who propose fusion cuisine in a modern ambiance, where design, music and drinks play a major role. The clientele, of course, is totally different: while Chinese restaurants are the best choice for people on a budget, these hip restaurants cater to more affluent and style-conscious customers. Italian chefs are exploring the possibility of integrating unusual ingredients and techniques into their dishes. Young culinary professionals do not only explore the ethnic restaurants around them, but they tend to travel extensively and get acquainted with foreign food traditions. Moreover, they create networks

Chinese restaurant
in Gorizia.

with other chefs from all over the world, exchanging recipes and tips, and even participate in formal meetings. Food enthusiasts and the media are paying attention to these trends, nurturing forms of culinary cosmopolitism that were unusual a few years ago. Cooking schools organize sushi classes and Mexican cuisine workshops, while publishers promote cookbooks on ethnic cuisines. However, greater knowledge of foreign food habits does not diminish the attachment and the pride that most Italians feel for their own culinary traditions. Globalization is negotiated at the personal level in complex and diverse ways, depending on cultural capital, financial means, personal experiences and interests, social environment and access. At the same time, individual dispositions and practices cannot be isolated from larger economic and political dynamics.

A few decades ago, Italians did not know what a kiwi was; now the country is one of the largest kiwi producers in the world. At the beginning of the twentieth century few were familiar with pizza, including in certain areas in Italy, but now the dish has turned into a global phenomenon. Words like carpaccio and risotto are no longer the exclusive domains of connoisseurs. As happens throughout history, Italian food is exposed to and affected by global influences, participating in wide networks of commercial and professional exchanges. It is difficult to make projections about the future, but we can safely affirm that any attempts to protect Italian food by isolating it from the world are unlikely to succeed. What is more Italian – a grandmother's traditional minestrone or the experimentations with miso soup by an up-and-coming chef? Only time will tell how Italians will mediate between the desire to maintain traditional practices, dishes and products and the inevitable realities of history and change.

# EIGHT

# A Nation of Towns and Regions: Italian *Campanilismo*

Pizza? That's old . . . New trends are all about Neapolitan-style pizza, Rome-style pizza, Apulia-style pizza. Spaghetti? Boring! How about some handmade *orecchiette* or some hardy *strozzapreti*? As growing scores of food lovers are in search of novelty to express and expand their culinary knowledge and cultural capital, an establishment advertised as simply 'Italian' risks being perceived as passé or lacking in 'authenticity'. Savvy restaurant-goers, who have access to expert information and are likely to have travelled to Italy, have become acutely aware of the complexity of its local food traditions. Our journey in the history of Italy has indicated how these dynamics are far from new, but at the same time they have affected the culinary landscape of the peninsula in different ways across time and place. Local culinary traditions were already established when Maestro Martino wrote his famous recipe book *Liber de arte coquinaria* (Book on the Art of Cooking) in the mid-1460s. Of course, certain areas were better known than others for their specialities, which were clearly identified in terms of geographical origins. The famous author was able to distinguish clearly among regional pasta traditions, as the recipes overleaf show.

The very existence of a national Italian cuisine is frequently called into question. In the United States, for instance, many restaurants started defining their food as 'northern Italian' as early as the late 1970s, distinguishing their cuisine from the seemingly old-school and immigrant-owned plain 'Italian' cooking, widely identified as southern Italian. In the 1980s, the craze for everything Tuscan exploded, fuelled by media, travel agencies and marketing. Recently the focus has shifted to once lesser-known culinary specialties from regions such as Apulia, Sardinia and Val D'Aosta, with renewed interest in local traditions of cities, towns and rural areas. This trend has been strengthened by the Italians' own renewed interest

### Roman Macaroni

Take some fine white flour, mix it with water and make a sheet a little thicker than lasagna, and wrap it around a rolling pin. Then take the pin out, and cut the pasta as wide as a little finger. It will end up looking like strips or strings. Cook them in fatty meat broth or in water, depending on the time of the year. If you cook them in water, add fresh butter and a little salt. As soon as they are cooked, pour them on a platter with good cheese, butter and sweet spices.[1]

### Sicilian Macaroni

Take some very fine white flour and knead it with egg whites or with rose water or plain water. If you want to make two platters don't put [in] more than one or two egg whites, and make the dough nice and firm. Make sticks the length of a handbreadth and as thin as hay. Take an iron wire the length of a handbreadth or more, and put it over the stick, and roll it with both hands on the table. Then take the iron out and pull the macaroni with a hole running through the centre. These macaroni need to dry in the sun, and will last two or three years, especially if you make them during the August moon. Cook them in water or in meat broth. Pour them in the platters with good-quality grated cheese, fresh butter and sweet spices. This kind of macaroni needs to boil for two hours.[2]

in their local culinary identities, a phenomenon that since the end of the 1980s has deeply changed food preferences and practices in Italy. Unusual wine varieties (known as *vitigni autoctoni*), frequently closely connected with specific locations, are now all the rage. Grapes such as *negroamaro*, *lagrein* and *cannonau*, which until twenty years ago belonged to the intimidating domain of wine experts and oenologists, have become current, while newly rediscovered varieties such as *pecorino* and *sagrantino* are receiving media and consumer attention. *Osterie*, small and usually unpretentious eateries that were once floundering in popularity, have enjoyed a renaissance. They are now appreciated as the strongholds of local dishes and customs against the invasion of mass-produced, globalized foods and

EU logo for DOP (*Denominazione d'Origine Protetta* or PDO, Protected Designation of Origin) products; (right) EU logo for IGP (*Indicazione Geografica Protetta* or PDO, Protected Geographical Indication) products.

fads. Young entrepreneurs are opening *osterie* to capitalize on the growing interest of patrons for these traditional public spaces and the sense of community they are supposed to foster. Geographical indications, a category of intellectual property that identifies foods with their places of origin, are widely perceived as markers of higher quality; both commercial entities and public institutions are putting great efforts into obtaining the coveted recognitions of protected designation of origin (PDO),

*Orecchiette*, a pasta from Apulia.

253

protected geographical indication (PGI) and traditional speciality guaranteed (TSG) from the European Union.

## THE EUROPEAN POLITICS OF EATING

It has become common for businessmen, media operators, administrators and politicians to exploit food-related trends to promote their own agendas, leveraging the most physical and intimate aspects of their fellow citizens' lives. Contemporary social issues have increasingly affected food debates at the local, national and international level, influencing the way traditions and typical ingredients are identified, protected and turned into development engines for the economy.

Italy and other European Union countries such as France and Spain have found themselves at the forefront of the establishment and the advancement of international regulations on Geographical Indications (GIs). Under the Agreement on Trade-Related Aspects of Intellectual Property Rights (TRIPs) of the World Trade Organization, signed in 1994, GIs are names or signs that identify a product with a specific place in a member state. Although they only certify a product's origin, consumers usually perceive GIs as a guarantee of high quality and reputation. Food manufacturers are aware that GIs can increase the value of their goods, protecting them from competitors selling similar products under the same name and creating entry barriers for producers who do not have the means to comply with the complex regulations. Consumers and authorities feel more protected from fraud.

The TRIPs agreement followed a regulation issued in 1992 by the European Union, the infamous 2082/92, that allowed the registration of specialities and products under two categories: the PDO and the PGI. The PDO refers to the name of a region, a specific place or a country from which a product originates, whose quality or other characteristics are essentially or exclusively a result of the specific geographical environment. This means that production and transformation must be carried out in the geographical area designated by the PDO regulations. Among PDOs from Italy we can cite Prosciutto di Parma, Asiago cheese and honey from the Lunigiana area in northern Tuscany. It should be noted that while some products have enjoyed century-long recognition among gourmets and average consumers, others are the result of anthropological research, commercial entrepreneurship and political initiatives that have revived disappearing practices, as long as there is some trace of their

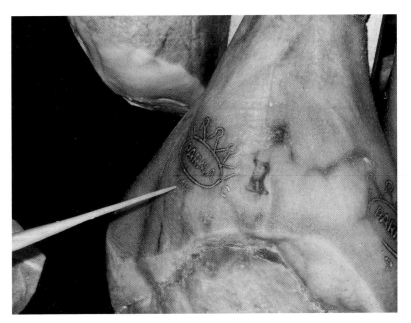

*Prosciutto di Parma*, among the most popular PDO products.

historical past. For instance, in the area of Siena, Tuscany, local producers, who already manufactured raw sheep's milk cheese under the Pecorino
Toscano PDO, have recently decided to revive the age-old tradition of
making cheese using wild cardoons (a Mediterranean species similar to
the artichoke) instead of veal rennet, to differentiate their offering and
to lure vegetarian consumers. The use of vegetarian curdling ingredients such as cardoons and fig sap is, according to the consortium of the
producers of Pecorino Toscano, a practice that was already common in
ancient Roman times.[3] The historical precedents and the connection
with the territory seem undisputed, supported by frequent mentions in
documents that had been written not by cheesemakers but by the local-
authority figures of the time.

The definition of PGI, on the other hand, is less strict than PDO,
including components such as traditional notoriety. For instance, Vialone
Nano rice, lemons from Sorrento and mortadella from Bologna all enjoy
PGI status, as their historical relevance and fame are considered to be
crucial factors in defining the products. Furthermore, not all phases of
production or transformation need take place in the geographical area indicated by the PGI regulations. In 2006, following a series of legislative acts
in 1997 and 1998, the European Union Council defined and regulated
the TSG (traditional speciality guaranteed) a third and less strict category

Although *Pizza Napoletana* has obtained the status of Traditional Specialty Guaranteed, pizza is being made in diverse and creative ways all over the world.

that, as outlined in the 1992 document, does not refer to any specific area of origin:

> An agricultural product or foodstuff shall either be produced using traditional raw materials or be characterized by a traditional composition or a mode of production and/or processing reflecting a traditional type of production and/or processing. Registration shall not be permitted in the case of an agricultural product or foodstuff the specific character of which is due to its provenance or geographic origin.[4]

For PDO and PGI products, as well as for TSG ones, only an association of producers can file the request for registration. So far in Italy, only mozzarella and pizza makers have managed to obtain TSG denominations, in 1998 and 2010 respectively. Other associations have applied for products such as Antico Cioccolato Artigianale (ancient artisanal chocolate) and Gallo Ruspante (free-range rooster), and it is quite likely that others will follow in the future. Italy and the southern members of the Union took advantage of the threefold EU system of classification, boosting the value of their agricultural products and transforming food-related traditions and local customs into relevant topics in public debates and national politics. Similar systems are in place for wine production, following the same general principles. However, since they were implemented before the unified EU regulations, they vary country by country.

### UNDER THE BELL TOWER: WHAT FOOD IS ITALIAN?

These relatively recent trends seem to feed off and strengthen a powerful element of Italian culture: *campanilismo*. This profoundly Italian expression refers to the love, pride and attachment to a certain place by those whose homes are located in the area metaphorically covered by the shadow of the local bell tower. *Campanilismo* expresses itself through food as well. Towns, cities and even tiny countryside or mountain villages boast traditions that are unique or shared only with the immediate surrounding territory, often reflecting artisanal skills and rural civilizations that are visibly changing and, some say, slowly disappearing.

The variety and complexity of Italian food culture can be traced back to the origin of civilization in the peninsula. The influence of

The bell tower (*campanile*) in my grandparents' village of Tossicia, Abruzzo. It's the origin of the expression *campanilismo*, referring to local pride.

# The classification of wine

The European Union system of geographical indications ultimately derives from the system of classification that France created in 1855 to rank winemakers in the Bordeaux area. Over time, the Appellation d'Origine Contrôlée (controlled appellation of origin) as a legal category was officially established in the 1930s. Following the French example, in 1963 the Italian government issued a law that introduced DOC (controlled denomination of origin, in Italian *Denominazione d'Origine Controllata*) and DOCG (denomination of controlled and guaranteed origin, in Italian *Denominazione d'Origine Controllata e Garantita*), with the goal of highlighting and protecting the best wine production just when mechanization was stimulating output with little attention to quality. Rules were established to determine who had the power to create new DOCs, and how. Production regulations (called *disciplinare*) delimit the zones in which the wines originate and specify type (or types, since a denomination may include a range of versions), colour, grape varieties, minimum alcohol levels, maximum yields in grapes per hectare and wine from grapes, basic sensory characteristics, fermentation (in wood or otherwise and possibly in sealed tanks), required minimum ageing periods and special designations identifying particular sub-zones, such as *classico* or *superiore*. A DOCG wine must meet standards that are stricter than those stipulated in DOC regulations. One of the main differences is the lower yields imposed by the DOCG rules. The limitations in output have probably done more to boost the quality of wines than any other provision in the regulations, which also require in-depth chemical analyses for all DOCG wines.

The first DOC, Vermaccia di San Gimignano in Tuscany, was declared only in 1966, and the first DOCG, Brunello di Montalcino in Tuscany, in 1980. A third category was established in 1992, in compliance with the European Union regulations: the IGT (typical geographic indication, Indicazione Geografica Tipica). The IGT regulations require use of authorized varieties, most of them establishing the use of one type only or in a ratio of at least 85 per cent to other approved grapes. The IGT wines are identified with specific territories, most of which are larger than the zones specified in the regulations for DOCGs and DOCs. Some are region-wide, as in the case of Toscano in Tuscany and Sicilia in Sicily, while others are limited to a valley or a range of hills. For consumers, the IGT denomination primarily indicates a wide range of wines of acceptable quality available at highly competitive prices. It also allowed many local wines to acquire a higher status than regular table wine (*vino da tavola*), which can come from anywhere in Italy and can be bottled anywhere or even sold in bulk (*sfuso*). In fact, Italy is still one of the most important producers of bulk wine in the world.

From the beginning, some innovative wine producers, who were particularly interested in experimenting with grape varieties and techniques, found these regulations too tight. Already in 1968, in the Maremma area of southern Tuscany, with the help of the oenologist Giacomo Tachis, Count Incisa della Rocchetta created Sassicaia, still considered by many to be one of the best Italian wines. In 1971, again in Tuscany, Antinori launched Tignanello. Though officially classified as *vini da tavola*, these wines, known in the English-speaking world as Supertuscans, gained global renown. In time, together with others such as Ornellaia or Guado al Tasso, they were able to compete with the great Bordeaux on the international market.

While these innovative trends were receiving widespread recognition, in 1986 Italy was struck by a scandal that had deep consequences for many years. Methanol, a poisonous substance, was added to a few Piedmont wines to raise the alcohol content, killing several people and causing intoxication and a few cases of blindness in Lombardy, Liguria and Piedmont. Although the Italian government issued many emergency regulations, the general perception of wine was profoundly tainted. Consumption fell to a historical low, while many Italians resorted, at least for a while, to beer. On the international market Italian wines were seen with growing suspicion. The economic damage was incalculable but at the same time forced wineries to improve their production and become more attentive to questions of safety, consumer perception and certification procedures, allowing Italian wine to acquire global fame.

the Mediterranean climate on Italian production and cuisine depends on the distance from the shoreline and on altitude. Precipitation varies greatly between the semi-arid plains and low hills of the south where rain can be limited or absent five to seven months a year, to the more humid hills and plains of central and northern Italy. Humidity and precipitation increases on the Apennines and in the areas located at the foot of the Alps.[5] The different soil, water and climate characteristics have affected customs, social structures and other cultural traits of the settled populations. While farmers, herders and fishermen developed practices adapted to their environments, they also applied customs and technologies that they had borrowed from elsewhere to the familiar landscapes.

We must keep in mind that the present-day environmental situation and the problems connected with it are the result of 4,000 years of long- and short-term interactions between humans and their surroundings, which at different times caused, accelerated or counteracted the degradation of the soils caused by agricultural exploitation, deforestation or water management. Despite the generally mild climate in vast areas of the peninsula, agricultural yields were often insufficient, especially in periods of demographic expansion. As a result, populations moved towards lands that could guarantee crops in the necessary amounts, as in Roman times, or intensified agricultural outputs through the application of new technologies, artisanal skills, trade and, later on, industrialization. As a result, Italy generated and still maintains a dazzling variety of products, now an important component of local identities. I distinctly remember that while growing up I was not aware of many fantastic products that I now love, including the squash *tortelli* from Mantova, the smoked pork *speck* from Alto Adige, or the luscious *burrata* cheese from Apulia. At the same time, my Roman friends had no clue about the *arrosticini* (tiny grilled skewers of mutton) or the *ventricina* (ground pork and pork fat with spices, encased in a pig bladder) that I grew accustomed to during my childhood vacations in Abruzzo, just 160 km away.

Due to this diversity, many wonder how to define Italian cuisine as a whole, or if it is even possible to do so. In his book about foreign invasions, historian Girolamo Arnaldi quotes poet Mario Luzi, saying, 'Italy is an illusion, indeed, a mirage, the stuff of wishes' with a 'terribly fragile' national identity.[6] Is there a set of ingredients, dishes, cultural attitudes and practices that can be identified as Italian? Does a coherent and clearly codified Italian culinary repertoire even exist, or is it the collection of interconnected but independent local traditions?

*Burrata* cheese from Apulia.

These questions became the object of public debates and media attention when in 2011 Italy celebrated the 150th anniversary of its unification as a sovereign state, a goal that many still consider unaccomplished or plainly unrealistic. Many deep-rooted issues continue to shape the political discourse about national identity, with important organizations and parties aiming at greater local autonomies, if not downright secession. While most of the anniversary celebrations focused on elements such as the flag, the constitution and the anthem, cuisine also received some consideration. In particular, events were organized to commemorate the role and relevance of cookbook author Pellegrino Artusi, who in 1891 published *La scienza in cucina e l'arte di mangiare bene* (Science in the Kitchen and the Art of Eating Well). As we discussed in chapter Four, this collection of recipes is still considered the first to imply the possibility of Italian cultural unification, without articulating any political agenda. Acknowledging varying local elements, Artusi treated the complex mosaic of Italian food as one entity that needed a cohesive approach and a unified language. In fact, right after the introductory chapters and before the recipes, he provides a glossary of terms that, 'belonging to the Tuscan dialect, not everybody would understand'.[7] At the time, common words like *lardo* (rendered pork fat), *matterello* (rolling pin), *mestolo* (ladle) and *tagliere* (chopping board) still needed an explanation. A few decades after

261

Bust of Pellegrino
Artusi in the cemetery
of San Miniato al
Monte, near Florence.

the publication of the book, the Fascist propaganda machine took it upon
itself to shape and reinforce the identity of Italian cuisine as a component of national identity and as a reason for national pride, enriched by
its variety and its regional characteristics.

Of course, the shared perception among Italians about what dishes
and ingredients should be included in a national inventory has changed
over time. On the occasion of the 150th anniversary of the unification,
the popular wine and food magazine *Gambero rosso* invited its readers
to identify what were, in their opinion, the most important Italian foods.
The online survey indicated Parmigiano Reggiano as the product with the
highest percentage of mentions (53.5 per cent), followed by extra-virgin
olive oil (43.8 per cent), pizza Napoletana (43.2 per cent) and buffalo
mozzarella (40 per cent). Surprisingly, rice (37.4 per cent) appeared to be
considered to be more 'Italian' than bread (36.7 per cent) and spaghetti
(34.1 per cent), the latter with the same percentage as panettone, a
Christmas dessert speciality from Milan that acquired national distribution only when it was industrially produced after the First World War.

*Panettone*, a Christmas dessert speciality from Milan.

The *Gambero rosso* top-fifteen items also included Florentine-style steak, Genovese-style pesto, lasagna, *pasta amatriciana* (a typical Roman dish with *guanciale* – cured pork cheek, *pecorino* cheese and tomato), mortadella and Barolo wine.[8] The list does not have scientific value as it was produced by the readers of a food magazine, and more specifically only by those who had online access. In fact, it seems to be skewed towards the north. At any

*Pasta amatriciana*, a typical Roman dish with *guanciale* (cured pork cheek), *pecorino* cheese and tomato.

263

rate, the list reflects the strong local character of Italian cuisine, even when specialities connected with particular places are embraced as national dishes. Some products, such as pesto and buffalo mozzarella, only recently acquired national renown, proving that Italian cuisine does not have a fixed or stable canon. Instead, what makes certain foods Italian is their strong connection with local identities, artisanal skills and traditions, even when these elements are heavily influenced by perception and marketing. Looking back at Artusi's book, *mozzarella di bufala* and *pasta amatriciana* were not even mentioned, the only Genoa-style sauce finding a place among his recipes included capers and eggs and was used with boiled fish, while Neapolitan pizza was a dessert with almonds, eggs and ricotta.

## Italians and Their Food Traditions

Practices and ideas about the definition of Italian food have changed since the late 1800s and are bound to keep on changing, despite any administrative effort to define and regulate products through the enthusiastic embrace of the European Union legislation on geographical indications. Similarly, what qualifies as traditional and what additions are acceptable is bound to evolve over time. More interesting to question, then, might not be which product or dish is traditional, but rather what do Italians mean by tradition and why do certain elements end up being perceived as traditional? Above all, the most crucial issue is why, at the beginning of the twenty-first century, do Italians care so much about tradition after having almost completely discarded it half a century ago when the country embarked on a path of fast and sweeping economic development? Why are values such as 'typical', 'artisanal' and 'authentic' so relevant in the contemporary cultural discourse on food? Why have the connections between specific places and local traditions acquired such relevance? And how do the various levels of this interest – from the very local, to the regional, to the national – interact with one another?

I would argue that Italians, like many other nationalities, tend to give attention to their past, including its material aspects, as a reaction to anxieties and priorities in their present. This renewed interest in culinary traditions, local products and artisanal delicacies is reaching new heights not only in Italy but also Western Europe, Japan and more recently the United States and Australia. Other countries are following right behind, such as Brazil, Mexico and Costa Rica, where a still-growing upper class is showing shifting sensitivity about the cultural relevance of food traditions.[9] Until a few years ago, many citizens in developing countries would have considered local ingredients and dishes embarrassing, uncouth and uncomfortably close to the rural realities and the ethnic groups often left at the margin of national projects of modernization. This was definitely the case in Italy, which in the late 1950s underwent a fast and widespread transition from rural to urban environments, from poverty to relative prosperity, from backwardness to modernity, from unsophisticated to cosmopolitan sensibilities (which, as we will see, do not coincide with actual multiculturalism). Only from the late 1980s, when the uncomfortable past seemed distant enough, were Italians able to look back with a certain sense of nostalgia, discovering an unprecedented appreciation of many aspects of their traditions such as foods that they had been eager to leave behind and that were at risk of extinction.

Over the past twenty years in many post-industrial societies there has been a growing appreciation for local food customs, as well as the manual skills and the know-how of food producers. *Terroir*, originally a French concept connecting the sensory quality of a food or wine to soil, climate and the geographical environment of production, is no longer exclusively applied to French traditions. Producers all over the world, including those in less developed countries, are becoming increasingly aware that the shift towards unique foodstuffs could help them move towards more rewarding value-added segments of the business, breaking free from the commodities market, recently plagued by international speculation and uncontrollable spikes in prices. Coffee beans connected with a specific area, grown in limited amounts, with recognizable sensory profiles and produced according to precise rules, can command much higher price tags on the global market – as long as international consumers are made aware of their existence and their distinctiveness. Renowned cocoa from specific locations is highly valued by experts, pastry chefs and well-informed consumers. In Italy, varieties of tomato from Pachino or San Marzano, known for their flavour, shape and culinary versatility, are now sold and bought at much higher prices than other less famous kinds. The trade of speciality products is growing in volume and relevance. This trend – quite visible in supermarkets, restaurants and around domestic tables – is promoted and exploited by the media, marketers and politicians, and it is inevitably reflected in tourism flows. Many of these products thrive precisely because they find buyers beyond the areas in which they are produced, not only nationally but often also internationally. However, while these dynamics can have a positive impact on rural communities, it is undeniable that participation in worldwide currents of people, money, goods and information frequently causes disruption and tension.

Contemporary Italians, the majority of whom live in cities and with little direct connection to food manufacturing, tend to perceive local traditional foods as deeply rooted in the rural world and a long history of artisanal activities. In fact, much of the appreciation of these products is fuelled by the fear that they might disappear under the assault of industrialization, globalization and corporate appropriation. As we discussed in chapter Six, a noticeable interest in organic produce, farmers' markets, CSAs and fair trade, together with the success of the Slow Food movement, demonstrates how consumers want to know where their food comes from, how it is made and how it lands on their tables. However, for many urban Italians with spending power, the countryside is little more than a picturesque background for their weekend outings and their vacations, a landscape dotted with *agriturismi*, where they can spend time enjoying a controlled and unthreatening connection with a world they identify with relaxation, calm and physical well-being. The harshness of land toiling, as well as the economic and structural problems plaguing agriculture, rarely become part of an approach to food that emphasizes leisure and entertainment. Now and in the past, rural activities are framed around urban consumption. Starting from the Middle Ages, some of the most pricey and sought-after specialties were not named after the places in the countryside where they were grown or manufactured, but rather were identified with the cities and towns that historically constituted their main markets and where merchants and consumers from outside their area of production got to know them. For instance, we are familiar with lentils from Castelluccio, chestnuts from Vallerano, *Ragusano* cheese (from the town of Ragusa) and traditional balsamic vinegars from Modena and Reggio Emilia, but none of these products is actually produced within the limits of the towns that give them their names. These denominations are the result of rural–urban connections that, in the thirteenth century and today, put Italian cities in a predominant – and often exploitative – position towards the surrounding countryside.

The rediscovery of local and artisanal foods emphasizes easily identifiable – and defendable – units, like cities or specific rural areas. This is the mechanism behind the geographical indications adopted by the European Union legislation and other forms of protection.

Nevertheless, in contemporary Italy the attachment and the defence of local identities can assume various forms and operate at different levels: the same individuals can be proud (and defensive) of the unique recipes of their town, but also of the products of the larger area in which their town is located, of the region to which both the town and the surrounding area belong, and of more general geographical categories, such as 'the north' and 'the south', which still play quite a relevant role in Italian cultural and political debates.

## REGIONAL FOODS

While the attachment to the food of specific areas, cities and even villages, dates back centuries, it is only recently that food traditions, ingredients and dishes have been discussed in terms of regions.[10] This might sound strange to foreign consumers who in the past two decades have grown used to understanding and classifying Italian food by region. Certain areas, such as Tuscany and Sicily, have been clearly identified in Italian culture for centuries and attributed specific and recognizable traits. Regions were already listed among the five elements forming the Italian Republic together with the Municipalities, the Provinces, the Metropolitan Cities and the State in the 1948 Italian constitution. Passed after the 1946 referendum that determined the end of the Reign of Italy and the beginning of the republican era, a substantial section of the constitution, articles 114 to 133, is dedicated to local autonomies and their relationships with the central government. The founding fathers of republican Italy emphasized this topic's importance by placing it among the fundamental principles of the new state. Article 5 reads:

> The Republic is one and indivisible. It recognizes and promotes local autonomies, and implements the fullest measure of administrative decentralization in those services that depend on the State. The Republic adapts the principles and methods of its legislation to the requirements of autonomy and decentralization.

After two decades of centralized administration by the Fascist government, politicians operating in post-war Italy found it was not easy to implement autonomies. Under Fascism, *Podestà*, appointed by Rome, had replaced elected mayors. When the 1948 constitution was approved, the text already mentioned the future twenty regions by name, but only four of them were established at the time: Sicily, Sardinia, Trentino-Alto Adige and Val d'Aosta, followed in 1963 by a fifth, Friuli-Venezia Giulia. Each of these regions was granted a special level of autonomy, as they had a unique past and were currently struggling with complex issues, often connected with the presence of ethnic minorities and with border negotiations. The remaining fifteen regions, foreseen in the constitution as regulated by 'ordinary statutes', were established as actual administrative entities only after 1970. Since then, their legislative and regulatory powers have increased. They cover matters such as tourism, agriculture, fisheries, forestry and food safety, all managed in coordination with the Ministero delle Politiche Agricole, Alimentari, e Forestali – the ministry for agricultural, food and forestry policies of the central government. (The ministry, temporarily abolished in 1993, was reinstated in 1999 in response to the need for an institutional representative of Italy in negotiations at the European Union level, including those about the establishment of geographical indications for food products.)

Despite their short history, Italian regions have acquired great relevance and visibility in the everyday life of Italians due to growing legislative reach. Over time, their influence has also been felt at cultural and social levels, including gastronomy and food traditions. The expression 'regional cuisine' has become quite common both in Italy and abroad, even if it is, at times, hard to define. What are these regional customs? Do they differ from local practices, do they include them all or is it possible to identify a specific set of culinary specificities, ingredients or techniques that would clearly mark a dish or a preparation as part of a regional tradition?

Regional cookbooks are now popular, and cookbooks on Italian cuisine often arrange recipes by region. This establishes a clear organizing principle that is easy to manage and helps make sense of a dazzling cultural and material variety. For Italians, this classification is extremely practical for identifying dishes and products that are not well known or that, at any rate, do not belong to one's own traditions. One of the first recipe collections that adopted this structure was *La nuova cucina delle specialità regionali*, published in 1909 by Vittorio Agnetti. However, his classification did not cover all twenty regions that exist today, while some regions were represented only by their major cities.[11] So while Agnetti dedicated sections to Piedmont, Lombardy, Emilia Romagna and Tuscany, we find Venice instead of Veneto and Rome as representing all of Latium. Naples stood for the whole south, although the author carved out subsections dedicated to Sicily and Sardinia. The overall goal of the

The 20 contemporary regions of Italy.

volume was to show that Italy's cuisine was as diverse as its inhabitants, from 'the people from Friuli, a little like Germans' to 'Sicilians, a little like Arabs', and that for that reason food 'is far superior, for variety and deliciousness, to the well-renowned French cuisine'.[12] At a time when the newly unified kingdom was striving to assume a relevant role in international politics, Agnetti was more motivated by national pride than by the desire to explore all of Italy. This attitude towards regional cuisines became prevalent during the Fascist regime, which approved the publication of the *Guida gastronomica d'Italia* (Gastronomic Guide to Italy) in 1931 by the Touring Club of Italy.[13] As mentioned in chapter Five, the volume's goal was not to present recipes but rather to provide information for travellers and tourists, as well as to promote Italian products, 'a good nationalistic activity'.[14] The list of regions provided in the guidebook is quite similar to the ones enshrined in the 1948 constitution of the Italian Republic, with a list of specialities, dishes and wines for the provinces composing each region, frequently with mentions of products from specific cities. To this day, the volume remains a precious tool to assess the state of food production and cuisine in Italy before the major changes that swept the country during the late 1950s.

Neither of these early twentieth-century volumes nor contemporary recipe collections confronts the issue of defining what regional cuisines are, using these large categories to organize dishes and ingredients that can also be identified by more specific places of origin. For instance, books, articles or TV shows discussing Tuscany often mention *cacciucco*, the fish and shellfish stew cooked in wine, tomatoes and herbs, as a typical dish from Livorno (one of the main Tuscan cities). Can *cacciucco's* classification as a Tuscan dish highlight common traits shared with completely different traditions that also happen to be located in Tuscany, such as Lunigiana or Chianti? How are the vastly different material cultures of these areas connected to each other, other than belonging to the same administrative unit? In some cases a budding regional identity, superimposed onto diverse realities, has managed to acquire its own life. A dish like *pasta amatriciana* in Latium is now widely perceived as regional, especially by people from other places. Debates rage about its origin: was it created in Rome or in the town of Amatrice, also in Latium, where many of the *osteria* cooks came from. Other specialities, like *caponata*, a sweet-and-sour vegetable relish, and *arancine*, fried stuffed rice balls, both from Sicily, are now widely identified with the whole region rather than with specific towns or provinces. The question of their origin within the island is mostly sidestepped by focusing on their connections to the Muslims who occupied the area in the Middle Ages. This is not the case for all Sicilian dishes of Muslim derivation: couscous, for instance, is still strongly identified with western Sicily, and in particular the province of Trapani.

## NORTH AND SOUTH

Apart from regions, there are even wider geographical identifications that still operate in Italian culture, reflecting themselves in areas from gastronomy to politics. The most relevant of these classifications is the generic, but nevertheless widespread, distinction between the north and the south. This separation was originally based on the abysmal social and economic disparities between the two areas at the time of Italy's unification. These differences turned into grave issues for the kingdom and then for the republic. Beginning in the late 1950s, southern Italians tried to escape poverty and underdevelopment by moving en masse towards northern cities. In particular, the so-called 'industrial triangle' between Milan, Turin and Genoa held promises of stable jobs and modernity. Quite suddenly, workers appeared in the north who did not share the same culture, bringing exotic food-related habits, culinary techniques and unheard-of ingredients and dishes. The newcomers – frequently from rural backgrounds – were often represented as unrefined, uneducated, noisy and not greatly concerned with hygiene, but their generosity and gregariousness were also noted. Their food was perceived as abundant, intensely seasoned and closely connected with their tight-knit family lives, yet at the same time unusual and somewhat threatening. These vast generalizations drew much of their power precisely from their vagueness; they could be applied at any scale and to comment on any set of problems.

Today, decades after the epochal migration, with the former new-comers largely assimilated into the host cultures, the distinctions between the north and the south still survive, having become effective, pervasive and apparently natural categories. Especially in popular culture and media, individuals are frequently pigeonholed into specific roles that fulfil common stereotypes. The Luca Miniero box-office blockbuster *Benvenuti al sud* (Welcome to the South, 2010), the Italian remake of the French hit movie *Bienvenue chez les Ch'tis* (2008), tells the story of a post-office manager from Milan who is transferred to a little village on the coast south of Naples. Despite the breathtaking beauty of the landscape, the newcomer cannot adapt to the local way of life, and a series of misunderstandings provides abundant fodder for easy comedy. Of course, food plays a huge role in emphasizing the differences between the south and the north. Northerners are represented as more modern, with social structures organized around work and the nuclear family. While attached to their traditional products like Gorgonzola cheese, they are also open to all kinds of cosmopolitan food including sushi, presented in the film as the litmus test for culinary adventurousness. Down south, young couples with children live with their parents, matriarchs

Gorgonzola, among the most famous Italian cheeses.

have control over others' lives, food is abundant, traditional (including *sanguinaccio*, a spread made with chocolate and pig's blood), almost always prepared by hand and consumed at a slow pace in settings that favour sharing and community. Over time, the northern functionary understands the true value behind such distinctive customs and finds his place in the village. While it can be argued that the narrative resolution invites viewers to look beyond the stereotypes, most of the comic effect is actually built by exploiting – and, by default, naturalizing – them. The movie's success spawned a sequel, *Benvenuti al nord* (Welcome to the North, 2012), where the same film-maker, Luca Miniero, flips the script by sending a southern post-office worker to the north, playing on the exact same stereotypes that have underlined many Italian comedies since the 1950s. This does not imply that all Italian films embrace this approach. For instance, Francesco Rosi's amazing *Cristo si è fermato a Eboli* (Christ Stopped in Eboli, 1979), about an intellectual from the north exiled to a tiny southern village during Fascist rule, provides a more nuanced and realistic description of cultural differences and social dynamics at a specific point in time. Recently, younger film-makers from the south are looking at their own culture with a critical but affec-tionate eye, often employing satire and a hyper-realistic style that manages to achieve bizarre, dreamlike results. These films are almost implying that only by embracing the contradictions, the dramatic problems and the seeming madness of the contemporary south can viewers hope to understand it beyond any stereotype. An interesting example of this approach is Rocco Papaleo's *Basilicata Coast to Coast* (2010), which describes the voyage of four young men through Basilicata, still one of the less developed regions in Italy. By travelling on foot, the protagonists are confronted with the productive landscape of their land and with its traditional dishes, such as bread with frittata, dried peppers and *gnummareddi*, pieces of offal meat tied with lamb's intestines. Eduardo de Angelis's *Mozzarella Stories* from 2011 focuses instead on the buffalo mozzarella industry in the areas south of Naples, highlighting the political and economic problems that plague those communities, from organized crime to corruption and the impact of Chinese competitors. These films reject nostalgia, highlighting instead the changing and shifting nature of local traditions and artisanal skills, threatened and at the same made more valuable by their exposure to globalization.

For historical, economic and cultural reasons, regional cuisines are fundamentally hybrids, as culinary expert Vincenzo Buonassisi affirmed at the 1983 convention of the Gruppo Ristoratori Italiani (GRI), the Italian Restaurateur Association in the United States. He stated to all participants,

> In Italy there is no longer such a thing as truly autonomous regional cuisines. This is a romantic American notion, not a modern reality. In the modern Italy that actually exists, regional cooking is traveling from region to region.[15]

In conclusion, are culinary identities in Italy to be understood as exclusively local and fragmented or are there elements that can be identified as national and Italian? Food historian Massimo Montanari tackles the question in his book *L'identità italiana in cucina* (Italian Identity in the Kitchen). He argues that since the rebirth of city life in the late Middle Ages, a shared set of food-related tastes, styles, practices and preferences, often adopted and adapted from nearby rural environments and lower classes, circulated among the upper classes in urban environments across Italy, far away from their places of origin.

> The upper strata of society, the aristocracy and the bourgeoisie, had been living for centuries in an 'Italian' dimension that superseded the political and administrative borders of the numerous states located in the peninsula and on the islands. That is to

say, at least for some Italy already existed. It was an Italy made
of lifestyles, daily practices, mental attitudes.[16]

Montanari maintains that it is not historically sound to look for a strictly
unitary model that includes and erases differences: local diversity constitutes instead one of the fundamental traits of Italian cuisine.[17]

## FOOD AND COMMUNITY

As much as they are increasingly appreciated, traditional foods and food
customs are not excluded from the dynamics of globalization that involve
many aspects of contemporary material culture. And not all its effects are
negative. By increasing demand and prices, international exposure can
revamp or even save disappearing ingredients or dishes, even if it exposes
producers to the uncertainties and caprices of worldwide markets. The
dichotomy that opposes global versus local, homogeneity versus diversity,
and universality versus particularity, comes across as an oversimplification.
When it comes to food, it is arguable that, in many cases, local identities
are the historical result of larger trade and contact networks, and are acknowledged and defined as local against the backdrop of other, different places.
Italian food historians Alberto Capatti and Massimo Montanari state:

> In the context of culinary traditions, one might assume as self-
> evident that identity has to do with belonging to a particular
> place and that it involves the products and recipes of a specific
> location. Thinking about it like this may cause one to forget that
> identity might also – perhaps primarily – be defined as difference,
> that is, difference in relation to others. In the case of gastron-
> omy, one thing is quite clear: 'local' identity is created as a
> function of exchange, at the moment when (and to the degree
> that) a product or recipe is brought into contact with different
> systems and cultures.[18]

Following this approach, the two historians argue that it is necessary to
move the roots of identity from production to exchange, emphasizing
contamination and hybridization among localities, classes and cultures.
If we adopt this perspective, we cannot continue to consider local identities as eternal and static elements but rather cultural and social constructions
that result from relations, tensions and ongoing negotiations between

different people, the places in which they live and the power structures that sustain them. Since both the local and the global are always developing, it is useful to abandon the naive point of view that considers the local as 'natural', original, connected to biodiversity and heterogeneity, as the last defence against the homogenizing forces of globalization.[19]

The Italian debates about local identities and traditions point to the potential conundrums faced by any attempts at defining and protecting food-related products and practices, which are often embraced as tools to oppose economic standardization, hyper-exploitation of the environment and commodification of local cultures. It does not matter whether customary eating habits, typical products and artisans are not so ancient or if they have been established quite recently with little or no connection to the past. They are often perceived as the contemporary expression of a long and living history, but at the same time they are described as at risk of extinction and in need of appreciation and protection.

The defence and promotion of local and traditional foods and eating habits contributes to a renewed and enhanced sense of communal identity that can be easily manipulated for political gain. This emotional investment is easy to exploit as a rallying cry for localized activism and political interests ranging from regional to national and international levels, often on both sides of the widening rift that divides conservatives and progressives in Italy. The very current concept of *terroir*, which considers the flavours and qualities of a food as a direct result of its connection to a territory and its inhabitants, has the potential to favour intercultural dialogue that stresses diversity and integration, but can also become a weapon for xenophobic attitudes and conservative agendas aimed at protecting the territory against immigrant penetration. Local communities are frequently fiercely attached to their food traditions, which are charged with emotional significance and passionately embraced by all the actors involved. These food-related debates are born out of specific situations, calling on individuals, communities and interest groups to create new and ever-evolving local identities. Through its intimate connection with bodies and their material survival, food constitutes a perfect anchor for these cultural processes, which can then be readily enlisted in wide-reaching social and political projects.[20] Referred to in terms of satisfactory and pleasant consumption, of potential danger or even of disgust, ingestion offers a set of structured and powerful metaphors that can easily inform political discourse about acceptance or refusal of multiculturalism and acceptance of outsiders. Food allows individuals

Tortellini are commonly identified with the regional cuisine of Emilia Romagna.

to experience the material and physical reality of integration and exclusion, much more directly and compellingly than any intellectual discussion.

We have focused on the historical dynamics that throughout the centuries have shaped food in Italy, from the beginning of agricultural production to the most recent trends. It has become apparent how different populations, diverse habits and a dazzling variety of products and dishes have interacted to shape local identities, connecting what people eat with specific places but also with economic structures and power relationships. Traditions and authenticity constitute an important part of the lived experience for many people.[21] For this reason, they cannot be considered as fabricated, artificial or simply dispensable. In fact, they constitute powerful categories that can be mobilized in social and political projects.

There's more to meals than the pleasures of the table, the flavours of the ingredients and the skills of the cooks. They can help us to understand individuals and communities, cultures and societies. That is the goal of this book. I hope that next time you travel to Italy, you'll look differently at the landscapes, the people and all the amazing food you will encounter.

# References

All translations are my own unless otherwise mentioned.

## Introduction: The Food of Italy: Beyond Myths and Stereotypes

1 David Kamp, *The United States of Arugula: How We Became a Gourmet Nation* (New York, 2006).
2 Frances Mayes, *Under the Tuscan Sun* (New York, 1997), p. 192.
3 Ibid., pp. 120–21.
4 François de Salignac de la Mothe-Fénelon, *Telemachus, Son of Ulysses*, trans. Patrick Riley [1699] (Cambridge, 1994), p. 131.
5 Mayes, *Under the Tuscan Sun*, p. 189.
6 Vito Teti, *Il colore del cibo* (Rome, 1999), pp. 33–45.
7 Barbara Haber, 'The Mediterranean Diet: A View from History', *American Journal of Clinical Nutrition*, 10 (1997), pp. 1053s–7s.
8 Marion Nestle, 'Mediterranean Diets: Historical and Research Overview', *American Journal of Clinical Nutrition*, 61 (1995), pp. 1313s–20s.
9 Patricia Crotty, 'The Mediterranean Diet as a Food Guide: The Problem of Culture and History', *Nutrition Today*, XXXIII/6 (1998), pp. 227–32.
10 Intergovernmental Committee for the Safeguarding of the Intangible Cultural Heritage, Fifth session Nairobi, Kenya November 2010, Nomination File No. 00394 for inscription on the Representative List of the Intangible Cultural Heritage in 2010, p. 7.
11 Massimo Mazzotti, 'Enlightened Mills: Mechanizing Olive Oil Production in Mediterranean Europe', *Technology and Culture*, XLV/2 (2004), pp. 277–304; Anne Meneley, 'Like an Extra Virgin', *American Anthropologist*, CIX/4 (2007), pp. 678–87; Tom Mueller, *Extra Virginity: The Sublime and Scandalous World of Olive Oil* (New York, 2012).
12 *New Yorker* (11 and 18 July 2011), p. CV3.
13 Barbara Kirshenblatt-Gimblett, 'Theorizing Heritage', *Ethnomusicology*, XXXIX/3 (1995), p. 369.
14 Eric Hobsbawm and Terence Ranger, eds, *The Invention of Tradition* (Cambridge, 1983), p. 1.
15 Information on the *presidia* can be found at www.slowfoodfoundation.com.
16 Alison Leitch, 'The Social Life of Lardo: Slow Food in Fast Times', *Asian Pacific Journal of Anthropology*, I/1 (2000), pp. 103–28; Fabio Parasecoli,

'Postrevolutionary Chowhounds: Food, Globalization, and the Italian Left', *Gastronomica*, III/3 (2003), pp. 29–39.

17 Alberto Capatti and Massimo Montanari, *Italian Cuisine: A Cultural History* (New York, 2003), p. xiv.

18 Peter Garnsey, *Food and Society in Classical Antiquity* (Cambridge, 1999), p. 5.

ONE: A Land in the Mediterranean

1 Marcel Mazoyer and Laurence Roudart, *A History of World Agriculture: From the Neolithic Age to the Current Crisis* (New York, 2006), pp. 71–100; Ian Morris, *Why the West Rules – for Now: The Patterns of History and What They Reveal about the Future* (New York, 2011), pp. 89–105.

2 Jared Diamond, *Guns, Germs, and Steel* (New York, 1997), p. 124.

3 Ron Pinhasi, Joaquim Fort and Albert Ammerman, 'Tracing the Origin and Spread of Agriculture in Europe', PLOS *Biology*, III/12 (2005), p. e410.

4 C. Hunt, C. Malone, J. Sevink and S. Stoddart, 'Environment, Soils and Early Agriculture in Apennine Central Italy,' *World Archaeology*, XXII/1 (1990), pp. 34–44; T. Douglas Price, ed., *Europe's First Farmers* (Cambridge, 2000).

5 Emilio Sereni, *History of the Italian Agricultural Landscape* (Princeton, NJ, 1997), p. 17.

6 John Robb and Doortje Van Hove, 'Gardening, Foraging and Herding: Neolithic Land Use and Social Territories in Southern Italy', *Antiquity*, 77 (2003), pp. 241–54.

7 Umberto Albarella, Antonio Tagliacozzo, Keith Dobney and Peter Rowley-Conwy, 'Pig Hunting and Husbandry in Prehistoric Italy: A Contribution to the Domestication Debate', *Proceedings of the Prehistoric Society*, 72 (2006), pp. 193–227.

8 Fernand Braudel, *Memory and the Mediterranean* (New York, 2001), pp. 111, 139–41.

9 Maria Bernabò Brea, Andrea Cardarelli and Mauro Cremaschi, eds, *Le terre-mare, la più antica civiltà padana* (Milan, 1997).

10 Mauro Cremaschi, Chiara Pizzi and Veruska Valsecchi, 'Water Management and Land Use in the Terramare and a Possible Climatic Co-factor in their Abandonment: The Case Study of the Terramara of Poviglio Santa Rosa (Northern Italy)', *Quaternary International*, CLI/1 (2006), pp. 87–98.

11 Sabatino Moscati, *Così nacque l'Italia: profili di popoli riscoperti* (Turin, 1998).

12 Robert Leighton, *Sicily before History: An Archaeological Survey from the Paleolithic to the Iron Age* (Ithaca, 1999), pp. 203–6.

13 Robert Leighton, 'Later Prehistoric Settlement Patterns in Sicily: Old Paradigms and New Surveys', *European Journal of Archaeology*, VIII/3 (2005), pp. 261–87.

14 Anna Grazia Russu, 'Power and Social Structure in Nuragic Sardinia', *Eliten in der Bronzezeit-Ergebnisse Zweier Kolloquien in Mainz und Athen-Teil*, 1 (1999), pp. 197–221, plates 17–22; Gary Webster, *Duos Nuraghes: A Bronze Age Settlement in Sardinia*: vol. 1: *The Interpretive Archaeology, Bar International Series 949* (Oxford, 2001), pp. 43, 48.

15 J. M. Roberts, *The Penguin History of the World* (London, 1995): pp. 85–90.

16 Morris, *Why the West Rules*, pp. 215–20.

17 Braudel, *Memory*, p. 179.

18 Massimo Pallottino, *The Etruscans* (Bloomington, 1975), p. 75.

19 Robert Beekes, 'The Prehistory of the Lydians, the Origin of the Etruscans, Troy and Aeneas', *Biblioteca Orientalis*, LIX/3–4 (2002), pp. 205–41.

20 Alessandro Achilli et al., 'Mitochondrial DNA Variation of Modern Tuscans Supports the Near Eastern Origin of Etruscans', *American Journal of Human Genetics*, LXXX/4 (2007), pp. 759–68; Cristiano Vernesi et al., 'The Etruscans: A Population-Genetic Study', *American Journal of Human Genetics*, LXXIV/4 (2004), pp. 694–704.

21 Marco Pellecchia et al., 'The Mystery of Etruscan Origins: Novel Clues from Bos Taurus Mitochondrial DNA', *Proceedings of the Royal Society B*, CCLXXIV/1614 (2007), pp. 1175–9.

22 Braudel, *Memory*, p. 201; Massimo Pallottino, *A History of Earliest Italy* (Ann Arbor, MI, 1991), p. 53.

23 Jodi Magness, 'A Near Eastern Ethnic Element among the Etruscan Elite?', *Etruscan Studies*, VIII/4 (2001), pp. 80–82.

24 Mauro Cristofani, 'Economia e societa', in *Rasenna: storia e civiltà degli Etruschi*, ed. Massimo Pallottino et al. (Milan 1986), pp. 79–156.

25 Daphne Nash Briggs, 'Metals, Salt, and Slaves: Economic Links between Gaul and Italy from the Eighth to the Late Sixth Centuries BC', *Oxford Journal of Archaeology*, XXII/3 (2003), pp. 243–59.

26 Diodorus Siculus, *Bibliotheca Historica* 5.40.3–5.

27 Catullus, *Poems* 39.11; Virgil, *Georgics* 2.194.

28 Anthony Tuck, 'The Etruscan Seated Banquet: Villanovan Ritual and Etruscan Iconography', *American Journal of Archaeology*, XCVIII/4 (1994), pp. 617–28.

29 Lisa Pieraccini, 'Families, Feasting, and Funerals: Funerary Ritual at Ancient Caere', *Etruscan Studies*, 7 (2000), Article 3.

30 Jocelyn Penny Small, 'Eat, Drink, and Be Merry: Etruscan Banquets', in *Murlo and the Etruscans: Art and Society in Ancient Etruria*, ed. Richard Daniel De Puma and Jocelyn Penny Small (Madison, WI, 1994), pp. 85–94.

31 Daphne Nash Briggs, 'Servants at a Rich Man's Feast: Early Etruscan Household Slaves and Their Procurement', *Etruscan Studies*, 9 (2002), Article 14; Giovanni Camporeale, 'Vita private', in *Rasenna: storia e civiltà degli Etruschi*, ed. Massimo Pallottino et al. (Milan, 1986), pp. 239–308.

32 Gregory Warden, 'Ritual and Representation on a Campana Dinos in Boston', *Etruscan Studies*, 11 (2008), Article 8.

33 Adrian Paul Harrison and E. M. Bartels, 'A Modern Appraisal of Ancient Etruscan Herbal Practices', *American Journal of Pharmacology and Toxicology*, I/1 (2006), pp. 21–4; Gianni Race, *La cucina del mondo classico* (Napoli, 1999), pp. 143–6.

34 Jean and Eve Gran-Aymerich, 'Les Etrusques en Gaule et en Iberie: Du Mythe a la Realite des Dernieres Decouvertes', *Etruscan Studies*, 9 (2002), Article 17.

35 Braudel, *Memory*, p. 181.

36 Leighton, *Sicily*, p. 230.

37 Braudel, *Memory*, p. 192.

38 Valerio Manfredi, *I greci d'Occidente* (Milan, 1996), p. 72.

39 Pliny, *Naturalis Historia* 18.5; Varro, *De Re Rustica* 1.1.10.

40 Columella, *De Re Rustica* 1.1.13; Braudel, *Memory*, p. 196; Columella, *De Re Rustica* 12.39.1–2.

41 Pliny the Elder, *Historia Naturalis* 18.51.188

42 Braudel, *Memory*, p. 191; Susan and Andrew Sherratt, 'The Growth of the Mediterranean Economy in the Early First Millennium BC', *World Archaeology*, XXIV/3 (1993), pp. 361–78.

43 Richard J. Clifford, 'Phoenician Religion', *Bulletin of the American Schools of Oriental Research,* 279 (1990), p. 58.

44 Antonella Spanò Giammellaro, 'The Phoenicians and the Carthaginians: The Early Mediterranean Diet', in *Food: A Culinary History from Antiquity to the Present*, ed. Jean-Louis Flandrin and Massimo Montanari (New York, 1999), pp. 55–64.

45 Sherratt and Sherratt, 'The Growth of the Mediterranean Economy'; Sally Grainger, 'A New Approach to Roman Fish Sauce', *Petits Propos Culinaires*, 83 (2007), pp. 92–111.

46 David S. Reese, 'Whale Bones and Shell Purple-dye at Motya (Western Sicily, Italy)', *Oxford Journal of Archaeology*, XXIV/2 (2005), pp. 107–14.

47 Robert Roesti, 'The Declining Economic Role of the Mediterranean Tuna Fishery', *American Journal of Economics and Sociology*, XXV/1 (1966), pp. 77–90; Rob Van Ginkel, 'Killing Giants of the Sea: Contentious Heritage and the Politics of Culture', *Journal of Mediterranean Studies*, XV/1 (2005), pp. 71–98.

48 Hesiod, *Works and Days* 306–13, 458–64, 586–96, 609–14.

49 Peter Garnsey, *Food and Society in Classical Antiquity* (Cambridge, 1999), p. 2.

50 Marie-Claire Amouretti, 'Urban and Rural Diets in Greece', in *Food: A Culinary History from Antiquity to the Present*, ed. Jean-Louis Flandrin and Massimo Montanari (New York, 1999), pp. 79–89; Garnsey, *Food*, pp. 6, 65.

51 Massimo Montanari, 'Food Systems and Models of Civilization', in *Food: A Culinary History from Antiquity to the Present*, ed. Jean-Louis Flandrin and Massimo Montanari (New York, 1999), pp. 55–64.

52 Andrew Dalby, *Siren Feasts: A History of Food and Gastronomy in Greece* (London, 1996), p. 6.

53 Pauline Schmitt-Pantel, 'Greek Meals: A Civic Ritual', in *Food: A Culinary History from Antiquity to the Present*, ed. Jean-Louis Flandrin and Massimo Montanari (New York, 1999), pp. 90–95.

54 Robert I. Curtis, 'Professional Cooking, Kitchens, and Service Work', in *A Cultural History of Food in Antiquity*, ed. Fabio Parasecoli and Peter Scholliers (London, 2012), pp. 113–32.

55 Massimo Vetta, 'The Culture of the Symposium', in *Food: A Culinary History from Antiquity to the Present*, ed. Jean-Louis Flandrin and Massimo Montanari, (New York, 1999), pp. 96–105.

56 Domenico Musti, *L'economia in Grecia* (Bari, 1999), pp. 88–94.

57 Manfredi, *I greci*, pp. 18–19, 99.

58 Ibid., pp. 214, 221, 229.

59 Leighton, *Sicily*, pp. 234–42.

60 Sereni, *History*, p. 22.

61 Franco De Angelis, 'Trade and Agriculture at Megara Hyblaia', *Oxford Journal of*

*Archaeology*, xxi/3 (2002), pp. 299–310; Franco De Angelis, 'Going against the Grain in Sicilian Greek Economics', *Greece and Rome*, liii/1 (2006), pp. 29–47; Robin Osborne, 'Pots, Trade, and the Archaic Greek Economy', *Antiquity*, 70 (1996), pp. 31–44.

62 Plato, *Gorgias* 518b; Athenaeus, *The Deipnosophists* 325f.

63 Dalby, *Siren Feasts*, p. 110.

64 Race, *La cucina*, p. 51.

65 Chadwick, *The Celts*, p. 30.

66 Ibid., p. 41.

67 Venceslas Kruta and Valerio M. Manfredi, *I Celti in Italia* (Milan, 1999), p. 51.

68 Ibid., p. 11.

69 Chadwick, *The Celts*, pp. 46, 141.

70 Peter J. Reynolds, 'Rural Life and Farming', in *The Celtic World*, ed. Miranda Green (New York, 1995), pp. 176–209.

71 Kruta and Manfredi, *I Celti*, p. 10.

72 Paolo Galloni, *Storia e cultura della caccia: dalla preistoria a oggi* (Bari, 2000), pp. 86–8.

73 Mark Kurlansky, *Salt: A World History* (New York, 2002), p. 65.

74 Ibid., p. 93.

75 Kruta and Manfredi, *I Celti*, p. 59.

76 Antonietta Dosi and François Schnell, *Le abitudini alimentari dei Romani* (Rome, 1992), p. 13.

77 Kimberly B. Flint-Hamilton, 'Legumes in Ancient Greece and Rome: Food, Medicine, or Poison?', *Hesperia: The Journal of the American School of Classical Studies at Athens*, lxviii/3 (1999), pp. 371–85.

78 Paul Halstead, 'Food Production', in *A Cultural History of Food in Antiquity*, ed. Fabio Parasecoli and Peter Scholliers (London, 2012), pp. 21–39.

79 Dosi and Schnell, *Le abitudini*, p. 17.

80 Florence Dupont, 'The Grammar of Roman Food', in *Food: A Culinary History from Antiquity to the Present*, ed. Jean-Louis Flandrin and Massimo Montanari (New York, 1999), pp. 113–27.

81 Valerie Huet, 'Le sacrifice disparu: les reliefs de boucherie', *Food and History*, v/1 (2007), pp. 197–223; Nicholas Tran, 'Le statut de travail des bouchers dans l'Occident romain de la fin de la Republique et du Haut-Empire', *Food and History*, v/1 (2007), pp. 151–67.

82 Galloni, *Storia*, pp. 71–4.

83 Brian Fagan, *Fish on Friday: Feasting, Fasting, and the Discovery of the New World* (New York, 2006), p. 7.

84 Race, *La cucina*, pp. 221–30.

85 Claire De Ruyt, 'Les produits vendus au macellum', *Food and History*, v/1 (2007), pp. 135–50.

86 Nicole Belayche, 'Religion et consommation de la viande dans le monde romain: des réalités voilées', *Food and History*, v/1 (2007), pp. 29–43; John Scheid, 'Le statut de la viande à Rome', *Food and History*, v/1 (2007), pp. 19–28.

87 Steven J. R. Ellis, 'Eating and Drinking Out', in *A Cultural History of Food in Antiquity*, ed. Fabio Parasecoli and Peter Scholliers (London, 2012), pp. 111–12.

88 Robin Nadeau, 'Stratégies de survie et rituels festifs dans le monde gréco-romain',

in *Profusion et pénurie: les hommes face à leurs besoins alimentaires*, ed. Martin Bruegel (Rennes, 2009), pp. 55–69.

89 Antonietta Dosi and François Schnell, *I Romani in cucina* (Rome, 1992), pp. 93–121.

90 Dosi Antonietta and François Schnell, *Pasti e vasellame da tavola* (Rome, 1992), p. 12.

91 Dosi and Schnell, *I Romani*, pp. 108–15.

92 J.H.C. Williams, *Beyond the Rubicon: Romans and Gauls in Republican Italy* (Oxford, 2001).

93 Emilio Sereni, 'Agricoltura e mondo rurale', in *Storia d'Italia: I caratteri originali*, vol. 1, eds Ruggiero Romano and Corrado Vivanti (Turin, 1989), pp. 143–5.

94 Ellen Churchill Semple, 'Geographic Factors in the Ancient Mediterranean Grain Trade', *Annals of the Association of American Geographers*, 11 (1921), p. 73.

95 Paul Erdkamp, *The Grain Market in the Roman Empire: A Social, Political and Economic Study* (Cambridge, 2005).

96 Dosi and Schnell, *Le abitudini*, pp. 43–7.

97 Paul Erdkamp, *Hunger and the Sword: Warfare and Food Supply in Roman Republican Wars (264–30 BC)* (Amsterdam, 1998).

98 Dalby, *Siren Feasts*, p. 198.

99 James Innes Miller, *The Spice Trade of the Roman Empire, 29 BC to AD 641* [1969] (Oxford, 1998).

100 Garnsey, *Food*, p. 23.

101 Horace, *Satires* 2.6.77–115.

102 Stéphane Solier, 'Manières de tyran à la table de la satire latine: l'institutionnalisation de l'excès dans la convivialité romaine', *Food and History*, iv/2 (2006), pp. 91–111.

103 Christophe Badel, 'Ivresse et ivrognerie à Rome (iie s av. J.-C. - iiie s ap. J.-C.)', *Food and History*, iv/2 (2006), p. 75–89.

104 Dosi and Schnell, *Le abitudini*, pp. 113–18.

105 Elizabeth Ann Pollard, 'Pliny's Natural History and the Flavian Templum Pacis: Botanical Imperialism in First-Century CE Rome', *Journal of World History*, xx/3 (2009), pp. 311.

106 Deborah Ruscillo, 'When Gluttony Ruled!', *Archaeology*, liv/6 (2001), pp. 20–24; John H. D'Arms, 'The Culinary Reality of Roman Upper-class Convivia: Integrating Texts and Images', *Comparative Studies in Society and History*, xlvi/3 (2004), pp. 428–50.

107 Konrad I. Vössing, 'Family and Domesticity', in *A Cultural History of Food in Antiquity*, ed. Fabio Parasecoli and Peter Scholliers (London, 2012), pp. 133–43.

108 Dosi and Schnell, *Pasti*, pp. 24–6.

109 Roy Strong, *Feast: A History of Grand Eating* (Orlando, 2002), p. 29.

110 Petronius, *Satyricon* 31–70.

111 Christopher Grocock, Sally Grainger and Dan Shadrake, *Apicius: A Critical Edition with an Introduction and English Translation* (Totnes, 2006).

112 Curtis, 'Professional Cooking', pp. 113–32.

113 Apicius, *Cooking and Dining in Imperial Rome*, trans. Joseph Dommers Vehling (Chicago, 1936), available at www.gutenberg.org.

114 Robin Nadeau, 'Body and Soul', in *A Cultural History of Food in Antiquity*, ed. Parasecoli and Scholliers, pp. 145–62.

115 Garnsey, *Food*, p. 110.

116 Gillian Feeley-Harnik, *The Lord's Table: The Meaning of Food in Early Judaism and Christianity* (Washington and London, 1994), pp. 153–64.

117 Wim Broekaert and Arjan Zuiderhoek, 'Food Systems in Classic Antiquity', in *A Cultural History of Food in Antiquity*, ed. Parasecoli and Scholliers, pp. 75–93.

118 Paul Erdkamp, 'Food Security, Safety, and Crises', in *A Cultural History of Food in Antiquity*, ed. Parasecoli and Scholliers, pp. 57–74.

119 Wim Broekaert and Arjan Zuiderhoek, 'Food and Politics in Classic Antiquity', in *A Cultural History of Food in Antiquity*, ed. Parasecoli and Scholliers, pp. 41–55; Garnsey, *Food*, pp. 30–33.

120 Broekaert and Zuiderhoek, 'Food Systems', p. 48.

121 Steven J. R. Ellis, 'The Pompeian Bar: Archaeology and the Role of Food and Drink Outlets in an Ancient Community', *Food and History*, II/1 (2004), pp. 41–58.

122 Dosi and Schnell, *Pasti*, pp. 36–58.

## TWO: Invaders

1 Jairus Banaji, *Agrarian Change in Late Antiquity: Gold, Labour, and Aristocratic Dominance* (Oxford, 2007).

2 Lin Foxhall, 'The Dependent Tenant: Land Leasing and Labour in Italy and Greece,' *Journal of Roman Studies*, 80 (1990), pp. 97–114.

3 Emilio Sereni, 'Agricoltura e mondo rurale', in *Storia d'Italia: I caratteri originali*, vol. I, ed. Ruggiero Romano and Corrado Vivanti (Turin, 1989), pp. 146–8.

4 Paolo Galloni, *Storia e cultura della caccia: dalla preistoria a oggi* (Bari, 2000), pp. 74–84.

5 Girolamo Arnaldi, *Italy and Its Invaders* (Cambridge, MA, 2005), p. 15.

6 Massimo Montanari, *Convivio* (Bari, 1989), p. 208.

7 Emilio Sereni, *History of the Italian Agricultural Landscape* (Princeton, NJ, 1997), pp. 58–61.

8 Alfio Cortonesi, 'Food Production', in *A Cultural History of Food: In the Medieval Age*, ed. Fabio Parasecoli and Peter Scholliers (Oxford, 2012), p. 22.

9 Galloni, *Storia*, pp. 93–109.

10 Lars Brownworth, *Lost to the West* (New York, 2009), pp. 67–113.

11 Arnaldi, *Italy*, p. 28.

12 Peter Charanis, 'Ethnic Changes in the Byzantine Empire in the Seventh Century', *Dumbarton Oaks Papers*, 13 (1959), pp. 23–44.

13 Lynn White, 'The Byzantinization of Sicily', *American Historical Review*, XLII/1 (1936), pp. 1–21.

14 Ann Wharton Epstein, 'The Problem of Provincialism: Byzantine Monasteries in Cappadocia and Monks in South Italy', *Journal of the Warburg and Courtauld Institutes*, 42 (1979), pp. 28–46.

15 Giovanni Haussmann, 'Il suolo d'Italia nella storia', in *Storia d'Italia: I caratteri original*, vol. I, ed. Ruggiero Romano and Corrado Vivanti (Turin, 1989), p. 79.

16 St Benedict, *Rule* 35.

17 St Benedict, *Rule* 39.

18 St Benedict, *Rule* 40.

19 Brian Fagan, *Fish on Friday: Feasting, Fasting, and the Discovery of the New World* (New York, 2006), p. 23.

20 Andrew Dalby, *Siren Feasts: A History of Food and Gastronomy in Greece* (London, 1996), p. 197.

21 Neil Christie, 'Byzantine Liguria: An Imperial Province against the Longobards, AD 568–643', *Papers of the British School at Rome*, 58 (1990), pp. 229–71.

22 Peter Sarris, 'Aristocrats, Peasants and the Transformation of Rural Society, *c.* 400–800', *Journal of Agrarian Change*, IX/1 (2009), p. 15.

23 Thomas Brown and Neil Christie, 'Was There a Byzantine Model of Settlement in Italy?', *Melanges de l'École francaise de Rome. Moyen-Age, Temps modernes*, CI/2 (1989), pp. 377–99.

24 Pere Benito, 'Food Systems', in *A Cultural History of Food: In the Medieval Age*, ed. Fabio Parasecoli and Peter Scholliers (Oxford, 2012), p. 52.

25 Daron Acemoglu and James A. Robinson, *Why Nations Fail: The Origin of Power, Prosperity, and Poverty* (New York, 2012), pp. 151–2.

26 Armand O. Citarella, 'Patterns in Medieval Trade: The Commerce of Amalfi before the Crusades', *Journal of Economic History*, XXVIII/4 (1968), pp. 531–55; Barbara M. Kreutz, 'Ghost Ships and Phantom Cargoes: Reconstructing Early Amalfitan Trade', *Journal of Medieval History*, 20 (1994), pp. 347–57; Patricia Skinner, *Family Power in Southern Italy: The Duchy of Gaeta and Its Neighbors, 850–1139* (Cambridge, MA, 1995).

27 Marios Costambeys, 'Settlement, Taxation and the Condition of the Peasantry in Post-Roman Central Italy', *Journal of Agrarian Change*, IX/1 (2009), pp. 92–119.

28 Lynn White Jr, 'Indic Elements in the Iconography of Petrarch's Trionfo Della Morte', *Speculum*, 49 (1974), pp. 204–5; ANASB, 'Le origini del bufalo', www.anasb.it.

29 André Guillou, 'Production and Profits in the Byzantine Province of Italy (Tenth to Eleventh Centuries): An Expanding Society', *Dumbarton Oaks Papers*, 28 (1974), p. 92.

30 John L. Teall, 'The Grain Supply of the Byzantine Empire, 330–1025', *Dumbarton Oaks Papers*, 13 (1959), pp. 137–8.

31 Dalby, *Siren Feasts*, pp. 189–99.

32 Anthony Bryer, 'Byzantine Agricultural Implements: The Evidence of Medieval Illustrations of Hesiod's "Works and Days"', *Annual of the British School at Athens*, 81 (1986), pp. 45–80.

33 Sereni, *History*, p. 49.

34 Arnaldi, *Italy*, p. 59.

35 Einhard, *Vita Karoli Magni*, (Hannover and Lipsia, 1905), p. 24, available at http://archive.org/stream.

36 Galloni, *Storia*, pp. 109–24.

37 Yann Grappe, *Sulle Tracce del Gusto: Storia e cultura del vino nel Medievo* (Bari, 2006), pp. 6–10.

38 Sereni, *History*, p. 69.

39 Massimo Montanari, 'Production Structures and Food Systems in the Early

Middle Ages', in *Food: A Culinary History from Antiquity to the Present*, ed. Jean-Louis Flandrin and Massimo Montanari (New York, 1999), pp. 168–77.

40 Montanari, *Convivio*, p. 255.

41 Giuliano Pinto, 'Food Safety', in *A Cultural History of Food: In the Medieval Age*, ed. Parasecoli and Scholliers, pp. 57–64.

42 Fagan, *Fish*, pp. 10–11.

43 Anthimus, *De observatione ciborum epistula ad Theudericum, regem Francorum. Bibliotheca scriptorum Graecorum et Romanorum Teubneriana*, ed. Valentin Rose (Lipsia, 1877).

44 *The Holy Rule of St Benedict*, trans. Rev. Boniface Verheyen, OSB (Atchison, KS, 1949).

45 Andrew Watson, *Agricultural Innovation in the Early Islamic World* (Cambridge, 1983); Michael Decker, 'Plants and Progress: Rethinking the Islamic Agricultural Revolution', *Journal of World History*, XX/2 (2009), pp. 197–206.

46 Clifford A. Wright, *A Mediterranean Feast* (New York, 1999).

47 Charles Perry, 'Sicilian Cheese in Medieval Arab Recipes', *Gastronomica*, I/I (2001), pp. 76–7.

48 Manuela Marìn, 'Beyond Taste', in *A Taste of Thyme: Culinary Cultures of the Middle East*, ed. Sami Zubaida and Richard Tapper (London, 2000), pp. 205–14.

49 Lilia Zaouali, *Medieval Cuisine of the Islamic World* (Berkeley, CA, 2007).

50 Janet L. Abu-Lughod, *Before European Hegemony: The World System, AD 1250–1350* (New York and Oxford, 1989); George F. Hourani, *Arab Seafaring in the Indian Ocean and In Ancient and Early Medieval Times* (Princeton, NJ, 1995).

51 Arnaldi, *Italy*, p. 71.

52 Francesco Gabrieli, 'Greeks and Arabs in the Central Mediterranean Area', *Dumbarton Oaks Papers*, 18 (1964), pp. 57–65.

53 Mohamed Ouerfelli, 'Production et commerce du sucre en Sicile au XVe siècle', *Food and History*, I/I (2003), p. 105.

54 David Abulafia, 'Pisan Commercial Colonies and Consulates in Twelfth-century Sicily', *English Historical Review*, XCIII/366 (1978), pp. 68–81.

55 David Abulafia, 'The Crown and the Economy under Roger II and his Successors', *Dumbarton Oaks Papers*, 37 (1983), pp. 1–14.

THREE: Rebirth

1 Giovanni Ceccarelli, Alberto Grandi and Stefano Magagnoli, 'The "Taste" of Typicality', *Food and History*, VIII/2 (2010), pp. 45–76.

2 Giovanni Boccaccio, *The Decameron*, Eighth Day, Novella 3; Pina Palma, 'Hermits, Husband and Lovers: Moderation and Excesses at the Table in the *Decameron*', *Food and History*, IV/2 (2006), pp. 151–62.

3 Emilio Sereni, *History of the Italian Agricultural Landscape* (Princeton, NJ, 1997), p. 114.

4 Ibid., pp. 81–6.

5 Ibid., p. 99, 110.

6 Pere Benito, 'Food Systems', in *A Cultural History of Food: In the Medieval Age*, ed. Fabio Parasecoli and Peter Scholliers (Oxford, 2012), p. 42.

7 Eric E. Dursteler, 'Food and Politics', in *A Cultural History of Food: In the Renaissance*, ed. Fabio Parasecoli and Peter Scholliers (London, 2012), pp. 84–5.

8 Silvano Serventi and Françoise Sabban, *Pasta: The Story of a Universal Food* (New York, 2002), pp. 9–62.

9 Evelyn Welch, *Shopping in the Renaissance: Consumer Cultures in Italy 1400–1600* (New Haven and London, 2005), pp. 70–103.

10 Federica Badiali, *Cucina medioevale italiana* (Bologna, 1999); Allen J. Grieco, 'Body and Soul', in *A Cultural History of Food: In the Medieval Age*, ed. Parasecoli and Scholliers, pp. 143–9.

11 Yann Grappe, *Sulle Tracce del Gusto: Storia e cultura del vino nel Medievo* (Bari, 2006), pp. 71–7.

12 Mohamed Ouerfelli, 'Production et commerce du sucre en Sicile au xve siècle', *Food and History*, 1/1 (2003), pp. 105–6.

13 Giuseppe Sperduti, *Riccardo di San Germano: La Cronaca* (Cassino, 1995), pp. 138–45.

14 Joshua Starr, 'The Mass Conversion of Jews in Southern Italy (1290–1293)', *Speculum*, xxi/2 (1946), pp. 203–11; Nadia Zeldes, 'Legal Status of Jewish Converts to Christianity in Southern Italy and Provence', *California Italian Studies Journal*, 1/1(2010), available at http://escholarship.org.

15 Sereni, *History*, p. 126.

16 Daron Acemoglu and James A. Robinson, *Why Nations Fail: The Origin of Power, Prosperity, and Poverty* (New York, 2012), pp. 155–6; E. Ashtor, 'Profits from Trade with the Levant in the Fifteenth Century', *Bulletin of the School of Oriental and African Studies*, xxxviii/2 (1975), pp. 250–75.

17 Sereni, *History*, p. 97.

18 Ibid., pp. 133–9.

19 Welch, *Shopping*, pp. 2–11.

20 Ibid., pp. 32–55.

21 Lino Turrini, *La cucina ai tempi dei Gonzaga* (Milan, 2002).

22 Jeremy Parzen, 'Please Play with Your Food: An Incomplete Survey of Culinary Wonders in Italian Renaissance Cookery', *Gastronomica*, iv/4 (2004), pp. 25–33.

23 Muriel Badet, 'Piero di Cosimo: d'une iconographie à l'autre. Rapt, repas de noce et pique-nique pour l'Enlèvement d'Hippodamie', *Food and History*, iv/1 (2006), pp. 147–67; John Varriano, 'At Supper with Leonardo', *Gastronomica*, viii/3 (2008), pp. 75–9; John Varriano, *Tastes and Temptations: Food and Art in Renaissance Italy* (Berkeley, CA, 2011); Gillian Riley, 'Food in Painting', in *A Cultural History of Food: In the Renaissance*, ed. Fabio Parasecoli and Peter Scholliers (London, 2012), pp. 171–82.

24 Antonella Campanini, 'La table sous contrôle: Les banquets et l'excès alimentaire dans le cadre des lois somptuaires en Italie entre le Moyen Âge et la Renaissance', *Food and History*, iv/2 (2006), pp. 131–50.

25 Ken Albala, *Food in Early Modern Europe* (Westport, CT, 2003), pp. 107–12.

26 Massimo Montanari, *Convivio* (Bari, 1989), pp. 363–8.

27 Darra Goldstein, 'Implements of Eating', in *Feeding Desire: Design and the Tools of the Table, 1500–2005*, ed. Sarah D. Coffin, Ellen Lupton, Darra Goldstein and Barbara Bloemink (New York, 2006), p. 118.

28 Daniele Alexandre-Bidon, 'La cigale et la fourmi: Céramique et conservation

des aliments et des médicaments (Moyen Age–XVI siècle)', in *Profusion et Pénurie: les hommes face à leurs besoins alimentaires*, ed. Martin Bruegel (Rennes, 2009), pp. 71–84.

29  Wendy Watson, *Italian Renaissance Ceramics* (Philadelphia, 2006).

30  Catherine Hess, George Saliba and Linda Komaroff, *The Arts of Fire: Islamic Influences on Glass and Ceramics of the Italian Renaissance* (Los Angeles, 2004).

31  Aldo Bova, *L'avventura del vetro dal Rinascimento al Novecento tra Venezia e mondi lontani* (Geneva, 2010).

32  Jutta-Annette Page, *Beyond Venice: Glass in Venetian Style, 1500–1750* (Manchester, VT, 2004).

33  Margaret Gallucci and Paolo Rossi, *Benvenuto Cellini: Sculptor, Goldsmith, Writer* (Cambridge, 2004).

34  Albala, *Food*, pp. 115–21.

35  Ariel Toaff, *Mangiare alla giudia* (Bologna, 2000), p. 67.

36  Jean François Revel, *Culture and Cuisine: A Journey through the History of Food* (New York, 1982), pp. 117–20.

37  Giovanna Giusti Galardi, *Dolci a corte: dipinti ed altro* (Livorno, 2001).

38  Grappe, *Sulle Tracce*, pp. 13–14; Luisa Cogliati Arano, *The Medieval Health Handbook: Tacuinum Sanitatis* (New York, 1976).

39  Montanari, *Convivio*, pp. 267–8.

40  Luciano Mauro and Paola Valitutti, *Il Giardino della Minerva* (Salerno, 2011).

41  Kenneth D. Keele, 'Leonardo da Vinci's Studies of the Alimentary Tract', *Journal of the History of Medicine*, XXVII/2 (1972), pp. 133–44.

42  Ken Albala, *Eating Right in the Renaissance* (Berkeley and Los Angeles, 2002), pp. 14–47.

43  Alberto Capatti and Massimo Montanari, *Italian Cuisine: A Cultural History* (New York, 2003), p. 9; Nancy Harmon Jenkins, 'Two Ways of Looking at Maestro Martino', *Gastronomica*, VII/2 (2007), pp. 97–103; Maestro Martino, *The Art of Cooking: The First Modern Cookery Book* (Berkeley and Los Angeles, 2005).

44  Laura Giannetti, 'Italian Renaissance Food-Fashioning or The Triumph of Greens', *California Italian Studies*, I/2 (2010), available at http://escholarship.org; Giovanna Bosi, Anna Maria Mercuri, Chiara Guarnieri and Marta Bandini Mazzanti, 'Luxury Food and Ornamental Plants at the 15th Century AD Renaissance Court of the Este Family (Ferrara, Northern Italy)', *Vegetation History and Archaeobotany*, XVIII/5 (2009), pp. 389–402.

45  David Gentilcore, *Pomodoro: A History of the Tomato in Italy* (New York, 2010), p. 32.

46  John Varriano, 'Fruits and Vegetables as Sexual Metaphor in Late Renaissance Rome', *Gastronomica*, V/4 (2005), pp. 8–14.

47  Montanari, *Convivio*, p. 504.

48  Maestro Martino, *The Art of Cooking*, p. 17; Jenkins, 'Two Ways', p. 97.

49  Cristoforo di Messisbugo, *Banchetti, compositioni di vivande et apparecchio generale* (Ferrara, 1549), p. 20. Available at http://books.google.com.

50  *The Opera of Bartolomeo Scappi (1570)*, trans. Terence Scully (Toronto, 2008); June di Schino and Furio Luccichenti, *Il cuoco segreto dei papi – Bartolomeo Scappi e la Confraternita dei cuochi e dei pasticceri* (Rome, 2008).

51 Bartolomeo Scappi, *Opera* (Venezia, 1570), p. 2. Available at http://archive.org.
52 Capatti and Montanari, *Italian Cuisine*, p. 13.
53 Albala, *Food*, pp. 122–33.
54 Ibid., pp. 89–99.
55 Alison A. Smith, 'Family and Domesticity', in *A Cultural History of Food: In the Renaissance*, ed. Parasecoli and Scholliers, p. 138.
56 Serventi and Sabban, *Pasta*, pp. 63–90.
57 Claudia Roden, *The Book of Jewish Food* (New York, 1998), p. 479.
58 Toaff, *Mangiare*, p. 17.
59 Henry Kamen, 'The Mediterranean and the Expulsion of Spanish Jews in 1492', *Past and Present*, CXIX/1 (1988), pp. 30–55.
60 Joyce Goldstein, *Cucina Ebraica* (San Francisco, 1998); Edda Servi Machlin, *Classic Italian Jewish Cooking: Traditional Recipes and Menus* (New York, 2005).
61 Lucia Frattarelli Fischer and Stefano Villani, '"People of Every Mixture": Immigration, Tolerance and Religious Conflicts in Early Modern Livorno', in *Immigration and Emigration in Historical Perspective*, ed. Ann Katherine Isaacs (Pisa, 2007), pp. 93–107; Matthias B. Lehmann, 'A Livornese "Port Jew" and the Sephardim of the Ottoman Empire', *Jewish Social Studies*, XI/2 (2005), pp. 51–76.
62 Howard Adelman, 'Rabbis and Reality: Public Activities of Jewish Women in Italy during the Renaissance and Catholic Restoration', *Jewish History*, V/1 (1991), pp. 27–40.
63 Toaff, *Mangiare*, pp. 26–7.
64 Maurizio Sentieri and Zazzu Guido, *I semi dell'Eldorado* (Bari, 1992); Alfred Crosby, *The Columbian Exchange: Biological and Cultural Consequences of 1492* (Westport, CT, 1972).
65 Valérie Boudier, 'Appropriation et représentation des animaux du Nouveau Monde chez deux artistes nord italiens de la fin du XVIe siècle. Le cas du dindon', *Food History*, VII/1 (2009), pp. 79–102.
66 Salvatore Marchese, *Benedetta patata: Una storia del '700, un trattato e 50 ricette* (Padova, 1999).
67 Gentilcore, *Pomodoro*, p. 4.
68 Dursteler, 'Food and Politics', p. 93.
69 Massimo Montanari, *Nuovo Convivio* (Bari, 1991), p. 183.

FOUR: Fragmentation and Unification

1 Brian Fagan, *The Little Ice Age: How Climate Made History, 1300–1850* (New York, 2001).
2 Emilio Sereni, *History of the Italian Agricultural Landscape* (Princeton, NJ, 1997), p. 187.
3 Ibid, pp. 189–98.
4 Ariel Toaff, *Mangiare alla giudia* (Bologna, 2000), p. 82.
5 Ibid., pp. 74–5.
6 Bartolomeo Stefani, *L'arte del ben cucinare ed instruire i meno periti in questa lodevole professione: dove anche s'insegna a far pasticci, sapori, salse, gelatine, torte, ed altro* (Mantova, 1662), p. 137. Available at www.academiabarilla.it.

7 Ken Albala, *Food in Early Modern Europe* (Westport, CT, 2003), pp. 133–6.

8 John Dickie, *Delizia: The Epic History of the Italians and Their Food* (New York, 2008), pp. 139–43.

9 Alberto Capatti and Massimo Montanari, *Italian Cuisine: A Cultural History* (New York, 2003), p. 21.

10 Antonio Latini, *Lo scalco alla moderna. Overo l'arte di ben disporre li conviti* (Napoli, 1693), intro., p. 2, available at www.academiabarilla.it.

11 David Gentilcore, *Pomodoro: A History of the Tomato in Italy* (New York, 2010), p. 48.

12 Albala, *Food*, pp. 13–8.

13 Giacomo Castelvetro, *The Fruit, Herbs, and Vegetables of Italy*, trans. Gillian Riley (London, 1989), p. 49.

14 Castelvetro, *The Fruit*, p. 65.

15 Massimo Montanari, *Nuovo Convivio* (Bari, 1991), pp. 355–6.

16 Ibid., p. 358.

17 Piero Camporesi, 'La cucina borghese dell'Ottocento fra tradizione e rinnovamento', in *La terra e la luna* (Garzanti, 1995), p. 233.

18 Sereni, *History*, p. 221.

19 Silvano Serventi and Françoise Sabban, *Pasta: The Story of a Universal Food* (New York, 2002), pp. 91–115.

20 Toaff, *Mangiare*, p. 111.

21 Mark Pendergrast, *Uncommon Grounds: The History of Coffee and How It Transformed Our World* (New York, 1999); Bennett A. Weinberg and Bonnie K. Bealer, *The World of Caffeine: The Science and Culture of the World's Most Popular Drug* (New York and London, 2002).

22 Sophie D. Coe, *America's First Cuisines* (Austin, 1994), p. 55.

23 Montanari, *Nuovo Convivio*, pp. 315–16.

24 Piero Camporesi, *Exotic Brew: The Art of Living in the Age of Enlightenment* (Malden, MA, 1998), p. 40.

25 Ibid., p. 48.

26 Montanari, *Nuovo Convivio*, p. 335.

27 Gentilcore, *Pomodoro*, p. 53.

28 Albala, *Food*, pp. 139–40.

29 Alberto Capatti, 'Il Buon Paese', in *Introduzione alla Guida Gastronomica Italiana 1931* (Milan, 2003), p. 6.

30 Vincenzo Corrado, *Il Credenziere di Buon Gusto* (Napoli, 1778), p. ix.

31 Maria Attilia Fabbri Dall'Oglio and Alessandro Fortis, *Il gastrononomo errante Giacomo Casanova* (Rome, 1998).

32 Louis Chevalier de Jaucourt, 'Cuisine', in *Encyclopédie ou Dictionnaire raisonné des sciences, des arts et des métiers*, vol. IV (Paris, 1754), p. 538.

33 Renato Mariani-Costantini and Aldo Mariani-Costantini, 'An Outline of the History of Pellagra in Italy', *Journal of Anthropological Sciences*, 85 (2007), pp. 163–71.

34 Athos Bellettini, 'Aspetti e problemi della ripresa demografica nell'Italia del Settecento', *Società e Storia*, 6 (1979), pp. 817–38.

35 Vera Zamagni, *Economic History of Italy, 1860–1990: Recovery after Decline* (Oxford, 1993), pp. 118–19.

36 Alberto Capatti, Alberto De Bernardi and Angelo Varni, 'Introduzione', in *Storia d'Italia, Annali 13: L'alimentazione*, p. xxxv.

37 'La falange noi siam de' mietitori, / E falciamo le messi a lor signori. / Ben venga il Sol cocente, il Sol di giugno / Che ci arde il sangue, ci annerisce il grugno / E ci arroventa la falce nel pugno, Quando falciam le messi a lor signori. . . / I nostri figlioletti non han pane, / E chi sa? Forse moriran domane, /I nvidiando il pranzo al vostro cane . . . / E noi falciamo le messi a lor signori. / Ebbre di sole ognun di noi barcolla; / Acqua ed aceto, un tozzo e una cipolla / Ci disseta, ci allena, ci satolla. / Falciam, falciam le messi a quei signori.' Mario Rapisardi, *Versi: scelti e riveduti da esso* (Milan, 1888), p. 167.

38 Francesco Taddei, 'Il cibo nell'Italia mezzadrile fra Ottocento and Novecento', in *Storia d'Italia, Annali 13: L'alimentazione*, ed. Alberto De Bernardi, Alberto Varni and Angelo Capatti (Turin, 1998), p. 32.

39 Giovanni Verga, *Cavalleria Rusticana and Other Stories*, trans. G. H. McWilliam (Harmondsworth, 1999), p. 169.

40 Alberto Caracciolo, *L'Inchiesta Agraria Jacini* (Turin, 1973).

41 Maria Luisa Betri, 'L'alimentazione popolare nell'Italia dell'Ottocento', in *Storia d'Italia, Annali 13: L'alimentazione*, ed. De Bernardi, Varni and Capatti, p. 7.

42 Giuliano Malizia, *La cucina romana e ebraico-romanesca* (Rome, 2001).

43 Carol Helstosky, *Garlic and Oil: Food and Politics in Italy* (Oxford, 2004), p. 22; Alfredo Niceforo, *Italiani del Nord, italiani del Sud* (Turin, 1901); Vito Teti, *La razza maledetta: origini del pregiudizio antimeridionale* (Rome, 2011).

44 Betri, 'L'alimentazione', p. 19.

45 Paolo Sorcinelli, *Gli Italiani e il cibo: dalla polenta ai cracker* (Milan, 1999), p. 47.

46 Giorgio Pedrocco, 'La conservazione del cibo: dal sale all'industria agro-alimentare', in *Storia d'Italia, Annali 13: L'alimentazione*, ed. De Bernardi, Varni and Capatti, pp. 401–19.

47 Ibid., pp. 423–6.

48 Serventi and Sabban, *Pasta*, pp. 162–9.

49 Stefano Somogyi, 'L'alimentazione nell'Italia unita', in *Storia d'Italia*, vol. v/1: *I documenti*, ed. Lellia Cracco Ruggini and Giorgio Cracco (Turin, 1973), pp. 841–87.

50 Francesco Chiapparino, 'L'industria alimentare dall'Unità al period fra le due guerre', in *Storia d'Italia, Annali 13: L'alimentazione*, ed. De Bernardi, Varni and Capatti, pp. 231–50.

51 Ada Lonni, 'Dall'alterazione all'adulterazione: le sofisticazioni alimentari nella società industriale', in *Storia d'Italia, Annali 13: L'alimentazione*, ed. De Bernardi, Varni and Capatti, pp. 531–84.

52 Giorgio Pedrocco, 'Viticultura e enologia in Italia nel XIX secolo', in *La vite e il vino: storia e diritto (secoli XI–XIX)*, ed. Maria Da Passano, Antonello Mattone, Franca Mele and Pinuccia F. Simbula (Rome, 2000), pp. 613–27.

53 Hugh Johnson, *Story of Wine* (London, 1989), p. 308.

54 Domenico Quirico, *Naja: storia del servizio di leva in Italia* (Milan, 2008).

55 Assunta Trova, 'L'approvvigionamento alimentare dell'esercito italiano', *Storia d'Italia, Annali 13: L'alimentazione*, ed. De Bernardi, Varni and Capatti, pp. 495–530.

56 Helstosky, *Garlic*, p. 31.

57 Sorcinelli, *Gli italiani*, pp. 59–62.

58 Pellegrino Artusi, *La scienza in cucina e l'arte di mangiar bene* [1891] (Florence, 1998), p. 93.

59 Artusi, *La scienza*, p. 168.

60 Eugenia Tognotti, 'Alcolismo e pensiero medico nell'Italia liberale', in *La vite e il vino: storia e diritto (secoli XI–XIX)*, ed. Maria Da Passano, Antonello Mattone, Franca Mele and Pinuccia F. Simbula (Rome, 2000), pp. 1237–48.

61 Sorcinelli, *Gli italiani*, pp. 50–52.

62 Penelope Francks, 'From Peasant to Entrepreneur in Italy and Japan', *Journal of Peasant Studies*, XXII/4 (1995), pp. 699–709.

63 Elizabeth D. Whitaker, 'Bread and Work: Pellagra and Economic Transformation in Turn-of-the-century Italy', *Anthropological Quarterly*, LXV/2 (1992), pp. 80–90.

## FIVE: From War to Miracle

1 Paolo Sorcinelli, *Gli Italiani e il cibo: dalla polenta ai cracker* (Milan, 1999), p. 168.

2 Carol Helstosky, *Garlic and Oil: Food and Politics in Italy* (Oxford, 2004), p. 40.

3 Riccardo Bachi, *L'alimentazione e la politica annonaria* (Bari, 1926).

4 Giovanna Tagliati, 'Olindo Guerrini gastronomo: Le rime romagnole de E' Viazze L'arte di utilizzare gli avanzi della mensa', *Storia e Futuro*, 20 (2009), available at www.storiaefuturo.com.

5 Olindo Guerrini, *L'arte di utilizzare gli avanzi della mensa* [1917] (Padova, 1993), p. 57.

6 Vera Zamagni, 'L'evoluzione dei consumi tra tradizione e innovazione', in *Storia d'Italia, Annali 13: L'alimentazione*, ed. Alberto De Bernardi, Alberto Varni and Angelo Capatti (Turin, 1998), p. 185.

7 The drink's ascent would be temporarily hampered after 1927 when the Fascist government imposed the use of at least 15 per cent of rice in beer brewing to boost local rice consumption in an attempt to limit imports of cereals.

8 Helstosky, *Garlic*, p. 51.

9 Pasquale Lucio Scandizzo, 'L'agricoltura e lo sviluppo economico', in *L'Italia Agricola nel XX secolo: Storia e scenari* (Corigliano Calabro, 2000), p. 16.

10 Amate il pane, cuore della casa, profumo della mensa, gioia del focolare. Rispettate il pane, sudore della fronte, orgoglio del lavoro, poema di sacrificio. Onorate il pane, gloria dei campi, fragranza della terra, festa della vita. Non sciupate il pane, ricchezza della patria, il più soave dono di Dio, il più santo premio alla fatica umana (Benito Mussolini, *Il popolo d'Italia*, 25 March 1928, p. 15).

11 Simonetta Falasca Zamponi, *Lo spettacolo del fascismo* (Rome, 2003), pp. 226–42.

12 Ernesto Laura, *Le stagioni dell'aquila: storia dell'Istituto Luce* (Rome, 2000).

13 The historical archives of the Istituto Luce are now available online at www.archivioluce.com.

14 Helstosky, *Garlic*, pp. 100–02.

15 Sorcinelli, *Gli Italiani*, pp. 200–01.

16 Stephen C. Bruner, 'Leopoldo Franchetti and Italian Settlement in Eritrea: Emigration, Welfare Colonialism and the Southern Question', *European History Quarterly*, xxxix/1 (2009), pp. 71–94.

17 Kate Ferris, '"Fare di ogni famiglia italiana un fortilizio": The League of Nations' Economic Sanctions and Everyday Life in Venice', *Journal of Modern Italian Studies*, xi/2 (2006), pp. 117–42.

18 'Mai come in quest'ora delicatissima, in cui tutto ciò che è forza morale attiva e fattiva acquista, sulla via del sacrificio, un potere trascendentale, la vostra missione di massaie ha avuto la suprema importanza che si riconnette, nel modo più diverso, cogli attuali urgenti interessi della Nazione. Perché specialmente da voi, massaie, che delle vostre attività e delle vostre possibilità spirituali fate il fulcro della vita familiare, si vuole che parta l'esempio capace di portare irre-sistibilmente anche gli indifferenti, anche gli incoscienti alla rigida osservanza della regola di parsimonia che ci siamo imposte e nella quale persevereremo fino al giorno della vittoria!' (Frida, 'Cucina Antisanzionista', *Cucina Italiana*, December 1935, p. 9.)

19 Perry R. Wilson, 'Cooking the Patriotic Omelette: Women and the Italian Fascist Ruralization Campaign', *European History Quarterly*, xxvii/4 (1993), pp. 351–47; Paul Corner, 'Women in Fascist Italy: Changing Family Roles in the Transition from an Agricultural to an Industrial Society', *European History Quarterly*, xxiii/1 (1997), pp. 51–68.

20 Jeffrey T. Schnapp, 'The Romance of Caffeine and Aluminum', *Critical Inquiry*, xxviii/1(2001), pp. 244–69; Jonathan Morris, 'Making Italian Espresso, Making Espresso Italian', *Food and History*, viii/2 (2010), pp. 155–84.

21 'Il caffe non e necessario alla nostra razza dinamica, attiva, svegliatissima, quin-di niente affatto bisognosa di eccitanti o stimolanti in genere . . . Il caffe non rappresenta per noi una necessità ma una ghiottoneria, un'abitudine, un pregiudizio che sia la panacea di molti mali o l'indispensabile aiuto di quel lavoro che non ci sgomenta mai neppure se snervante o continuo o identico a se stesso, quel lavoro che per essere da noi integralmente e sanamente compiuto non ha bisogno delle pause al banco degli espressi' (Eleonora della Pura, 'Vini tipici e frutta invece di caffè', *La cucina italiana*, June 1939, p. 164).

22 Gian Franco Vené, *Mille lire al mese: vita quotidiana della famiglia nell'Italia Fascista* (Milan, 1988).

23 Gianni Isola, *Abbassa la tua radio per favore . . . Storia dell'ascolto radiofonico nell'italia fascista* (Florence, 1990).

24 Adam Ardvisson, 'Between Fascism and the American Dream: Advertising in Interwar Italy', *Social Science History*, xxv/2 (2001), p. 176.

25 Giampaolo Gallo, Renato Covino and Roberto Monicchia, 'Crescita, crisi, riorganizzazione: l'industria alimentare dal dopoguerra a oggi', in *Storia d'italia, Annali 13: L'alimentazione*, ed. De Bernardi, Varni and Capatti, p. 172.

26 Alberto Capatti, 'La nascita delle associazioni vegetariane in Italia', *Food and History*, ii/1 (2004), pp. 167–90.

27 Ada Bonfiglio Krassich, *Almanacco della cucina 1937: La cucina economica e sana: consigli preziosi per la massaia* (Milan, 1936), p. 25.

28 Bonfiglio Krassich, *Almanacco*, p. 34.

29 Steve Siporin, 'From Kashrut to Cucina Ebraica: The Recasting of Italian Jewish

Foodways', *Journal of American Folklore*, CVII/424 (1994), pp. 268–81.

30 Agnese Portincasa, 'Il Touring Club Italiano e la Guida Gastronomica d'Italia. Creazione, circolazione del modello e tracce della sua evoluzione (1931–1984)', *Food and History*, VI/1 (2008), pp. 83–116.

31 Touring Club Italiano, *Guida Gastronomica d'Italia* (Milan, 1931); Massimo Montanari, 'Gastronomia e Cultura', in *Introduzione alla Guida Gastronomica Italiana 1931* (Milan, 2003), pp. 4–5.

32 Alberto Capatti, *L'osteria nuova: una storia italiana del XX secolo* (Bra, 2000), p. 65.

33 Alberto Capatti, 'Il Buon Paese', in *Introduzione alla Guida Gastronomica Italiana 1931* (Milan, 2003), p. 16.

34 Federazione Nazionale Fascista Pubblici Esercizi, *Trattorie d'Italia 1939* (Rome, 1939).

35 Capatti, *L'osteria*, pp. 34–5.

36 Ibid., pp. 19–22.

37 Hans Barth, *Osteria: Guida spirituale delle osterie italiane da Verona a Capri* (Florence, 1921).

38 Filippo Tommaso Marinetti and Fillia [Luigi Colombo], *La cucina futurista* (Milan 1932), pp. 28–30

39 Ibid., p. 5.

40 Ibid., pp. 218–19.

41 Enrico Cesaretti, 'Recipes for the Future: Traces of Past Utopias in the Futurist Cookbook', *European Legacy*, XIV/7 (2009), pp. 841–56.

42 Marinetti and Fillia, *La cucina futurista*, p. 146.

43 Maria Paola Moroni Salvatori, 'Ragguaglio bibliografico sui ricettari del primo Novecento', in *Storia d'Italia, Annali 13: L'alimentazione*, ed. De Bernardi, Varni and Capatti, p. 900.

44 Pietro Luminati, *La Borsa Nera* (Rome, 1945).

45 Pierpaolo Luzzato Fegiz, *Alimentazione e Prezzi in tempo di Guerra, 1942–43* (Trieste, 1948).

46 Sorcinelli, *Gli italiani*, p. 137.

47 Rinaldo Chidichimo, 'Un secolo di agricoltura italiana: uno sguardo d'insieme', in *L'Italia Agricola nel XX secolo: Storia e scenari*, ed. Società Italiana degli Agricoltori (Corigliano Calabro, 2000), p. 5.

48 Paul Ginsborg, *A History of Contemporary Italy: Society and Politics 1943–1988* (New York, 2003), pp. 121–40.

49 Scandizzo, 'L'agricoltura', pp. 30–31.

50 Cao Pinna, 'Le classi povere', in *Atti della commissione parlamentare di inchiesta sulla miseria in Italia e sui mezzi per combatterla*, vol. II (Rome, 1954).

51 Sorcinelli, *Gli italiani*, p. 212.

52 Viviana Lapertosa, *Dalla fame all'abbondanza: Gli italiani e il cibo nel cinema dal dopoguerra ad oggi* (Turin, 2002).

53 Fabio Carlini, Donata Dinoia and Maurizio Gusso, *C'è il boom o non c'è. Immagini dell'Italia del miracolo economico attraverso film dell'epoca (1958–1965)* (Milan, 1998).

54 Helstosky, *Garlic*, p. 127.

55 Luisa Tasca, '"The Average Housewife" in Post-World War II Italy', *Journal of Women's History*, XVI/2 (2004), pp. 92–115; Adam Arvidsson, 'The Therapy of

Consumption Motivation Research and the New Italian Housewife, 1958–62',
*Journal of Material Culture*, v/3 (2000), pp. 251–74.

56 Scandizzo, 'L'agricoltura', p. 35.

57 Paolo Malanima, 'Urbanisation and the Italian Economy During the Last
Millennium', *European Review of Economic History*, 9 (2005), p. 106.

58 Sorcinelli, *Gli italiani*, p. 219.

59 Scandizzo, 'L'agricoltura', p. 22.

60 Gianpaolo Fissore, 'Gli italiani e il cibo sul grande schermo dal secondo
dopoguerra a oggi', in *Il cibo dell'altro: movimenti migratori e culture
alimentari nella Torino del Novecento*, ed. Marcella Filippa (Rome, 2003),
pp. 163–79.

61 Mara Anastasia and Bruno Maida, 'I luoghi dello scambio', in *Il cibo dell'altro:
movimenti migratori e culture alimentary nella Torino del Novecento*, ed. Marcella
Filippa (Rome, 2003), pp. 3–52.

62 Rachel E. Black, *Porta Palazzo: The Anthropology of an Italian Market*
(Philadelphia, 2012).

63 Paolo Sorcinelli, 'Identification Process at Work: Virtues of the Italian
Working-class Diet in the First Half of the Twentieth Century', in *Food, Drink
and Identity*, ed. Peter Scholliers (Oxford, 2001), p. 81.

64 Istituto Italiano Alimenti Surgelati, *I surgelati: amici di famiglia* (Rome, 2011),
p. 30.

65 Gian Paolo Ceserani, *Storia della pubblicità in Italia* (Bari, 1988); Gianni
Canova, *Dreams: i sogni degli italiani in 50 anni di pubblicità televisiva* (Milan,
2004); Gian Luigi Falabrino, *Storia della pubblicità in Italia dal 1945 a oggi*
(Rome, 2007).

66 Emanuela Scarpellini, 'Shopping American-style: The Arrival of the Supermarket
in Postwar Italy', *Enterprise and Society*, v/4 (2004), pp. 625–68.

67 Bernando Caprotti, *Falce e carrello: Le mani sulla spesa degli italiani* (Venezia,
2007).

68 Morris, 'Making Italian Espresso', p. 164.

## SIX: Now and the Future

1 Piero Camporesi, *La terra e la luna* (Garzanti, 1995), p. 339.

2 Pasquale Lucio Scandizzo, 'L'agricoltura e lo sviluppo economico', in *L'Italia
Agricola nel xx secolo: Storia e scenari* (Corigliano Calabro, 2000), p. 41.

3 Ibid., p. 21.

4 Aida Turrini, Anna Saba, Domenico Perrone, Eugenio Cialfa and Amleto
D'Amicis, 'Food Consumption Patterns in Italy: the INN-CA Study 1994–1996',
*European Journal of Clinical Nutrition*, LV/7 (2001), pp. 571–88.

5 ISTAT, *Rapporto Annuale 2012: La situazione del Paese* (Rome, 2012).

6 Fondazione Qualivita – Ismea, *Rapporto 2011 sulle produzioni agroalimentari
italiane dop igp stg* (Siena, 2012).

7 Monica Giulietti, 'Buyer and Seller Power in Grocery Retailing: Evidence from
Italy', *Revista de Economía del Rosario*, x/2 (2007), pp. 109–25.

8 Ulf Johansson and Steve Burt, 'The Buying of Private Brands and Manufacturer
Brands in Grocery Retailing: a Comparative Study of Buying Processes in

the UK, Sweden and Italy', *Journal of Marketing Management*, XX/7–8 (2004), pp. 799–824.

9 Lucio Sicca, *Lo straniero nel piatto* (Milan, 2002).

10 Rachel Eden Black, *Porta Palazzo: The Anthropology of an Italian Market* (Philadelphia, 2012), pp. 93–118.

11 Riccardo Vecchio, 'Local Food at Italian Farmers' Markets: Three Case Studies', *International Journal of Sociology of Agriculture and Food*, XVII/2 (2010), pp. 122–39.

12 Anna Carbone, Marco Gaito and Saverio Senni, 'Consumer Attitudes toward Ethical Food: Evidence from Social Farming in Italy', *Journal of Food Products Marketing*, XV/3 (2009), pp. 337–50.

13 Paolo C. Conti, *La leggenda del buon cibo italiano* (Rome, 2006), pp. 102–12.

14 Maria Paola Ferretti and Paolo Magaudda, 'The Slow Pace of Institutional Change in the Italian Food System', *Appetite*, LXVII/2 (2006), pp. 161–9; Bente Halkier, Lotte Holm, Mafalda Domingues, Paolo Magaudda, Annemette Nielsen and Laura Terragni, 'Trusting, Complex, Quality-conscious or Unprotected?' *Journal of Consumer Culture*, VII/3 (2007), pp. 379–402; Roberta Sassatelli and Alan Scott, 'Novel Food, New Markets and Trust Regimes: Responses to the Erosion of Consumers' Confidence in Austria, Italy and the UK', *European Societies*, III/2 (2001), pp. 213–44; Andrew Fearne, Susan Hornibrook and Sandra Dedman, 'The Management of Perceived Risk in the Food Supply Chain: A Comparative Study of Retailer-led Beef Quality Assurance Schemes in Germany and Italy', *International Food and Agribusiness Management Review*, IV/1 (2001), pp. 19–36.

15 See http://gmofree-euroregions.regione.marche.it.

16 Johanna Gibson, 'Markets in Tradition – Traditional Agricultural Communities in Italy and the Impact of GMOs', *Script-ed*, III/3 (2006), pp. 243–52.

17 Ferruccio Trabalzi, 'Crossing Conventions in Localized Food Networks: Insights from Southern Italy', *Environment and Planning A*, XXXIX/2 (2007), pp. 283–300; Andrés Rodríguez-Pose and Maria Cristina Refolo, 'The Link Between Local Production Systems and Public and University Research in Italy', *Environment and Planning A*, XXXV/8 (2003), pp. 1477–92.

18 Felice Adinolfi, Marcello De Rosa, Ferruccio Trabalzi, 'Dedicated and Generic Marketing Strategies: The Disconnection between Geographical Indications and Consumer Behavior in Italy', *British Food Journal*, CXIII/3 (2011), pp. 419–35.

19 Conti, *La leggenda*, pp. 200–02.

20 Directorate-General for Agriculture and Rural Development, *An Analysis of the EU Organic Sector* (Brussels, 2010).

21 Achille Mingozzi and Rosa Maria Bertino, *Rapporto Bio Bank 2012: prosegue la corsa per accorciare la filiera* (Forlí, 2012). See www.biobank.it.

22 Roberta Sonnino, 'Quality Food, Public Procurement, and Sustainable Development: The School Meal Revolution in Rome', *Environment and Planning A*, XLI/2 (2009), pp. 425–40; Stefano Bocchi, Roberto Spigarolo, Natale Marcomini and Valerio Sarti, 'Organic and Conventional Public Food Procurement for Youth in Italy', *Bioforsk Report*, III/42 (2008), pp. 1–45.

23 Carole Counihan, *Around the Tuscan Table: Food, Family, and Gender in Twentieth-century Florence* (New York and London, 2004).

24 Angelo Presenza, Antonio Minguzzi and Clara Petrillo, 'Managing Wine Tourism in Italy', *Journal of Tourism Consumption and Practice*, II/1 (2010), pp. 46–61.

25 Filippo Ceccarelli, *Lo stomaco della Repubblica* (Milan, 2000).

26 Fabio Parasecoli, 'Postrevolutionary Chowhounds: Food, Globalization, and the Italian Left', *Gastronomica*, III/3 (2003), pp. 29–39.

27 Mara Miele and Jonathan Murdoch, 'The Practical Aesthetics of Traditional Cuisines: Slow Food in Tuscany', *Sociologia Ruralis*, XLII/4 (2002), pp. 312–28; Costanza Nosi and Lorenzo Zanni, 'Moving From "Typical Products" to "Food-related services": The Slow Food Case as a New Business Paradigm', *British Food Journal*, CVI/10–11 (2004), pp. 779–92.

28 Corby Kummer, *The Pleasures of Slow Food: Celebrating Authentic Traditions, Flavors, and Recipes* (San Francisco, 2002).

29 Heather Paxson, 'Slow Food in a Fat Society: Satisfying Ethical Appetites', *Gastronomica*, V/2 (2005), pp. 14–18; Narie Sarita Gaytàn, 'Globalizing Resistance: Slow Food and New Local Imaginaries', *Food, Culture and Society*, VII/2 (2004), pp. 97–116.

30 Carlo Petrini, ed., *Slow Food: Collected Thoughts on Taste, Tradition, and the Honest Pleasures of Food* (White River Junction, VT, 2001); Carlo Petrini, *Slow Food: The Case of Taste* (New York, 2003); Carlo Petrini and Gigi Padovani, *Slow Food Revolution* (New York, 2006).

31 Janet Chrzan, 'Slow Food: What, Why, and to Where?', *Food, Culture and Society*, VII/2 (2004), pp. 117–32.

32 Rachel Laudan, 'Slow Food: The French Terroir Strategy, and Culinary Modernism', *Food, Culture and Society*, VII/2 (2004), pp. 133–44.

SEVEN: The Globalization of Italian Food

1 Jeffrey M. Pilcher, *Food in World History* (New York, 2006), p. 87.

2 David Gentilcore, *Pomodoro: A History of the Tomato in Italy* (New York, 2010), p. 100; Ercole Sori, *L'emigrazione italiana dall'unità alla seconda guerra mondiale* (Bologna, 1980).

3 Alberto Pecorini, 'The Italian as an Agricultural Laborer', *Annals of the American Academy of Political and Social Science*, XXXIII/2 (1909), p. 158.

4 Ibid., p. 159.

5 Nancy Tregre Wilson, *Louisiana's Food, Recipes, and Folkways* (Gretna, LA, 2005).

6 Joel Denker, *The World on a Plate: A Tour through the History of America's Ethnic Cuisines* (Boulder, CO, 2003), pp. 14–20.

7 Dick Rosano, *Wine Heritage: The Story of Italian American Vintners* (San Francisco, 2000); Simone Cinotto, *Terra soffice uva nera: Vitivinicoltori piemontesi in California prima e dopo il Proibizionismo* (Turin, 2008).

8 Carol Helstosky, *Garlic and Oil: Food and Politics in Italy* (Oxford, 2004), p. 28.

9 Gentilcore, *Pomodoro*, p. 114.

10 Julia Lovejoy Cuniberti, *Practical Italian Recipes for American Kitchens* (Gazette Printing Company, 1918), p. 27, available at http://books.google.com.

11 Donna Gabaccia, *We Are What We Eat: Ethnic Food and the Making of Americans* (Cambridge, MA, 1998), p. 52.

12 Hasia Diner, *Hungering for America: Italian, Irish, and Jewish Foodways in the Age of Migration* (Cambridge, MA, 2001), p. 64.

13 Naomi Guttman and Roberta L. Krueger, 'Utica Greens: Central New York's Italian–American Specialty', *Gastronomica*, IX/3 (2009), pp. 62–7.

14 Maddalena Tirabassi, *Il Faro di Beacon Street: Social Workers e immigrate negli Stati Uniti, 1910–1939* (Milan, 1990).

15 Jane Ziegelman, *97 Orchard: An Edible History of Five Immigrant Families in One New York Tenement* (New York, 2010), pp. 183–227.

16 Fernando Devoto, Gianfausto Rosoli and Diego Armus, *La inmigración italiana en la Argentina* (Buenos Aires, 2000); Fernando Devoto, *La Historia de los Italianos en la Argentina* (Buenos Aires, 2008); Franco Cenni, *Italianos no Brasil: 'Andiamo in Merica'* (São Paulo, 2002).

17 Paola Corti, 'Emigrazione e consuetudini alimentari', in *Storia d'Italia, Annali 13: L'alimentazione*, ed. Alberto De Bernardi, Alberto Varni and Angelo Capatti (Turin, 1998), pp. 696–702.

18 Diner, *Hungering*, pp. 48–83.

19 Roberta James, 'The Reliable Beauty of Aroma: Staples of Food and Cultural Production among Italian Australians', *Australian Journal of Anthropology*, XV/1 (2004), pp. 23–39; Harvey Levenstein, *Paradox of Plenty: A Social History of Eating in Modern America* (Berkeley and Los Angeles, 2003), p. 29.

20 Simone Cinotto, 'La cucina diasporica: il cibo come segno di identita culturale', in *Storia d'Italia, Annali 24: Migrazioni*, ed. Alberto De Bernardi, Alberto Varni and Angelo Capatti (Turin, 2009), pp. 653–72.

21 Lara Pascali, 'Two Stoves, Two Refrigerators, Due Cucine: The Italian Immigrant Home with Two Kitchens', *Gender, Place and Culture*, XIII/6 (2006), pp. 685–95.

22 Leen Beyers, 'Creating Home: Food, Ethnicity and Gender among Italians in Belgium since 1946', *Food, Culture and Society*, XI/1 (2008), pp. 7–27.

23 Maren Möhring, 'Staging and Consuming the Italian Lifestyle: The Gelateria and the Pizzeria-Ristorante in Post-war Germany', *Food and History*, VII/2 (2009), pp. 181–202.

24 Jonathan Morris, 'Imprenditoria italiana in Gran Bretagna Il consumo del caffè "stile italiano"', *Italia Contemporanea*, 241 (2005), pp. 540–52.

25 Taken from http://japaneats.tv.

26 Rossella Ceccarini, *Pizza and Pizza Chefs in Japan: A Case of Culinary Globalization* (Leiden, 2011); Corky White, 'Italian Food: Japan's Unlikely Culinary Passion', *The Atlantic* (6 October 2010), available at www.theatlantic.com.

27 Robbie Swinnerton, 'Italian Cucina Meets 21st-century Tokyo', *Japan Times* online (18 June 2004), available at www.japantimes.co.jp.

28 Luigi Cembalo, Gianni Cicia, Teresa Del Giudice, Riccardo Scarpa and Carolina Tagliafierro, 'Beyond Agropiracy: The Case of Italian Pasta in the United States Retail Market', *Agribusiness*, XXIV/3 (2008), pp. 403–13.

29 Gabaccia, *We Are What We Eat*, p. 150.

30 John F. Mariani, *How Italian Food Conquered the World* (New York, 2011), pp. 44–5.

31 Hasimu Huliyeti, Sergio Marchesini and Maurizio Canavari, 'Chinese Distribution Practitioners' Attitudes towards Italian Quality Foods', *Journal of*

*Chinese Economic and Foreign Trade Studies*, I/3 (2008), pp. 214–31.

32  Davide Girardelli, 'Commodified Identities: The Myth of Italian Food in the United States', *Journal of Communication Inquiry*, XXVIII/4 (2004), pp. 307–24.

33  itchefs, GVCI, 'IDIC 2010: An Unforgettable Day in the Name of Tagliatelle al Ragù Bolognese', www.itchefs-gvci.com.

34  Dwayne Woods, 'Pockets of Resistance to Globalization: The Case of the Lega Nord', *Patterns of Prejudice*, XLIII/2(2009), pp. 161–77.

35  Laura Chadwick, *The Celts* (London, 1997), p. 19.

36  Michael Dietler, 'Our Ancestors the Gauls: Archaeology, Ethnic Nationalism, and the Manipulation of Celtic Identity in Modern Europe', *American Anthropologist,* New Series, XCVI/3 (1994), p. 584.

37  E. Ma, 'La polenta uncia contro il "cous cous"', *La Provincia di Como* (7 February 2004).

38  'Straniera la polenta uncia: L'accusa arriva dallo chef', *La Provincia di Como* (1 Feburary 2010), available at www.laprovinciadicomo.it.

39  Flavia Krause-Jackson, 'Tuscan Town Accused of Culinary Racism for Kebab Ban', www.bloomberg.com, 27 January 2009.

40  Maria Sorbi, '"Coprifuoco" notturno per kebab e gelati', www.ilgiornale.it, 22 April 2009.

41  Matthew Fort, 'McDonald's Launch McItaly', *The Guardian* (28 January 2010).

42  Ibid.

43  Carlo Petrini, 'Lettera al panino McItaly', *La Repubblica* (3 February 2010).

44  'Gualtiero Marchesi firma due nuovi panini per Mcdonald's', www.italianfood-net.com, 11 October 2011.

45  Luca Zaia, *Adottare la terra (per non morire di fame)* (Milan, 2010), p. 9.

46  Ibid., p. 20.

47  Ibid., p. 57.

48  Rosario Scarpato, 'Pizza: An Organic Free Range. Tale in Four Slices', *Divine*, 20 (2001), pp. 30–41.

49  European Union Commission, 'Commission Regulation (EU) no 97/2010', *Official Journal of the European Union*, VI/2 (2010), pp. L34/7–16.

50  Ian Fisher, 'Is Cuisine Still Italian Even if the Chef Isn't?', *New York Times* (7 April 2008).

51  Pina Sozio, 'Fornelli d'Italia', *Gambero Rosso*, XIX/221 (2010), pp. 86–91.

52  Marco Delogu, 'Due Migrazioni', *Sguardi online*, 54 (2007), available at www.nital.it; Marco Delogu, *Pastori*, vol. II (Rome, 2009).

53  Lorenzo Cairoli, 'Pigneto: Etnico senza trucchi', *Gambero Rosso*, XIX/220 (2010), pp. 76–83.

54  Jonathan Leake, 'Global Warming Threatens to Rob Italy of Pasta', *Sunday Times* (15 November 2009), p. 9.

55  Rudy Ruitenberg, 'Italian Grain Imports Rise 11% on Soft-Wheat, Barley Purchases, Group Says', www.bloomberg.com, 13 August 2010.

56  Barilla, *FAQS* (2010), available at www.barillaus.com.

57  Coldiretti, 'Rosarno: Coldiretti, nei campi oltre 90mila extracomunitari regolari', *NewsColdiretti* (24 January 2010), available at www.coldiretti.it.

58  Giuseppe Salvaggiulo, 'La rivolta nera di Rosarno', *La Stampa* (8 January 2010).

59  Massimo Ferrara, 'Food, Migration, and Identity: Halal Food and Muslim

Immigrants in Italy', masters thesis, Center for Global and International
Studies, University of Kansas, 2011, pp. 25–6.

60 Pierpaolo Mudu, 'The People's Food: The Ingredients of "Ethnic" Hierarchies
and the Development of Chinese Restaurants in Rome', *GeoJournal*, 68 (2007),
pp. 195–210.


EIGHT: A Nation of Towns and Regions: Italian *Campanilismo*

1 Emilio Faccioli, ed., *Arte della cucina. Libri di ricette, testi sopra lo scalco, i
trincianti e i vini. Dal XIV al XIX secolo*, vol. 1 (Milan, 1966), p. 143.

2 Faccioli, *Arte*, p. 146.

3 Pecorino Toscano DOP, *Viaggio nella storia* [Travel history] (2008), available at
www.pecorinotoscanodop.it.

4 European Union Council, 'Council Regulation (EC) no 510/2006', *Official
Journal* L 93, XXXI/3 (2006), pp. 12–25.

5 Giovanni Haussmann, 'Il suolo d'Italia nella storia', in *Storia d'Italia: I caratteri
originali*, vol. 1, ed. Ruggiero Romano and Corrado Vivanti (Turin, 1989),
p. 66.

6 Girolamo Arnaldi, *Italy and Its Invaders* (Cambridge, MA, 2005), p. vii.

7 Pellegrino Artusi, *La scienza in cucina e l'arte di mangiare bene* [1891]
(Florence, 1998), p. 29.

8 '150 anni di sapori', *Gambero Rosso*, XX/228 (2011), pp. 23–36.

9 Julio Paz Cafferata and Carlos Pomareda, *Indicaciones geográficas y
denominaciones de origen en Centroamerica: situacion y perspectivas* (Geneva,
2009); Leonardo Granados and Carols Álvarez, 'Viabilidad de establecer el
sistema de denominaciones de origen de los productos agroalimentarios en
Costa Rica', *Agronomía Costarricense*, XXVI/1 (2002), p. 63–72.

10 Vito Teti, *Il colore del cibo* (Rome, 1999), pp. 107–114.

11 Vittorio Agnetti, *La nuova cucina delle specialità regionali* (Milan, 1909).

12 Ibid., pp. 5–6.

13 Touring Club Italiano, *Guida Gastronomica d'Italia* (Milan, 1931).

14 Ibid., p. 5.

15 John F. Mariani, *How Italian Food Conquered the World* (New York, 2011),
p. 163.

16 Massimo Montanari, *L'identità Italiana in Cucina* (Rome, 2010), p. vii.

17 Ibid., p. 17.

18 Alberto Capatti and Massimo Montanari, *Italian Cuisine: A Cultural History*
(New York, 2003), p. xiv.

19 Michael Hardt and Antonio Negri, *Empire* (Cambridge, MA, 2001), pp. 44–5.

20 Davide Panagia, *The Political Life of Sensation* (Durham, NC, and London, 2009).

21 Regina Bendix, *In Search of Authenticity: The Formation of Folklore Studies*
(Madison, WI, 1997); Meredith Abarca, 'Authentic or Not, It's Original', *Food
and Foodways*, XII/1 (2004), pp. 1–25.

# Select Bibliography

Abarca, Meredith, 'Authentic or Not, it's Original', *Food and Foodways*, XII/1 (2004), pp. 1–25

Abulafia, David, 'Pisan Commercial Colonies and Consulates in Twelfth-century Sicily', *English Historical Review*, XCIII/366 (1978), pp. 68–81

——, 'The Crown and the Economy under Roger II and his Successors', *Dumbarton Oaks Papers*, 37 (1983), pp. 1–14

Abu-Lughod, Janet, *Before European Hegemony: The World System, AD 1250–1350* (New York and Oxford, 1989)

Acemoglu, Daron, and James A. Robinson, *Why Nations Fail: The Origin of Power, Prosperity, and Poverty* (New York, 2012)

Achilli, Alessandro et al., 'Mitochondrial DNA Variation of Modern Tuscans Supports the Near Eastern Origin of Etruscans', *American Journal of Human Genetics*, LXXX/4 (2007), pp. 759–68

Adelman, Howard, 'Rabbis and Reality: Public Activities of Jewish Women in Italy during the Renaissance and Catholic Restoration', *Jewish History*, V/1 (1991), pp. 27–40

Adinolfi, Felice, Marcello De Rosa and Ferruccio Trabalzi, 'Dedicated and Generic Marketing Strategies: The Disconnection between Geographical Indications and Consumer Behavior in Italy', *British Food Journal*, CXIII/3 (2011), pp. 419–35

Agnetti, Vittorio, *La nuova cucina delle specialità regionali* (Milan, 1909). Available at www.academiabarilla.it

Albala, Ken, *Eating Right in the Renaissance* (Berkeley and Los Angeles, 2002)

——, *Food in Early Modern Europe* (Westport, CT, 2003)

Albarella, Umberto, Antonio Tagliacozzo, Keith Dobney and Peter Rowley-Conwy, 'Pig Hunting and Husbandry in Prehistoric Italy: A Contribution to the Domestication Debate', *Proceedings of the Prehistoric Society*, 72 (2006), pp. 193–227

Alexandre-Bidon, Daniele, 'La cigale et la fourmi: Céramique et conservation des aliments et des médicaments (Moyen Age–XVI siècle)', in *Profusion et Pénurie: Les hommes face à leurs besoins alimentaires*, ed. Martin Bruegel (Rennes, 2009), pp. 71–84

Amouretti, Marie-Claire, 'Urban and Rural Diets in Greece', in *Food: A Culinary History from Antiquity to the Present*, ed. Jean-Louis Flandrin and Massimo Montanari (New York, 1999), pp. 79–89

Anastasia, Mara, and Bruno Maida, 'I luoghi dello scambio', in *Il cibo dell'altro: movimenti migratori e culture alimentary nella Torino del Novecento*, ed. Marcella Filippa (Roma, 2003), pp. 3–52

Ardvisson, Adam, 'Between Fascism and the American Dream: Advertising in Interwar Italy', *Social Science History*, xxv/2 (2001), pp. 151–84

——, 'The Therapy of Consumption Motivation Research and the New Italian Housewife, 1958–62', *Journal of Material Culture*, v/3 (2000), pp. 251–74

Arnaldi, Girolamo, *Italy and Its Invaders* (Cambridge, MA, 2005)

Artusi, Pellegrino, *La scienza in cucina e l'arte di mangiare bene* [1891] (Firenze, 1998)

Ashtor, E., 'Profits from Trade with the Levant in the Fifteenth Century', *Bulletin of the School of Oriental and African Studies*, xxxviii/2 (1975), pp. 250–75

Bachi, Riccardo, *L'alimentazione e la politica annonaria* (Bari, 1926)

Badel, Christophe, 'Ivresse et ivrognerie a Rome (iie s av. J.-C.– iiie s ap. J.-C.)', *Food and History*, iv/2 (2006), pp. 75–89

Badet, Muriel, 'Piero di Cosimo: d'une iconographie a l'autre. Rapt, repas de noce et pique-nique pour l'Enlevement d'Hippodamie', *Food and History*, iv/1 (2006), pp. 147–67

Badiali, Federica, *Cucina mediaevale italiana* (Bologna, 1999)

Banaji, Jairus, *Agrarian Change in Late Antiquity: Gold, Labour, and Aristocratic Dominance* (Oxford, 2007)

Barker, Graeme, *The Agricultural Revolution in Prehistory: Why Did Foragers Become Farmers?* (Oxford, 2006)

Barth, Hans, *Osteria: Guida spirituale delle osterie italiane da Verona a Capri* (Firenze, 1921)

Beekes, Robert, 'The Prehistory of the Lydians, the Origin of the Etruscans, Troy and Aeneas', *Biblioteca Orientalis*, lix/3–4 (2002), pp. 205–41

Belayche, Nicole, 'Religion et consommation de la viande dans le monde romain: des réalités voilées', *Food and History*, v/1 (2007), pp. 29–43

Bellettini, Athos, 'Aspetti e problemi della ripresa demografica nell'Italia del Settecento', *Società e Storia*, 6 (1979), pp. 817–38

Bendix, Regina, *In Search of Authenticity: The Formation of Folklore Studies* (Madison, WI, 1997)

Benito, Pere, 'Food Systems', in *A Cultural History of Food: In the Medieval Age*, ed. Fabio Parasecoli and Peter Scholliers (Oxford, 2012), pp. 37–56

Bernabò Brea, Maria, Andrea Cardarelli and Mauro Cremaschi, eds, *Le terremare, la più antica civiltà padana* (Milan, 1997)

Betri, Maria Luisa, 'L'alimentazione popolare nell'Italia dell'Ottocento', in *Storia d'Italia, Annali 13: L'alimentazione*, ed. Alberto De Bernardi, Alberto Varni and Angelo Capatti (Torino, 1998), pp. 7–38

Beyers, Leen, 'Creating Home: Food, Ethnicity and Gender among Italians in Belgium since 1946', *Food, Culture and Society*, xi/1 (2008), pp. 7–27

Black, Rachel Eden, *Porta Palazzo: The Anthropology of an Italian Market* (Philadelphia, 2012)

Bocchi, Stefano, Roberto Spigarolo, Natale Marcomini and Valerio Sarti, 'Organic and Conventional Public Food Procurement for Youth in Italy', *Bioforsk Report*, III/42 (2008), pp. 1–45

Bosi, Giovanna, Anna Maria Mercuri, Chiara Guarnieri and Marta Bandini Mazzanti, 'Luxury Food and Ornamental Plants at the 15th-century AD Renaissance Court of the Este Family (Ferrara, Northern Italy)', *Vegetation History and Archaeobotany*, XVIII/5 (2009), pp. 389–402

Boudier, Valérie, 'Appropriation et représentation des animaux du Nouveau Monde chez deux artistes nord italiens de la fin du XVIe siècle: Le cas du dindon', *Food History*, VII/1 (2009), pp. 79–102

Bova, Aldo, *L'avventura del vetro dal Rinascimento al Novecento tra Venezia e mondi lontani* (Geneva, 2010)

Braudel, Fernand, *Memory and the Mediterranean* (New York, 2001)

Briggs, Daphne Nash, 'Metals, Salt, and Slaves: Economic Links between Gaul and Italy from the Eighth to the Late Sixth Centuries BC', *Oxford Journal of Archaeology*, XXII/3 (2003), pp. 243–59

——, 'Servants at a Rich Man's Feast: Early Etruscan Household Slaves and Their Procurement', *Etruscan Studies*, 9, Article 14 (2002). Available at: http://scholarworks.umass.edu

Broekaert, Wim, and Arjan Zuiderhoek, 'Food and Politics in Classic Antiquity', in *A Cultural History of Food in Antiquity*, ed. Fabio Parasecoli and Peter Scholliers (London, 2012), pp. 41–55

——, 'Food Systems in Classic Antiquity', in *A Cultural History of Food in Antiquity*, ed. Fabio Parasecoli and Peter Scholliers (London, 2012), pp. 75–93

Brothwell, Don, and Patricia Brothwell, *Food in Antiquity: A Survey of the Diet of Early Peoples* (Baltimore and London, 1998)

Brown, Thomas and Neil Christie, 'Was There a Byzantine Model of Settlement in Italy?', *Melanges de l'École française de Rome: Moyen-Age, Temps modernes*, CI/2 (1989), pp. 377–99

Brownworth, Lars, *Lost to the West* (New York, 2009)

Bruegel, Martin, 'Pénurie et profusion: de la crise alimentaire à l'alimentation en crise', in *Profusion et penurie: les hommes face à leurs besoins alimentaires*, ed. Martin Bruegel (Rennes, 2009), pp. 9–34

Bruner, Stephen C., 'Leopoldo Franchetti and Italian Settlement in Eritrea: Emigration, Welfare Colonialism and the Southern Question', *European History Quarterly*, XXXIX/1 (2009), pp. 71–94

Bryer, Anthony, 'Byzantine Agricultural Implements: The Evidence of Medieval Illustrations in Hesiod's "Works and Days"', *Annual of the British School at Athens*, 81 (1986), pp. 45–80

Cafferata, Julio Paz and Carlos Pomareda, *Indicaciones geograficas y denominaciones de origen en Centroamerica: situacion y perspectivas* (Geneva, 2009)

Cairoli, Lorenzo, 'Pigneto: Etnico senza trucchi', *Gambero Rosso*, XIX/220 (2010), pp. 76–83

Campanini, Antonella, 'La table sous controle: Les banquets et l'exces alimentaire dans le cadre des lois somptuaires en Italie entre le Moyen Age et la Renaissance', *Food and History*, IV/2 (2006), pp. 131–50

Camporeale, Giovanni, 'Vita privata', in *Rasenna: storia e civiltà degli Etruschi*, ed. Massimo Pallottino et al. (Milan, 1986), pp. 239–308

Camporesi, Piero, *Exotic Brew: The Art of Living in the Age of Enlightenment* (Malden, MA, 1998)

——, 'La cucina borghese dell'Ottocento fra tradizione e rinnovamento', in *La terra e la luna* (Garzanti, 1995), pp. 209–72

Canova, Gianni, *Dreams: i sogni degli italiani in 50 anni di pubblicità televisiva* (Milan, 2004)

Capatti, Alberto, 'Il Buon Paese', in *Introduzione alla Guida Gastronomica Italiana 1931* (Milan, 2003), pp. 6–31

——, 'La nascita delle associazioni vegetariane in Italia', *Food and History*, II/1 (2004), pp. 167–90

——, *L'osteria nuova: una storia italiana del xx secolo* (Bra, 2000)

Capatti, Alberto, Alberto de Bernardi and Angelo Varni, 'Introduzione', in *Storia d'Italia, Annali 13: L'alimentazione* (Torino, 1998), pp. xvii–lxiv

Capatti, Alberto, and Massimo Montanari, *Italian Cuisine: A Cultural History* (New York, 2003)

Caprotti, Bernando, *Falce e carrello: Le mani sulla spesa degli italiani* (Venezia, 2007)

Carbone, Anna, Marco Gaito and Saverio Senni, 'Consumer Attitudes toward Ethical Food: Evidence from Social Farming in Italy', *Journal of Food Products Marketing*, XV/3 (2009), pp. 337–50

Carlini, Fabio, Donata Dinoia and Maurizio Gusso, *C'è il boom o non c'è: Immagini dell'Italia del miracolo economico attraverso film dell'epoca (1958–1965)* (Milan, 1998)

Ceccarelli, Filippo, *Lo stomaco della Repubblica* (Milan, 2000)

Ceccarelli, Giovanni, Alberto Grandi and Stefano Magagnoli, 'The "Taste" of Typicality', *Food and History*, VIII/2 (2010), pp. 45–76

Ceccarini, Rossella, *Pizza and Pizza Chefs in Japan: A Case of Culinary Globalization* (Leiden, 2011)

Cembalo, Luigi, Gianni Cicia, Teresa Del Giudice, Riccardo Scarpa and Carolina Tagliafierro, 'Beyond Agropiracy: The Case of Italian Pasta in the United States Retail Market', *Agribusiness*, XXIV/3 (2008), pp. 403–13

Cenni, Franco, *Italianos no Brasil: 'Andiamo in Merica'* (São Paulo, 2002)

Cesaretti, Enrico, 'Recipes for the Future: Traces of Past Utopias in The Futurist Cookbook', *The European Legacy*, XIV/7 (2009), pp. 841–56

Ceserani, Gian Paolo, *Storia della pubblicità in Italia* (Bari, 1988)

Chadwick, Nora, *The Celts* (London, 1997)

Charanis, Peter, 'Ethnic Changes in the Byzantine Empire in the Seventh Century', *Dumbarton Oaks Papers*, 13 (1959), pp. 23–44

Chiapparino, Francesco, 'L'industria alimentare dall'Unità al period fra le due guerre', in *Storia d'Italia, Annali 13: L'alimentazione*, ed. Alberto De Bernardi, Alberto Varni and Angelo Capatti (Torino, 1998), pp. 206–68

Chidichimo, Rinaldo, 'Un secolo di agricoltura italiana: uno sguardo d'insieme', in *L'Italia Agricola nel xx secolo: Storia e scenari*, ed. Società Italiana degli Agricoltori (Corigliano Calabro, 2000), pp. 3–7

Christie, Neil, 'Byzantine Liguria: An Imperial Province against the Longobards, AD 568–643', *Papers of the British School at Rome*, 83 (1990), pp. 229–71

Chrzan, Janet, 'Slow Food: What, Why, and to Where?', *Food, Culture and Society*, VII/2 (2004), pp. 117–32

Churchill Semple, Ellen, 'Geographic Factors in the Ancient Mediterranean Grain Trade', *Annals of the Association of American Geographers*, 11 (1921), pp. 47–74

Cinotto, Simone, 'La cucina diasporica: il cibo come segno di identità culturale', in *Storia d'Italia, Annali 24: Migrazioni*, ed. Alberto De Bernardi, Alberto Varni and Angelo Capatti (Turin, 2009), pp. 653–72

——, *Terra soffice uva nera: Vitivinicoltori piemontesi in California prima e dopo il Proibizionismo* (Turin, 2008)

Citarella, Armand O., 'Patterns in Medieval Trade: The Commerce of Amalfi before the Crusades', *The Journal of Economic History*, xxviii/4 (1968), pp. 531–55

Clifford, Richard J., 'Phoenician Religion', *Bulletin of the American Schools of Oriental Research*, 279 (1990), pp. 55–64

Coe, Sophie D., *America's First Cuisines* (Austin, 1994)

Cogliati Arano, Luisa, *The Medieval Health Handbook: Tacuinum Sanitatis* (New York, 1976)

Conti, Paolo C., *La leggenda del buon cibo italiano* (Rome, 2006)

Corner, Paul, 'Women in Fascist Italy: Changing Family Roles in the Transition from an Agricultural to an Industrial Society', *European History Quarterly*, xxiii/1 (1997), pp. 51–68

Corrado, Vincenzo, *Il Credenziere di Buon Gusto* (Naples, 1778)

Corti, Paola, 'Emigrazione e consuetudini alimentary, in *Storia d'Italia, Annali 13: L'alimentazione*, ed. Alberto De Bernardi, Alberto Varni and Angelo Capatti (Turin, 1998), pp. 681–719

Cortonesi, Alfio, 'Food Production', in *A Cultural History of Food: In the Medieval Age*, ed. Fabio Parasecoli and Peter Scholliers (Oxford, 2012), pp. 19–36

Costambeys, Marios, 'Settlement, Taxation and the Condition of the Peasantry in Post-Roman Central Italy', *Journal of Agrarian Change*, ix/1 (2009), pp. 92–119

Counihan, Carole, *Around the Tuscan Table: Food, Family, and Gender in Twentieth-century Florence* (New York and London, 2004)

Cremaschi, Mauro, Chiara Pizzi and Veruska Valsecchi, 'Water Management and Land Use in the Terramare and a Possible Climatic Co-factor in their Abandonment: The Case Study of the Terramara of Poviglio Santa Rosa (Northern Italy)', *Quaternary International*, cli/1 (2006), pp. 87–98

Cristofani, Mauro, 'Economia e società', in Massimo Pallottino et al., *Rasenna: Storia e civiltà degli Etruschi* (Milan, 1986), pp. 79–156

Crosby, Alfred, *The Columbian Exchange: Biological and Cultural Consequences* of 1492 (Westport, CT, 1972)

Crotty, Patricia, 'The Mediterranean Diet as a Food Guide: The Problem of Culture and History', *Nutrition Today*, xxxiii/6 (1998), pp. 227–32

Curtis, Robert I., 'Professional Cooking, Kitchens, and Service Work', in *A Cultural History of Food in Antiquity*, ed. Fabio Parasecoli and Peter Scholliers (London, 2012), pp. 113–32

Dalby, Andrew, *Siren Feasts: A History of Food and Gastronomy in Greece* (London, 1996)

D'Arms, John H., 'The Culinary Reality of Roman Upper-class Convivia: Integrating Texts and Images', *Comparative Studies in Society and History*, xlvi/3 (2004), pp. 428–50

Davidson, James, *Courtesans and Fishcakes: The Consuming Passions of Classical Athens* (New York, 1997)

De Angelis, Franco, 'Going against the Grain in Sicilian Greek Economics', *Greece and Rome*, LIII/1 (2006), pp. 29–47

——, 'Trade and Agriculture at Megara Hyblaia', *Oxford Journal of Archaeology*, XXI/3 (2002), pp. 299–310

Decker, Michael, 'Plants and Progress: Rethinking the Islamic Agricultural Revolution', *Journal of World History*, XX/2 (2009), pp. 197–206

Delogu, Marco, 'Due Migrazioni', *Sguardi online*, 54 (2007), available at www.nital.it

——, *Pastori*, vol. II (Roma, 2009)

Denker, Joel, *The World on a Plate: A Tour through the History of America's Ethnic Cuisines* (Boulder, CO, 2003)

De Ruyt, Claire, 'Les produits vendus au macellum', *Food and History*, V/1 (2007), pp. 135–50

Devoto, Fernando, *La Historia de los Italianos en la Argentina* (Buenos Aires, 2008)

Devoto, Fernando, Gianfausto Rosoli and Diego Armus, *La inmigración italiana en la Argentina* (Buenos Aires, 2000)

Diamond, Jared, *Guns, Germs, and Steel* (New York, 1997)

Dickie, John, *Delizia: The Epic History of the Italians and Their Food* (New York, 2008)

Dietler, Michael, 'Our Ancestors the Gauls: Archaeology, Ethnic Nationalism, and the Manipulation of Celtic Identity in Modern Europe', *American Anthropologist, New Series*, XCVI/3 (1994), pp. 584–605

Diner, Hasia, *Hungering for America: Italian, Irish, and Jewish Foodways in the Age of Migration* (Cambridge, MA, 2001)

Directorate-General for Agriculture and Rural Development, *An Analysis of the EU Organic Sector* (Brussels, 2010)

di Schino, June, and Furio Luccichenti, *Il cuoco segreto dei papi – Bartolomeo Scappi e la Confraternita dei cuochi e dei pasticceri* (Roma, 2008)

Dosi, Antonietta and François Schnell, *Le abitudini alimentari dei Romani* (Rome, 1992)

——, *Pasti e vasellame da tavola* (Rome, 1992)

——, *I Romani in cucina* (Rome, 1992)

Dupont, Florence, 'The Grammar of Roman Food', in *Food: A Culinary History from Antiquity to the Present*, ed. Jean-Louis Flandrin and Massimo Montanari (New York, 1999), pp. 113–27

Dursteler, Eric E., 'Food and Politics', in *A Cultural History of Food: In the Renaissance*, ed. Fabio Parasecoli and Peter Scholliers (London, 2012), pp. 83–100

Ellis, Steven J. R., 'Eating and Drinking Out', in *A Cultural History of Food in Antiquity*, ed. Fabio Parasecoli and Peter Scholliers (London, 2012), pp. 95–112

——, 'The Pompeian Bar: Archaeology and the Role of Food and Drink Outlets in an Ancient Community', *Food and History*, II/1 (2004), pp. 41–58

Erdkamp, Paul, 'Food Security, Safety, and Crises', in *A Cultural History of Food in Antiquity*, ed. Fabio Parasecoli and Peter Scholliers (London, 2012), pp. 57–74

——, *The Grain Market in the Roman Empire: A Social, Political and Economic Study* (Cambridge, 2005)

——, *Hunger and the Sword: Warfare and Food Supply in Roman Republican Wars (264–30 BC)* (Amsterdam, 1998)

European Commission, 'Commission Regulation (EU) no 97/2010', *Official Journal of the European Union*, V/2 (2010), pp. L34/7–16

Faas, Patrick, *Around the Roman Table: Food and Feasting in Ancient Rome* (New York, 1994)

Fabbri Dall'Oglio, Maria Attilia, and Alessandro Fortis, *Il gastrononomo errante Giacomo Casanova* (Rome, 1998)

Fagan, Brian, *Fish on Friday: Feasting, Fasting, and the Discovery of the New World* (New York, 2006)

——, *The Little Ice Age: How Climate Made History, 1300–1850* (New York, 2001)

Falabrino, Gian Luigi, *Storia della pubblicità in Italia dal 1945 a oggi* (Rome, 2007)

Falasca Zamponi, Simonetta, *Lo Spettacolo del Fascismo* (Rome, 2003)

Fearne, Andrew, Susan Hornibrook and Sandra Dedman, 'The Management of Perceived Risk in the Food Supply Chain: A Comparative Study of Retailer-led Beef Quality Assurance Schemes in Germany and Italy', *International Food and Agribusiness Management Review*, IV/1 (2001), pp. 19–36

Federazione Nazionale Fascista Pubblici Esercizi, *Trattorie d'Italia 1939* (Rome, 1939)

Feeley-Harnik, Gillian, *The Lord's Table: The Meaning of Food in Early Judaism and Christianity* (Washington and London, 1994)

Fernàndez-Armesto, Felipe, *Near a Thousand Tables* (New York, 2002)

Ferrara, Massimo, 'Food, Migration, and Identity: Halal Food and Muslim Immigrants in Italy', masters thesis, Center for Global and International Studies, University of Kansas, 2011

Ferretti, Maria Paola, and Paolo Magaudda, 'The Slow Pace of Institutional Change in the Italian Food System', *Appetite*, LXVII/2 (2006), pp. 161–9

Ferris, Kate, '"Fare di ogni famiglia italiana un fortilizio": The League of Nations' Economic Sanctions and Everyday Life in Venice', *Journal of Modern Italian Studies*, XI/2 (2006), pp. 117–42

Fissore, Gianpaolo, 'Gli italiani e il cibo sul grande schermo dal secondo dopoguerra a oggi', in *Il cibo dell'altro: movimenti migratori e culture alimentari nella Torino del Novecento*, ed. Marcella Filippa (Rome, 2003), pp. 163–79

Flint-Hamilton, Kimberly B., 'Legumes in Ancient Greece and Rome: Food, Medicine, or Poison?', *Hesperia: The Journal of the American School of Classical Studies at Athens*, LXVIII/3 (1999), pp. 371–85

Fondazione Qualivita – Ismea, *Rapporto 2011 sulle produzioni agroalimentari italiane dop igp stg* (Siena, 2012)

Foxhall, Lin, 'The Dependent Tenant: Land Leasing and Labour in Italy and Greece', *The Journal of Roman Studies*, 80 (1990), pp. 97–114

Francks, Penelope, 'From Peasant to Entrepreneur in Italy and Japan', *Journal of Peasant Studies*, XXII/4 (1995), pp. 699–709

Frattarelli Fischer, Lucia, and Stefano Villani, '"People of Every Mixture": *Immigration and Emigration in Historical Perspective*, ed. Ann Katherine Isaacs (Pisa, 2007), pp. 93–107

Gabaccia, Donna, *We Are What We Eat: Ethnic Food and the Making of Americans* (Cambridge, MA, 1998)

Gabrieli, Francesco, 'Greeks and Arabs in the Central Mediterranean Area', *Dumbarton Oaks Papers*, 18 (1964), pp. 57–65

Gallo, Giampaolo, Renato Covino and Roberto Monicchia, 'Crescita, crisi, riorganizzazione: l'industria alimentare dal dopoguerra a oggi', in *Storia d'italia, Annali 13: L'alimentazione*, ed. Alberto De Bernardi, Alberto Varni and Angelo Capatti (Turin, 1998), pp. 269–343

Galloni, Paolo, *Storia e cultura della caccia: dalla preistoria a oggi* (Bari, 2000)

Gallucci, Margaret, and Paolo Rossi, *Benvenuto Cellini: Sculptor, Goldsmith, Writer* (Cambridge, 2004)

Garnsey, Peter, *Food and Society in Classical Antiquity* (Cambridge, 1999)

Gaytàn, Narie Sarita, 'Globalizing Resistance: Slow Food and New Local Imaginaries', *Food, Culture and Society*, VII/2 (2004), pp. 97–116

Gentilcore, David, *Pomodoro: A History of the Tomato in Italy* (New York, 2010)

Giannetti, Laura, 'Italian Renaissance Food-fashioning or the Triumph of Greens', *California Italian Studies*, I/2 (2010), available at http://escholarship.org

Gibson, Johanna, 'Markets in Tradition – Traditional Agricultural Communities in Italy and the Impact of GMOs', *Script-ed*, III/3 (2006), pp. 243–52

Ginsborg, Paul, *A History of Contemporary Italy: Society and Politics 1943–1988* (New York, 2003)

Girardelli, Davide, 'Commodified Identities: The Myth of Italian Food in the United States', *Journal of Communication Inquiry*, XXVIII/4 (2004), pp. 307–24

Giulietti, Monica, 'Buyer and Seller Power in Grocery Retailing: Evidence from Italy', *Revista de Economía del Rosario*, X/2 (2007), pp. 109–25

Giusti Galardi, Giovanna, *Dolci a corte: dipinti ed altro* (Livorno, 2001)

Goldstein, Darra, 'Implements of Eating', in *Feeding Desire: Design and the Tools of the Table, 1500–2005*, ed. Sarah D. Coffin, Ellen Lupton, Darra Goldstein and Barbara Bloemink (New York, 2006), pp. 115–63

Goldstein, Joyce, *Cucina Ebraica* (San Francisco, 1998)

Grainger, Sally, 'A New Approach to Roman Fish Sauce', *Petits Propos Culinaires*, 83 (2007), pp. 92–111

Granados, Leonardo, and Carlos Álvarez, 'Viabilidad de establecer el sistema de denominaciones de origen de los productos agroalimentarios en Costa Rica', *Agronomía Costarricense*, XXVI/1 (2002), pp. 63–72

Gran-Aymerich, Jean, and Eve Gran-Aymerich, 'Les Etrusques en Gaule et en Ibérie: Du Mythe à la Réalité des Dérnieres Decouvertes', *Etruscan Studies*, 9, Article 17 (2002), available at: http://scholarworks.umass.edu

Grappe, Yann, *Sulle Tracce del Gusto: Storia e cultura del vino nel Medievo* (Bari, 2006)

Greif, Avner, 'On the Political Foundations of the Late Medieval Commercial Revolution: Genoa during the Twelfth and Thirteenth Centuries', *The Journal of Economic History*, LIV/2 (1994), pp. 271–87

Grieco, Allen J., 'Body and Soul', in *A Cultural History of Food: In the Medieval Age*, ed. Fabio Parasecoli and Peter Scholliers (London, 2012), pp. 143–9

Grocock, Christopher, Sally Grainger and Dan Shadrake, *Apicius: A Critical Edition with an Introduction and English Translation* (Totnes, 2006)

Guerrini, Olindo, *L'arte di utilizzare gli avanzi della mensa* [1917] (Padua, 1993)

Guillou, André, 'Production and Profits in the Byzantine Province of Italy (Tenth to Eleventh Centuries): An Expanding Society', *Dumbarton Oaks Papers*, 28 (1974), pp. 89–109

Guttman, Naomi, and Roberta L. Krueger, 'Utica Greens: Central New York's Italian–American Specialty', *Gastronomica*, IX/3 (2009), pp. 62–7

Haber, Barbara, 'The Mediterranean Diet: A View From History', *American Journal of Clinical Nutrition*, 10 (1997), pp. 1053S–7S

Halkier, Bente, Lotte Holm, Mafalda Domingues, Paolo Magaudda, Annemette Nielsen and Laura Terragni, 'Trusting, Complex, Quality Conscious or Unprotected?', *Journal of Consumer Culture*, VII/3 (2007), pp. 379–402

Halstead, Paul, 'Food Production', in *A Cultural History of Food in Antiquity*, ed. Fabio Parasecoli and Peter Scholliers (London, 2012), pp. 21–39

Hardt, Michael, and Antonio Negri, *Empire* (Cambridge, MA, 2001)

Harrison, Adrian Paul, and E. M. Bartels, 'A Modern Appraisal of Ancient Etruscan Herbal Practices', *American Journal of Pharmacology and Toxicology*, I/1 (2006), pp. 21–4

Haussmann, Giovanni, 'Il suolo d'Italia nella storia', in *Storia d'Italia: I caratteri original*, vol. 1, ed. Ruggiero Romano and Corrado Vivanti (Turin, 1989), pp. 61–132

Helstosky, Carol, *Garlic and Oil: Food and Politics in Italy* (Oxford, 2004)

Hess, Catherine, George Saliba and Linda Komaroff, *The Arts of Fire: Islamic Influences on Glass and Ceramics of the Italian Renaissance* (Los Angeles, 2004)

Hobsbawm, Eric, and Terence Ranger, eds, *The Invention of Tradition* (Cambridge, 1983)

Hourani, George F., *Arab Seafaring in the Indian Ocean and In Ancient and Early Medieval Times* (Princeton, NJ, 1995)

Huet, Valérie, 'Le sacrifice disparu: Les reliefs de boucherie', *Food and History*, V/1 (2007), pp. 197–223

Huliyeti, Hasimu, Sergio Marchesini and Maurizio Canavari, 'Chinese Distribution Practitioners' Attitudes towards Italian Quality Foods', *Journal of Chinese Economic and Foreign Trade Studies*, I/3 (2008), pp. 214–31

Hunt, C., C. Malone, J. Sevink and S. Stoddart, 'Environment, Soils and Early Agriculture in Apennine Central Italy', *World Archaeology*, XXII/1 (1990), pp. 34–44

Isola, Gianni, *Abbassa la tua radio per favore . . . Storia dell'ascolto radiofonico nell'italia fascista* (Firenze, 1990)

ISTAT, *Rapporto Annuale 2012: La situazione del Paese* (Rome, 2012)

Istituto Italiano Alimenti Surgelati, *I surgelati: amici di famiglia* (Rome, 2011)

James, Roberta, 'The Reliable Beauty of Aroma: Staples of Food and Cultural Production among Italian Australians', *Australian Journal of Anthropology*, XV/1 (2004), pp. 23–39

Jaucourt, Louis, Chevalier de, 'Cuisine', in *Encyclopédie ou Dictionnaire raisonné des sciences, des arts et des métiers*, vol. IV (Paris, 1754), p. 538

Jenkins, Nancy Harmon, 'Two Ways of Looking at Maestro Martino', *Gastronomica*, VII/2 (2007), pp. 97–103

Johansson, Ulf, and Steve Burt, 'The Buying of Private Brands and Manufacturer Brands in Grocery Retailing: a Comparative Study of Buying Processes in the UK, Sweden and Italy', *Journal of Marketing Management*, XX/7–8 (2004), pp. 799–824

Johnson, Hugh, *Story of Wine* (London, 1989)

Kamen, Henry, 'The Mediterranean and the Expulsion of Spanish Jews in 1492', *Past and Present*, CXIX/1 (1988), pp. 30–55

Keele, Kenneth D., 'Leonardo da Vinci's Studies of the Alimentary Tract', *Journal of the History of Medicine*, XXVII/2 (1972), pp. 133–44

Kirshenblatt-Gimblett, Barbara, 'Theorizing Heritage', *Ethnomusicology*, XXXIX/3 (1995), pp. 367–80

Kreutz, Barbara M., 'Ghost Ships and Phantom Cargoes: Reconstructing Early Amalfitan Trade', *Journal of Medieval History*, 20 (1994), pp. 347–57

Krondl, Michael, *The Taste of Conquest: The Rise and Fall of the Three Great Cities of Spice* (New York, 2007)

Kruta, Venceslas and Valerio M. Manfredi, *I Celti in Italia* (Milan, 1999)

Kummer, Corby, *The Pleasures of Slow Food: Celebrating Authentic Traditions, Flavors, and Recipes* (San Francisco, 2002)

Kurlansky, Mark, *Salt: A World History* (New York, 2002)

Lane, Frederic, 'The Mediterranean Spice Trade: Further Evidence of its Revival in the Sixteenth Century', *The American Historical Review*, XLV/3 (1940), pp. 581–90

Lapertosa, Viviana, *Dalla fame all'abbondanza: Gli italiani e il cibo nel cinema dal dopoguerra ad oggi* (Turin, 2002)

Latini, Antonio, *Lo scalco alla moderna. Overo l'arte di ben disporre li conviti* (Naples, 1693)

Laudan, Rachel, 'Slow Food: The French Terroir Strategy, and Culinary Modernism', *Food, Culture and Society*, VII/2 (2004), pp. 133–44

Laura, Ernesto, *Le stagioni dell'aquila: storia dell'Istituto Luce* (Rome, 2000)

Lehmann, Matthias B., 'A Livornese "Port Jew" and the Sephardim of the Ottoman Empire', *Jewish Social Studies*, XI/2 (2005), pp. 51–76

Leighton, Robert, 'Later Prehistoric Settlement Patterns in Sicily: Old Paradigms and New Surveys', *European Journal of Archaeology*, VIII/3 (2005), pp. 261–87

——, *Sicily before History: An Archaeological Survey from the Paleolithic to the Iron Age* (Ithaca, 1999)

Leitch, Alison, 'The Social Life of Lardo: Slow Food in Fast Times', *Asian Pacific Journal of Anthropology*, I/1 (2000), pp. 103–28

Levenstein, Harvey, *Paradox of Plenty: A Social History of Eating in Modern America* (Berkeley and Los Angeles, 2003)

Lonni, Ada, 'Dall'alterazione all'adulterazione: le sofisticazioni alimentari nella società industriale', in *Storia d'Italia, Annali 13: L'alimentazione*, ed. Alberto De Bernardi, Alberto Varni and Angelo Capatti (Turin, 1998), pp. 531–84

Luminati, Pietro, *La Borsa Nera* (Rome, 1945)

Luzzato Fegiz, Pierpaolo, *Alimentazione e Prezzi in tempo di Guerra, 1942–43* (Trieste, 1948)

Maestro Martino, *The Art of Cooking: The First of Modern Cookery Book* (Berkeley and Los Angeles, 2005)

Magness, Jodi, 'A Near Eastern Ethnic Element Among the Etruscan Elite?', *Etruscan Studies*, VIII/4 (2001), pp. 79–117

Malanima, Paolo, 'Urbanisation and the Italian Economy during the Last Millennium', *European Review of Economic History*, 9 (2005), pp. 97–122

Manfredi, Valerio M., *I greci d'Occidente* (Milan, 1996)

Marchese, Salvatore, *Benedetta patata: Una storia del '700, un trattato e 50 ricette* (Padu, 1999)

Mariani, John F., *How Italian Food Conquered the World* (New York, 2011)

Mariani-Costantini, Renato, and Aldo Mariani-Costantini, 'An Outline of the History of Pellagra in Italy', *Journal of Anthropological Sciences*, 85 (2007), pp. 163–71

Marìn, Manuela, 'Beyond Taste', in *A Taste of Thyme: Culinary Cultures of the Middle East*, ed. Sami Zubaida and Richard Tapper (London, 2000), pp. 205–14

Mauro, Luciano, and Paola Valitutti, *Il Giardino della Minerva* (Salerno, 2011)

Mayes, Frances, *Under the Tuscan Sun* (New York, 1997)

Mazoyer, Marcel and Laurence Roudart, *A History of World Agriculture: From the Neolithic Age to the Current Crisis* (New York, 2006)

Mazzotti, Massimo, 'Enlightened Mills: Mechanizing Olive Oil Production in Mediterranean Europe', *Technology and Culture*, XLV/2 (2004), pp. 277–304

Meneley, Anne, 'Like an Extra Virgin', *American Anthropologist*, CIX/4 (2007), pp. 678–87

Miele, Mara and Jonathan Murdoch, 'The Practical Aesthetics of Traditional Cuisines: Slow Food in Tuscany', *Sociologia Ruralis*, XLII/4 (2002), pp. 312–28

Miller, James Innes, *The Spice Trade of the Roman Empire, 29 BC to AD 641* [1969] (Oxford, 1998)

Mingozzi, Achille, and Rosa Maria Bertino, *Rapporto Bio Bank 2012: Prosegue la corsa per accorciare la filiera* (Forlí, 2012)

Mohring, Maren, 'Staging and Consuming the Italian Lifestyle: The Gelateria and the Pizzeria-Ristorante in Post-war Germany', *Food and History*, VII/2 (2009), pp. 181–202

Monelli, Paolo, *Il Ghiottone Errante* (Milan, 1935)

Montanari, Massimo, *Convivio* (Bari, 1989)

——, 'Food Systems and Models of Civilization', in *Food: A Culinary History from Antiquity to the Present*, ed. Jean-Louis Flandrin and Massimo Montanari (New York, 1999), pp. 55–64

——, 'Gastronomia e Cultura', in *Introduzione alla Guida Gastronomica Italiana 1931* (Milan, 2003), pp. 4–5

——, *L'identità Italiana in Cucina* (Rome, 2010)

——, *Nuovo Convivio* (Bari, 1991)

——, 'Production Structures and Food Systems in the Early Middle Ages Civilization', in *Food: A Culinary History from Antiquity to the Present*, ed. Jean-Louis Flandrin and Massimo Montanari (New York, 1999), pp. 168–77

Moroni Salvatori, Maria Paola, 'Ragguaglio bibliografico sui ricettari del primo Novecento', in *Storia d'Italia, Annali 13: L'alimentazione*, ed. Alberto De Bernardi, Alberto Varni and Angelo Capatti (Turin, 1998), pp. 887–925

Morris, Ian, *Why the West Rules – for Now: The Patterns of History and What They Reveal about the Future* (New York, 2011)

Morris, Jonathan, 'Imprenditoria italiana in Gran Bretagna. Il consumo del caffè "stile italiano"', *Italia Contemporanea*, 241 (2005), pp. 540–52

——, 'Making Italian Espresso, Making Espresso Italian', *Food and History*, VIII/2 (2010), pp. 155–84

Moscati, Sabatino, *Così nacque l'Italia: profili di popoli riscoperti* (Turin, 1998)

Mudu, Pierpaolo, 'The People's Food: The Ingredients of "Ethnic" Hierarchies and the Development of Chinese Restaurants in Rome', *GeoJournal*, 68 (2007), pp. 195–210

Mueller, Tom, *Extra Virginity: The Sublime and Scandalous World of Olive Oil* (New York, 2012)

Musti, Domenico, *L'economia in Grecia* (Bari, 1999)

Nadeau, Robin, 'Body and Soul', in *A Cultural History of Food in Antiquity*, ed. Fabio Parasecoli and Peter Scholliers (London, 2012), pp. 145–62

——, 'Stratégies de survie et rituels festifs dans le monde gréco-romain', in *Profusion et pénurie: Les hommes face à leurs besoins alimentaires*, ed. Martin Bruegel (Rennes, 2009), pp. 55–69

Nestle, Marion, 'Mediterranean Diets: Historical and Research Overview', *American Journal of Clinical Nutrition*, 61 (1995), pp. 1313S–20S

Niceforo, Alfredo, *Italiani del Nord, italiani del Sud* (Turin, 1901)

Nosi, Costanza and Lorenzo Zanni, 'Moving from "Typical Products" to "Food-related Services": The Slow Food Case as a New Business Paradigm', *British Food Journal*, CVI/10–11 (2004), pp. 779–92

Osborne, Robin, 'Pots, Trade, and the Archaic Greek Economy', *Antiquity*, 70 (1996), pp. 31–44

Ouerfelli, Mohamed, 'Production et commerce du sucre en Sicile au XVe siècle', *Food and History*, I/1 (2003), pp. 103–22

Page, Jutta-Annette, *Beyond Venice: Glass in Venetian Style, 1500–1750* (Manchester, VT, 2004)

Pallottino, Massimo, *The Etruscans* (Bloomington, 1975)

——, *A History of Earliest Italy* (Ann Arbor, MI, 1991)

Palma, Pina, 'Hermits, Husband and Lovers: Moderation and Excesses at the Table in the *Decameron*', *Food and History*, IV/2 (2006), pp. 151–62

Panagia, Davide, *The Political Life of Sensation* (Durham and London, 2009)

Parasecoli, Fabio, 'Postrevolutionary Chowhounds: Food, Globalization, and the Italian Left', *Gastronomica*, III/3 (2003), pp. 29–39

Parzen, Jeremy, 'Please Play with Your Food: An Incomplete Survey of Culinary Wonders in Italian Renaissance Cookery', *Gastronomica*, IV/4 (2004), pp. 25–33

Pascali, Lara, 'Two Stoves, Two Refrigerators, Due Cucine: The Italian Immigrant Home with Two Kitchens', *Gender, Place and Culture*, XIII/6 (2006), pp. 685–95

Paxson, Heather, 'Slow Food in a Fat Society: Satisfying Ethical Appetites', *Gastronomica*, V/2 (2005), pp. 14–18

Pecorini, Alberto, 'The Italian as an Agricultural Laborer', *Annals of the American Academy of Political and Social Science*, XXXIII/2 (1909), pp. 156–66

Pedrocco, Giorgio, 'La conservazione del cibo: dal sale all'industria agro-alimentare', in *Storia d'Italia, Annali 13: L'alimentazione*, ed. Alberto De Bernardi, Alberto Varni and Angelo Capatti (Torino, 1998), pp. 377–447

——, 'Viticultura e enologia in Italia nel XIX secolo', in *La vite e il vino: storia e diritto (secoli XI–XIX)*, ed. Maria Da Passano, Antonello Mattone, Franca Mele and Pinuccia F. Simbula (Rome, 2000), pp. 613–27

Pellecchia, Marco et al., 'The Mystery of Etruscan Origins: Novel Clues from Bos Taurus Mitochondrial DNA', *Proceedings of the Royal Society B*, CCLXXIV/1614 (2007), pp. 1175–9

Pendergrast, Mark. *Uncommon Grounds: The History of Coffee and How It Transformed Our World* (New York, 1999)

Perry, Charles, 'Sicilian Cheese in Medieval Arab Recipes', *Gastronomica*, I/I (2001), pp. 76–7

Petrini, Carlo, ed., *Slow Food: Collected Thoughts on Taste, Tradition, and the Honest Pleasures of Food* (White River Junction, VT, 2001)

——, *Slow Food: The Case of Taste* (New York, 2003)

Petrini, Carlo, and Gigi Padovani, *Slow Food Revolution* (New York, 2006)

Pieraccini, Lisa, 'Families, Feasting, and Funerals: Funerary Ritual at Ancient Caere', *Etruscan Studies*, 7/Article 3 (2000), available at http://scholarworks.umass.edu

Pilcher, Jeffrey M., *Food in World History* (New York, 2006)

Pinhasi, Ron, Joaquim Fort and Albert Ammerman, 'Tracing the Origin and Spread of Agriculture in Europe', *PLOS Biology*, III/12 (2005), e410, doi:10.1371/journal.pbio.0030410

Pinna, Cao, 'Le classi povere', in *Atti della commissione parlamentare di inchiesta sulla miseria in Italia e sui mezzi per combatterla*, vol. II (Rome, 1954)

Pinto, Giuliano, 'Food Safety', in *A Cultural History of Food: In the Medieval Age*, ed. Fabio Parasecoli and Peter Scholliers (London, 2012), pp. 57–72

Pollard, Elizabeth Ann, 'Pliny's Natural History and the Flavian Templum Pacis: Botanical Imperialism in First-century CE Rome', *Journal of World History*, XX/3 (2009), pp. 309–38

Portincasa, Agnese, 'Il Touring Club Italiano e la Guida Gastronomica d'Italia. Creazione, circolazione del modello e tracce della sua evoluzione (1931–1984)', *Food and History*, VI/1 (2008), pp. 83–116

Presenza, Angelo, Antonio Minguzzi and Clara Petrillo, 'Managing Wine Tourism in Italy', *Journal of Tourism Consumption and Practice*, II/1 (2010), pp. 46–61

Price, T. Douglas, ed., *Europe's First Farmers* (Cambridge, 2000)

Purcell, N., 'Wine and Wealth in Ancient Italy', *Journal of Roman Studies*, 75 (1985), pp. 1–19

Quirico, Domenico, *Naja: Storia del servizio di leva in Italia* (Milan, 2008)

Race, Gianni, *La cucina del mondo classic* (Naples, 1999)

Rapisardi, Mario, *Versi: scelti e riveduti da esso* (Milan, 1888)

Rebora, Giovanni, *Culture of the Fork* (New York, 2001)

Reese, David S., 'Whale Bones and Shell Purple-dye at Motya (Western Sicily, Italy)', *Oxford Journal of Archaeology*, XXIV/2 (2005), pp. 107–14

Revel, Jean François, *Culture and Cuisine: A Journey through the History of Food* (New York, 1982)

Reynolds, Peter J., 'Rural Life and Farming', in *The Celtic World*, ed. Miranda Green (New York, 1995), pp. 176–209

Riley, Gillian, 'Food in Painting', in *A Cultural History of Food: In the Renaissance*, ed. Fabio Parasecoli and Peter Scholliers (London, 2012), pp. 171–82

Robb, John, and Doortje Van Hove, 'Gardening, Foraging and Herding: Neolithic Land Use and Social Territories in Southern Italy', *Antiquity*, 77 (2003), pp. 241–54

Roberts, J. M., *The Penguin History of the World* (London, 1995)

Roden, Claudia, *The Book of Jewish Food* (New York, 1998)

Rodríguez-Pose, Andrés, and Maria Cristina Refolo, 'The Link between Local Production Systems and Public and University Research in Italy', *Environment and Planning A*, xxxv/8 (2003), pp. 1477–92

Roesti, Robert, 'The Declining Economic Role of the Mediterranean Tuna Fishery', *American Journal of Economics and Sociology*, xxv/1 (1966), pp. 77–90

Rosano, Dick, *Wine Heritage: The Story of Italian American Vintners* (San Francisco, 2000)

Ruscillo, Deborah, 'When Gluttony Ruled!', *Archaeology*, LIV/6 (2001), pp. 20–24

Russu, Anna Grazia, 'Power and Social Structure in Nuragic Sardinia', *Eliten in der Bronzezeit-Ergebnisse Zweier Kolloquien in Mainz und Athen-Teil*, 1 (1999), pp. 197–221, plates 17–22

Sabatino Lopez, Roberto, 'Market Expansion: The Case of Genoa', *The Journal of Economic History*, xxiv/4 (1964), pp. 445–64

Salignac de la Mothe-Fénelon, François de, *Telemachus, Son of Ulysses*, trans. Patrick Riley [1699] (Cambridge, 1994)

Sarris, Peter, 'Aristocrats, Peasants and the Transformation of Rural Society, c. 400–800', *Journal of Agrarian Change*, ix/1 (2009), pp. 3–22

Sassatelli, Roberta, and Alan Scott, 'Novel Food, New Markets and Trust Regimes: Responses to the Erosion of Consumers' Confidence in Austria, Italy and the UK', *European Societies*, iii/2 (2001), pp. 213–44

Scandizzo, Pasquale Lucio, 'L'agricoltura e lo sviluppo economico', in *L'Italia Agricola nel xx secolo: Storia e scenari* (Corigliano Calabro, 2000), pp. 9–55

Scarpato, Rosario, 'Pizza: An Organic Free Range: Tale in Four Slices', *Divine*, 20 (2001), pp. 30–41

Scarpellini, Emanuela, 'Shopping American-style: The Arrival of the Supermarket in Postwar Italy', *Enterprise and Society*, v/4 (2004), pp. 625–68

Scheid, John, 'Le statut de la viande à Rome', *Food and History*, v/1 (2007), pp. 19–28

Schmitt-Pantel, Pauline, 'Greek Meals: A Civic Ritual', in *Food: A Culinary History from Antiquity to the Present*, ed. Jean-Louis Flandrin and Massimo Montanari (New York, 1999), pp. 90–95

Schnapp, Jeffrey T., 'The Romance of Caffeine and Aluminum', *Critical Inquiry*, xxviii/1 (2001), pp. 244–69

Sentieri, Maurizio, and Zazzu Guido, *I semi dell'Eldorado* (Bari, 1992)

Sereni, Emilio, 'Agricoltura e mondo rurale', in *Storia d'Italia: I caratteri originali*, vol. 1, ed. Ruggiero Romano and Corrado Vivanti (Torino, 1989), pp. 133–252

——, *History of the Italian Agricultural Landscape* (Princeton, NJ, 1997)

Serventi, Silvano, and Françoise Sabban, *Pasta: The Story of a Universal Food* (New York, 2002)

Servi Machlin, Edda, *Classic Italian Jewish Cooking: Traditional Recipes and Menus* (New York, 2005)

Sherratt, Susan, and Andrew Sherratt, 'The Growth of the Mediterranean Economy in the Early First Millennium BC', *World Archaeology*, xxiv/3 (1993), pp. 361–78

Sicca, Lucio, *Lo straniero nel piatto* (Milan, 2002)

Siporin, Steve, 'From Kashrut to Cucina Ebraica: The Recasting of Italian Jewish Foodways', *The Journal of American Folklore*, CVII/424 (1994), pp. 268–81

Skinner, Patricia, *Family Power in Southern Italy: The Duchy of Gaeta and Its Neighbors, 850–1139* (Cambridge, 1995)

Small, Jocelyn Penny, 'Eat, Drink, and Be Merry: Etruscan Banquets', in *Murlo and the Etruscans: Art and Society in Ancient Etruria*, ed. Richard Daniel De Puma and Jocelyn Penny Small (Madison, 1994), pp. 85–94

Smith, Alison A., 'Family and Domesticity', in *A Cultural History of Food: In the Renaissance*, ed. Fabio Parasecoli and Peter Scholliers (London, 2012), pp. 135–50

Solier, Stéphane, 'Manières de tyran à la table de la satire latine: l'institutionnalisation de l'excès dans la convivialité romaine', *Food and History*, IV/2 (2006), pp. 91–111

Somogyi, Stefano, 'L'alimentazione nell'Italia unita', in *Storia d'Italia*, vol. V/1: *I documenti*, ed. Lellia Cracco Ruggini and Giorgio Cracco (Turin, 1973), pp. 841–87

Sonnino, Roberta, 'Quality Food, Public Procurement, and Sustainable Development: The School Meal Revolution in Rome', *Environment and Planning A*, XLI/2 (2009), pp. 425–40

Sorcinelli, Paolo, *Gli Italiani e il cibo: dalla polenta ai cracker* (Milan, 1999)

——, 'Identification Process at Work: Virtues of the Italian Working-class Diet in the First Half of the Twentieth Century', in *Food, Drink and Identity*, ed. Peter Scholliers (Oxford, 2001), pp. 81–97

Sori, Ercole, *L'emigrazione italiana dall'unità alla seconda guerra mondiale* (Bologna, 1980)

Sozio, Pina, 'Fornelli d'Italia', *Gambero Rosso*, XIX/221 (2010), pp. 86–91

Spanò Giammellaro, Antonella, 'The Phoenicians and the Carthaginians: The Early Mediterranean Diet', in *Food: A Culinary History from Antiquity to the Present*, ed. Jean-Louis Flandrin and Massimo Montanari (New York, 1999), pp. 55–64

Sperduti, Giuseppe, *Riccardo di San Germano: La Cronaca* (Cassino, 1995)

Starr, Joshua, 'The Mass Conversion of Jews in Southern Italy (1290–1293)', *Speculum*, XXI/2 (1946), pp. 203–11

Strong, Roy, *Feast: A History of Grand Eating* (Orlando, FL, 2002)

Taddei, Francesco, 'Il cibo nell'Italia mezzadrile fra Ottocento and Novecento', in *Storia d'Italia, Annali 13: L'alimentazione*, ed. Alberto De Bernardi, Alberto Varni and Angelo Capatti (Turin, 1998), pp. 25–38

Tagliati, Giovanna, 'Olindo Guerrini gastronomo: Le rime romagnole de E' Viazze L'arte di utilizzare gli avanzi della mensa', *Storia e Futuro*, 20 (2009), available at www.storiaefuturo.com

Tasca, Luisa, 'The "Average Housewife" in Post-World War II Italy', *Journal of Women's History*, XVI/2 (2004), pp. 92–115

Teall, John L., 'The Grain Supply of the Byzantine Empire, 330–1025', *Dumbarton Oaks Papers*, 13 (1959), pp. 87–139

Teti, Vito, *Il colore del cibo* (Rome, 1999)

——, *La razza maledetta: origini del pregiudizio antimeridionale* (Rome, 2011)

Tirabassi, Maddalena, *Il Faro di Beacon Street. Social Workers e immigrate negli Stati Uniti (1910–1939)* (Milan, 1990)

Toaff, Ariel, *Mangiare alla giudia* (Bologna, 2000)

Tognotti, Eugenia, 'Alcolismo e pensiero medico nell'Italia liberale', in *La vite e il vino: storia e diritto (secoli XI–XIX)*, ed. Maria Da Passano, Antonello Mattone, Franca Mele and Pinuccia F. Simbula (Rome, 2000)

Touring Club Italiano, *Guida Gastronomica d'Italia* (Milan, 1931)

Trabalzi, Ferruccio, 'Crossing Conventions in Localized Food Networks: Insights from Southern Italy', *Environment and Planning A*, XXXIX/2 (2007), pp. 283–300

Tran, Nicholas, 'Le statut de travail des bouchers dans l'Occident romain de la fin de la République et du Haut-Empire', *Food and History*, V/1 (2007), pp. 151–67

Tregre Wilson, Nancy, *Louisiana's Food, Recipes, and Folkways* (Gretna, LA, 2005)

Trova, Assunta, 'L'approvvigionamento alimentare dell'esercito italiano', in *Storia d'Italia, Annali 13: L'alimentazione*, ed. Alberto De Bernardi, Alberto Varni and Angelo Capatti (Turin, 1998), pp. 495–530

Tuck, Anthony, 'The Etruscan Seated Banquet: Villanovan Ritual and Etruscan Iconography', *American Journal of Archaeology*, XCVIII/4 (1994), pp. 617–28

Turrini, Aida, Anna Saba, Domenico Perrone, Eugenio Cialfa and Amleto D'Amicis, 'Food Consumption Patterns in Italy: The INN-CA Study 1994–1996', *European Journal of Clinical Nutrition*, LV/7 (2001), pp. 571–88

Turrini, Lino, *La cucina ai tempi dei Gonzaga* (Milan, 2002)

Van Ginkel, Rob, 'Killing Giants of the Sea: Contentious Heritage and the Politics of Culture', *Journal of Mediterranean Studies*, XV/1 (2005), pp. 71–98

Varriano, John, 'At Supper with Leonardo', *Gastronomica*, VIII/3 (2008), pp. 75–9

——, 'Fruits and Vegetables as Sexual Metaphor in Late Renaissance Rome', *Gastronomica*, V/4 (2005), pp. 8–14

——, *Tastes and Temptations: Food and Art in Renaissance Italy* (Berkeley, CA, 2011)

Vecchio, Riccardo, 'Local Food at Italian Farmers' Markets: Three Case Studies', *International Journal of Sociology of Agriculture and Food*, XVII/2 (2010), pp. 122–39

Vené, Gian Franco, *Mille lire al mese: vita quotidiana della famiglia nell'Italia Fascista* (Milan, 1988)

Verga, Giovanni, *Cavalleria Rusticana and Other Stories*, trans. G. H. McWilliam (Harmondsworth, 1999)

Vernesi, Cristiano et al., 'The Etruscans: A Population-Genetic Study', *American Journal of Human Genetics*, LXXIV/4 (2004), pp. 694–704

Vetta, Massimo, 'The Culture of the Symposium', in *Food: A Culinary History from Antiquity to the Present*, ed. Jean-Louis Flandrin and Massimo Montanari (New York, 1999), pp. 96–105

Vössing, Konrad I., 'Family and Domesticity', in *A Cultural History of Food in Antiquity*, ed. Fabio Parasecoli and Peter Scholliers (London, 2012), pp. 133–43

Warden, Gregory, 'Ritual and Representation on a Campana Dinos in Boston', *Etruscan Studies*, 11/Article 8 (2008), available at http://scholarworks.umass.edu

Watson, Andrew, *Agricultural Innovation in the Early Islamic World* (Cambridge, 1983)

Watson, Wendy, *Italian Renaissance Ceramics* (Philadelphia, 2006)

Webster, Gary, *Duos Nuraghes: A Bronze Age Settlement in Sardinia, vol. 1:*
*The Interpretive Archaeology,* BAR *International Series 949* (Oxford, 2001)

Weinberg, Bennett A., and Bonnie K. Bealer, *The World of Caffeine: The Science and*
*Culture of the World's Most Popular Drug* (New York and London, 2002)

Welch, Evelyn, *Shopping in the Renaissance: Consumer Cultures in Italy, 1400–1600*
(New Haven and London, 2005)

Wharton Epstein, Ann, 'The Problem of Provincialism: Byzantine Monasteries in
Cappadocia and Monks in South Italy', *Journal of the Warburg and Courtauld*
*Institutes,* 42 (1979), pp. 28–46

Whitaker, Elizabeth D., 'Bread and Work: Pellagra and Economic Transformation
in Turn-of-the-century Italy', *Anthropological Quarter,* LXV/2 (1992), pp. 80–90

White, Lynn, 'The Byzantinization of Sicily', *American Historical Review,* XLII/1
(1936), pp. 1–21

White, Corky, 'Italian Food: Japan's Unlikely Culinary Passion', *The Atlantic*
(6 October 2010), available at www.theatlantic.com

White, Lynn Jr, 'Indic Elements in the Iconography of Petrarch's Trionfo Della
Morte', *Speculum,* 49 (1974), pp. 201–21

Williams, J.H.C., *Beyond the Rubicon: Romans and Gauls in Republican Italy*
(Oxford, 2001)

Wilson, Perry R., 'Cooking the Patriotic Omelette: Women and the Italian
Fascist Ruralization Campaign', *European History Quarterly,* XXVII/4 (1993),
pp. 351–47

Woods, Dwayne, 'Pockets of Resistance to Globalization: The Case of the Lega
Nord', *Patterns of Prejudice,* XLIII/2 (2009), pp. 161–77

Wright, Clifford A., *A Mediterranean Feast* (New York, 1999)

Zaia, Luca, *Adottare la terra (per non morire di fame)* (Milan, 2010)

Zamagni, Vera, *Economic History of Italy, 1860–1990: Recovery after Decline* (Oxford,
1993)

——, 'L'evoluzione dei consumi tra tradizione e innovazione', in *Storia d'Italia,*
*Annali 13: L'alimentazione,* ed. Alberto De Bernardi, Alberto Varni and Angelo
Capatti (Turin, 1998), pp. 169–204

Zaouali, Lilia, *Medieval Cuisine of the Islamic World* (Berkeley, CA, 2007)

Zeldes, Nadia, 'Legal Status of Jewish Converts to Christianity in Southern Italy and
Provence', *California Italian Studies Journal,* I/1 (2010), available at
http://escholarship.org

Ziegelman, Jane, *97 Orchard: An Edible History of Five Immigrant Families in One*
*New York Tenement* (New York, 2010)

# Acknowledgements

In good Italian form, I have to start by thanking my family. My mother, grand-mothers and aunts taught my sisters and me to cook. I am amazed that the strong women in my family were always in good spirits even when slaving at the stove for dozens of people (I am not exaggerating). Our Sunday meals in Rome are a tradition that I still thoroughly appreciate, and the numerous foreign friends who partook over the years seem to agree with me. Hopefully, my nephew Flavio and my niece Grazia will want to continue the tradition.

Author Andy Smith at the New School Food Studies Program deserves a special acknowledgement for putting me in contact with the publisher and for being a great example of discipline and professionalism. The New School has provided me with a great working environment, amazing colleagues and institutional support that has allowed me to work with Amy Orr, who had my back at work while I was writing, Eve Turow, a great editor, and Helen Kwok, who worked on the iconography.

I also want to thank all the students who have shared their passion for Italian food with me at The New School, the University of Gastronomic Sciences, Gustolab, *Gambero Rosso*, ALMA Graduate School at the University of Bologna, University of Illinois Champaign-Urbana, University of Massachusetts Amherst and New York University. Many of them have become close friends, a constant reminder of why I decided to quit journalism to teach. Their questions and curiosity have always pushed me ahead and made me grow as a human and a scholar. There are too many individuals to mention, but they know who they are.

My former co-workers at *Gambero rosso* magazine, especially Annalisa Barbagli, with her infinite knowledge of Italian food, and Stefano Bonilli, who bet on me when I was still writing about international affairs, have played a huge role in my professional development.

Many have shared the burden of this book's effort. Doran Ricks has patiently put up with me through various phases of excitement, panic, elation and fatigue. Sonia Massari, Pier Alberto Merli, Roberto Ludovico, Mitchell Davis, Lisa Sasson, Marion Nestle, Max Bergami, Ludovica Leone, Diana Mincyte, Peter Asaro, Janet Chrzan, Rachel Black, Carole Counihan, Ken Albala, Meryl Rosowsky, Paulo de Abreu e Lima and Roberta Alberotanza have regaled me with me ideas, laughter and many pleasurable moments around the table, providing unmatched stimulation for my research.

A great number of food scholars have inspired me and influenced my work: Arlene Avakian, Warren Belasco, Annie Bellows, Amy Bentley, Jennifer Berg, Antonella Campanini, Alberto Capatti, Simone Cinotto, Paul Freedman, Darra Goldstein, Yann Grappe, Allen Grieco, Lisa Heldke, Alice Julier, Laura Lindenfeld, Xavier Medina, Massimo Montanari, Beatrice Morandina, Priscilla Parkhurst Ferguson, Nicola Perullo, Andrea Pieroni, Krishnendu Ray, Signe Rousseau, Amy Trubek, Kyla Wazana Tompkis, Harry West, Rick Wilk and Psyche Williams-Forson.

The experience of co-editing the six-volume *Cultural History of Food* with Peter Scholliers and an incredible group of historians and scholars has renewed my passion for the topic and energized me when I was being pulled in many different directions by other projects.

I am deeply grateful to have had the opportunity and the luxury to choose my own idiosyncratic path in life, both personally and professionally. I am still working on it. Who knows what's next?

# Photo Acknowledgements

The author and publishers wish to express their thanks to the below sources of illustrative material and/or permission to reproduce it. Some locations of artworks are also given below.

Photo AIMare: p. 34; The Ashmolean Museum, Oxford: p. 110; photo BKP: p. 129; photo Giovanni Dall'Orto: p. 119; I. DeFrancisci & Son catalogue, c. 1914: p. 234; © duncan1890/iStock: pp. 77, 150; from *Gourmet Traveler*, 88 (2010) p. 233; from Jean-Pierre Houël, *Voyage pittoresque des Isles de Sicile, de Malte et de Lipari . . .* (Paris, 1782–7): p. 38; photo Jastrow: p. 43; photo Richard W. M. Jones: p. 16; photo Lewenstein: p. 111; photo LII324: p. 116; photos Library of Congress, Washington, DC: pp. 151, 229, 231; photo MChew: p. 69; from Cristoforo Messisbugo, *Banchetti, compositioni di vivande, et apparecchio generale* (Ferrara, 1549): p. 115; Musée du Louvre, Paris: pp. 40, 43; Musei di Strada Nuova, Genoa: p. 127; Museo Archeologico Nazionale di Napoli: pp. 51, 58; photo National Archives and Records Administration, College Park: pp. 185, 187 (top), 192; photo New York Public Library: p. 227; © nicoolay/iStock: p. 104; Österreichische Nationalbibliothek, Vienna: p. 111; © Fabio Parasecoli: pp. 91, 107; private collections: pp. 133, 137; photos Doran Ricks: pp. 9, 47, 51, 58, 61, 73, 102, 123, 141, 205, 257; photo Bibi Saint-Pol: p. 40; San Zeno, Verona: p. 92; from Bartolomeo Scappi, *Opera* (Venice, 1574): p. 116; © sergeyussr/iStock: p. 55; Statens Museum for Kunst, Copenhagen: p. 162; from François-Pierre La Varenne, *Le Vrai Cuisinier François . . .* (The Hague, 1721): p. 145; photo Volina/Shutterstock.com: p. 269; photo courtesy Walters Art Museum, Baltimore: p. 108; photo YQEdTTOFOX3lfQ: p. 127.

Scott Brenner, the copyright holder of the image on p. 255, Ben Hanbury, copyright holder of the image on p. 263 (top), jules:stonesoup, the copyright holder of the image on p. 218, Megan Mallen, the copyright holder of the image on p. 20, tomislav medak, the copyright holder of the image on p. 261, and j. c. winkler, the copyright holder of the image on p. 226, have published these online under conditions imposed by a Creative Commons Attribution 2.0 Generic license; Marco Bernardini, the copyright holder of the image on p. 11, Tom Chance, copyright holder of the image on

# Index